Archbishop Willi ple

Archbishop William Temple

A Study of Servant Leadership

Stephen Spencer

scm press

© Stephen Spencer 2022

Published in 2022 by SCM Press
Editorial office
3rd Floor, Invicta House,
108–114 Golden Lane,
London EC1Y 0TG, UK

www.scmpress.co.uk

SCM Press is an imprint of Hymns Ancient & Modern Ltd
(a registered charity)

Hymns Ancient & Modern® is a registered trademark of
Hymns Ancient & Modern Ltd
13A Hellesdon Park Road, Norwich,
Norfolk NR6 5DR, UK

Scripture quotations are from New Revised Standard Version Bible: Anglicized
Edition, copyright © 1989, 1995 National Council of the Churches of Christ in
the United States of America. Used by permission. All rights reserved worldwide.

British Library Cataloguing in Publication data
A catalogue record for this book is available
from the British Library

978-0-334-06167-0

Typeset by Regent Typesetting
Printed and bound by
CPI Group (UK) Ltd

Contents

Foreword

Stephen Cottrell, Archbishop of York

When I first approached my parish priest, blurting out that I thought God might be calling me to the priesthood, he gave me two books to read. One of them was Iremonger's famous biography of William Temple. Reading that book and learning about Temple shaped my thinking about Christian faith, Christian ministry and the way the Christian story can shape and guide the narrative of the world. Forty years later, my thinking has not moved on that much. Temple is still an inspiration and a compass point. This new book is a fitting contribution to the library of rich resources on William Temple. The emphasis on Temple's leadership is particularly welcome.

Leadership is a subject much written about in recent years. Temple's leadership highlights and embodies a call to fellowship, a recognition of the humanity of all people, the importance of community within society and, of course, the centrality of faith in all of life. The particular focus on servant leadership is very timely when we cannot help but note the lack of integrity that surrounds so much secular leadership. At its best, the church offers a counter-narrative to the pride and arrogance that is often modelled elsewhere. This call to care for the other before the self, to self-sacrifice and to service of others is a reminder of the leadership and, indeed, lifestyle that all Christians should seek to embody, emulating the way in which Jesus himself lived.

Temple faced challenges to his calling and he wrestled with the way in which the Christian faith was understood and taught. He also offered sharp critique of the way in which the church engaged with social conditions of the time. His passion for social justice is carefully analysed by Spencer and we would do well to engage with this more deeply.

The biographical details interwoven with theological development and struggles offer the reader a chance to engage with Temple in the way one might over dinner with a stranger who is to become a friend. He is not held up as the example of perfect leadership but of a fallible human being who struggled to know how God was calling him to be in a world that so often rejected the goodness and hope of the Gospel message.

Here is the story of a man who did not shy away from the daunting task to which he was called. Temple addressed the necessary changes that he saw as essential to the flourishing of the church, asking for financial commitments to support the work, with diocesan reorganization and the reforming of structures. Ahead of his time, he was a supporter of women's ordination and campaigned tirelessly for equal rights for women in civic life.

Spencer also captures the great delight that Temple took in his ministry despite the many challenges he faced. He relished teaching theology but also thoroughly enjoyed preaching, as is evidenced through the numerous quotations from lectures, sermons and books. Throughout it all was a deep personal faith, a journey to understand God more. The prophetic nature of Temple's later theology has much to say to our prophetic witness in the world today: his warning that our task is not to explain the world but to convert it invites us to participate in preaching the good news and allowing the kingdom of God to come near.

Here is the story of a holy man, one who shaped the Church of England and English theology throughout a lifetime of wrestling with the complexity of God, the gospels, the church and the world. Here is the story of an archbishop who refused to allow the church to be relegated to the private sphere: his faith informed his politics, driving him to campaign for justice and equality of opportunity. Even though his name is not well known today outside church circles, the influence of his leadership lives on.

Ecumenism also played an important part in Temple's leadership, as this book shows. He fostered relationships with other churches where he could, although he remained committed to episcopal leadership throughout his ministry and believed episcopal ordination was necessary for eucharistic ministry.

The mission and ministry, the servant leadership, the passion for the gospel, the earnest seeking of God are all characteristic of Temple's ministry and are gathered together here in a book that is enjoyable to read and invites us to reconsider our ministry in our time.

A call from one of his pastoral letters written just before his death remains as relevant today as then. Temple wrote that God

was putting before us a great opportunity. Let us all dedicate ourselves anew and pray for the guidance and strength of His Holy Spirit that we may use this time, when a new fashion of life must needs be formed, in the way that will most set forward His glory and the true welfare of all His people. (Temple, *Some Lambeth Letters*, p. 185, quoted on p. 184)

Preface

As this book reflects on the contribution of William Temple to our understanding of servant leadership it draws together and develops themes
from my earlier books and articles on this figure, especially *William
Temple: A Calling to Prophecy* (2001) and *Christ in All Things: William
Temple and His Writings* (2015). The first of these, published just over
20 years ago, brought together a description of Temple's work as teacher,
reformer and bishop with an introduction to the main contours of his
philosophy and theology. Overall it was asking a question about the
ongoing significance of Temple's life and thought for church and society
at large. It quoted Adrian Hastings, who at the end of a 1992 lecture
compared Temple with Charles Gore and Michael Ramsey, two other
twentieth-century Anglican figures who combined theological influence
with practical leadership: 'Temple remains the man "in the middle", his
time cut off in war, still the most enigmatic of the three, the most difficult to make up one's mind about.'[1] My book offered my first attempt
to make up my mind about Temple but was never more than that. Since
then, other scholars have published important studies on aspects of his
work, such as Matthew Grimley on his political theory,[2] Wendy Dackson
on his ecclesiology[3] and Edward Loane on his ecumenism,[4] but there has
been no further appraisal of his ministry and thought as a whole.

Meanwhile I have continued to reflect on Temple in a number of articles
and chapters in larger collections, especially taking forward analysis of
his social thought, and have continued to reflect on how to respond to
Hastings' challenge today.[5] My second book on Temple, *Christ in All
Things: William Temple and His Writings*, collected together some of the
key passages in his writings, with introductory notes and commentary,
but was not itself an analysis of his significance, though it did reveal the
compelling reason and wisdom at the heart of his ministry.

In this book I build on my earlier work to draw out what I now believe
to be a key contribution of Temple to church and society. This book
began life as a second edition of *William Temple: A Calling to Prophecy*
but has evolved since then, more than doubling in size and developing a
specific focus on the nature of the leadership he provided. This focus arises

out of current interest and debate about leadership in church and society and, especially, what authentic Christian leadership might be. There is now an extensive literature on both leadership in general and Christian leadership in particular, and this book is written in the conviction that study of exemplary figures from the past can make helpful contributions to all of this. For Anglicans there is little doubt that from the last century William Temple was one of the most exemplary of these. As the literature on him shows, his impact was huge and reckoned by many historians today to be greater than that of any other twentieth-century archbishop of Canterbury. Yet, as his life and writings show, he exercised leadership in a varied and extensive set of ways which together pose the question of what the nature of that leadership actually was. It is this question that this book addresses. Furthermore, in a year in which the bishops of the Anglican Communion are gathering for a Lambeth Conference and in which the scope and limits of episcopal authority are once again in the spotlight, a fresh exploration of Temple's leadership is very timely.

It is important to register at the outset that much of what Temple published in his 34 books and other pieces returned to themes he had already considered. This is because he was constantly asked to preach and speak within his busy life as a bishop and archbishop and this made it inevitable that there would be some repetition in what he said. What is impressive is that he never simply reused what he had said before but always came to themes and arguments in fresh ways. This shows how he was a systematic thinker with a well-developed philosophical and theological infrastructure that he could draw on whenever he was offered a pulpit or lectern. This book, then, does not look at each of his books in turn but, rather, draws out central and key themes, especially those which show his growth in leadership in church and society. It also makes a special point of tracing the change and development in his thinking and ministry. Even though he was a very stable personality and a systematic thinker, there was important and illuminating growth in his ministry and thought, and this provides much of the central subject matter of this book. Other studies of Temple have noted some changes and development but have not made this their primary focus. This book breaks new ground in this respect.

In order to capture the character and tone of what Temple was saying, he is quoted in his own words wherever possible. He is, in fact, eminently quotable. Hugh Warner, one of his chaplains and an editor of his writings, explains why:

> More than most people of his day, Archbishop Temple had the gift of expressing in a sentence or two the most profound conceptions of reli-

gion and philosophy. To hear him speak was always an intellectual joy; the turn of his sentences, their cadence, and the amazing way the chain of thought resolved itself in a single complex whole with never a word out of place, or the slightest hesitation in delivery – this is unforgettable.[6]

Temple's own writings are therefore the primary source for this book, both published and unpublished letters and papers at Lambeth Palace library. (The modern reader needs to be prepared for the way in which Temple comes from an era of non-inclusive language and that his writing reflects this, and that he has a habit of capitalizing the first letter of key concepts.) For secondary sources the authorized biography by F. A. Iremonger retains a special place because of the wealth of letters and other papers that it contains, letters by Temple and by those who corresponded with him.[7] Iremonger was a colleague of Temple's in the Life and Liberty movement and his biography was published only four years after his death, so was too close to him to offer a properly critical perspective but, nevertheless, until another fully comprehensive biography is published it remains a key source for students of Temple's life.

In what follows, the first two chapters provide introductory background to Temple's early life and career, setting the scene and putting all that follows in context, drawing especially on Iremonger's biography. The subsequent chapters look at Temple's growing leadership in various areas of church and national life, drawing especially on his own his writings.

I have been studying William Temple for around 30 years, beginning with my doctoral studies at Oxford on his political philosophy and ethics and then broadening my focus to his life and thought as a whole, with a number of publications along the way. It is a pleasure as well as a privilege to offer these chapters as the fruit of all that. I am very grateful to David Shervington and the team at SCM Press for providing the opportunity to do this.

This book is dedicated to the bishops of the Anglican Communion who in the very different and challenging circumstances of the twenty-first century must strive, like William Temple, to express a leadership that inspires and equips God's people for their discipleship in the world.

Notes

1 'William Temple', in Adrian Hastings, *The Shaping of Prophecy: Passion, Perception and Practicality*, London: Geoffrey Chapman, 1995, p. 68.

2 Matthew Grimley, *Citizenship, Community and the Church of England*, Oxford: Oxford University Press, 2004. Temple is one among a group of Anglicans that Grimley studies.

3 Wendy Dackson, *The Ecclesiology of Archbishop William Temple*, Lewiston, NY: Edwin Mellen Press, 2004.

4 Edward Loane, *William Temple and Church Unity: The Politics and Practice of Ecumenical Theology*, London: Palgrave Macmillan, 2016.

5 See 'William Temple and the "Temple Tradition"' in Stephen Spencer (ed.), *Theology Reforming Society: Rediscovering Anglican Social Theology*, London: SCM Press, 2017; 'R. H. Tawney and Anglican Social Theology', *Crucible: The Journal of Christian Social Ethics*, January 2018; 'John Neville Figgis and William Temple: A Common Tradition of Anglican Social Theology?' in Paul Avis (ed.), *Churches in a Pluralist World: The Thought and Legacy of John Neville Figgis, CR*, Leiden: Brill, 2022; 'William Temple and the Beveridge Report', *Crucible: The Journal of Christian Social Ethics*, July 2022; '*Christianity and Social Order* as a model of collaborative leadership in the public arena', *Theology*, July 2022.

6 Hugh C. Warner (ed.), *Daily Readings from William Temple*, London and Oxford: Mowbray, 1981, p. iv.

7 F. A. Iremonger, *William Temple, Archbishop of Canterbury: His Life and Letters*, Oxford, Oxford University Press, 1948.

Introduction

The idea of servant leadership has roots deep in the Hebrew Bible and in the New Testament, not least in Jesus' radical and subversive teaching to the disciples that 'whoever wishes to become great among you must be your servant, and whoever wishes to be first among you must be slave of all' (Mark 10.43–44). In recent times the idea of servant leadership has been revived and promoted in churches across the world, as seen in the Arusha Declaration of the World Council of Churches, which affirmed that 'We are called to be formed as servant leaders who demonstrate the way of Christ in a world that privileges power, wealth, and the culture of money' (Luke 22.25–27).[1]

It has also been developed into a comprehensive approach to leading organizations by Robert K. Greenleaf, beginning with his influential article of 1970, 'The Servant as Leader'. Greenleaf proposed that servant leaders are those who make serving others their main priority and find success and satisfaction in the growth of others. He described how servant leaders seek to be servants first, to care for the needs of the others around them, helping them become healthier and wiser, guiding them towards self-improvement. Eventually, those who are served take on the traits of a servant leader as well, continuing the spread of this leadership style.[2]

Greenleaf believed the betterment of others to be the true intention of a servant leader: an 'I serve' mentality in opposition to the usual 'I lead' mentality. This can be seen in politicians and government administrators who define their role as one of public service and seek to embody this ideal. It is especially prevalent in the teaching and caring professions. He argued that servant leadership develops in the context of serving others and *wanting* to serve others. In fact, only through the act of serving does the leader lead other people to be what they are capable of.

Another more recent exponent is Kenneth Blanchard who has made a cogent and popular case for servant leadership in talks and books that contrast self-serving leaders with servant leaders, people who are there 'to serve first and lead second'. His case is based on his observation that 'The most effective leaders I know are first and foremost good human beings – they care about people, they listen more than they talk, they want to help people win.'[3]

Blanchard has drawn out some of the practical implications of this approach by describing the two parts of servant leadership, the first providing vision and direction, the 'leadership part' of going somewhere and letting others know what is needed to do that. He describes the need to answer the following kind of questions to do this: what business are they in and why are they doing what they are doing; if they commit to this what will happen and where will they go; what are the values that will guide their journey; what are the immediate goals? Blanchard therefore understands a compelling vision to encompass both the present and the future, a vision of the way things are and of what they can become.

He then describes 'the implementation part', in which the traditional pyramid of a hierarchical organization is turned upside down and the leader comes to serve everyone else in the organization as they turn the vision into reality. The leader is the one who provides the caring, listening and appropriate support.[4]

Later he summarizes all this by describing 'three key aspects of being a leader: having clear goals, so that people around you know what you are trying to accomplish; acknowledging what others have done and of its importance; [and] offering clear and concise support when changes are needed', or of being a 'one-minute manager' (the title of one of his bestselling books) to help others get back on track.[5]

What might this simple yet compelling model of leadership look like in a Christian context and, specifically, within the corporate life of the church where historically the model of a hierarchical pyramid has been dominant? And how might servant leadership in this context adjust and deepen the insights of exponents like Greenleaf and Blanchard?

Joseph Galgalo provides one answer:

> Servant leadership is about the disposition of the leader, which should always be 'other centred' as opposed to self-centredness. It is oriented towards God and humanity, the two 'others' who the leader is privileged to serve. The shift from 'self' to the 'other' calls for self-sacrifice in that leadership is not about power to rule, and enrich oneself, but the power to give service; it should never be about self except in expending that self in serving.[6]

Malcolm Grundy adds to this when he writes that the servant leader 'in diocese and denomination, parish and congregation will lead by example. Their values, and often the source of those values, will be experienced in a leadership style with the actions which flow from it encouraging imitation and a certain mixture of aspiration and admiration.'[7] Jude Padfield highlights the centrality of hope within servant leadership, a hope and trust in what God is bringing to the world.[8]

This book seeks to build on these answers by turning to a prominent and influential church leader from recent church history who provides a rich and engaging example of servant leadership, one which encouraged imitation, aspiration and admiration. This is someone who self-evidently cared about others and gave his all in the service of church and society, and who did this by providing hopeful vision and direction, and help with its implementation, the parts of servant leadership described by Blanchard. Furthermore, this book shows how his example extends, enriches and deepens what is described by advocates and writers like Greenleaf and Blanchard. But how?

William Temple

A British news film report from September 1942 opens a window onto a remarkable moment in church history and specifically in the history of Anglicanism.[9] The Pathé clip begins with some urgent background music that suggests we must stop whatever we are doing and pay attention. The title of the clip then comes into view, 'The Church and Social Problems', not an immediately arresting one, yet the music will not allow us to turn away. The curtain then rises on a packed Royal Albert Hall on a Saturday afternoon in September 1942 with William Temple, the recently installed Archbishop of Canterbury, addressing the audience. He is at first almost lost in the crowds, with clergy and people on the platform behind him and in the arena in front of him. Some can be seen leaning forward listening intently to what is being said. There is a palpable sense of occasion, something important is happening.

All this is remarkable: that a church leader should fill a hall of 6,000 people to hear a speech on such a topic. Furthermore, Temple has gathered around him not only other church leaders (including, in a follow-up meeting, Cardinal Hinsley, the leader of the Roman Catholic Church in England and Wales) but also politicians, including a senior government minister, Sir Stafford Cripps, a future Chancellor of the Exchequer, who would speak after the archbishop in support of what he was saying.

Temple is at the centre of all this and an aura of authority becomes clear when he speaks, beginning with an unambiguous statement that 'we are here to affirm the right and the duty of the Church to declare its judgement upon social facts and social movements and to lay down principles which should govern the ordering of society'. Temple's voice is strongly projected, high-pitched, unapologetic, with an upper-class inflection that makes the word 'facts' sound like 'fects' and 'land' like 'lend'. He is not, then, offering one opinion among others, as a contribution to a debate, in the way that church leaders today must do when they speak in public, but speaking with recognized authority to the nation as well as to the church. It is an awe-inspiring moment.

The film then cuts to a later moment in the speech when Temple does not just talk about general political principles but takes aim at the economic system undergirding British society, no less. He begins with a general philosophical observation that is unarguable, expressed in the idioms of his time: 'There are four requisites for life which are given by the bounty of God – air, light, land and water. These exist before man's labour is expended upon them, and upon air and light man can do nothing except spoil them.' At this point it is clear Temple has the attention of his audience and with a touch of irony he is ready to take aim at his target: 'I suppose if it were possible to have established property rights in air, somebody would have done it before now, and then he would demand of us that we should pay him if we wanted to breathe what he called *his* air.' Now the audience breaks out in laughter: they recognize the absurd truth that capitalists would turn the air that we breathe into a commodity to buy and sell if they could. Temple has touched a nerve in his audience; now they are with him and he can land the decisive blow:

> Well, it couldn't be done, so it hasn't been done. But it could be done with land, and it has been done with land; and, as it seems to me, we have been far too tender towards the claims that have been made by the owners of land and of water as compared with the interests of the public, who need that land and water for the ordinary purposes of human life.

At this point applause erupts and spreads through the hall. The audience is behind him: private owners of land and water supplies should not just levy whatever rents and charges they like: private ownership has no over-riding rights and Temple is implying that the state should constrain and control what owners do with their natural resources so that the interests of the public at large always come first. This, in turn, is implying a radical overhaul of the capitalist system on which British economic life is based! It was no wonder that a right-wing commentator, the diarist Henry 'Chips' Channon, described him as 'positively dangerous. He now openly preaches Socialism from a platform which he shares with Cripps – Is England mad, and doomed?'[10] But Temple says in the next sentence he is not advocating nationalization and nowhere does he mention socialism.

But all this shows how strongly he had weighed into public debate and with what authority he had done so.

This speech was not an isolated event but part of a bigger campaign to mobilize support for reconstruction after the Second World War. It was being waged against the backdrop of long-term mass unemployment, poverty and hunger in the industrial areas of pre-war Britain. There had never been less than a million unemployed in the 1920s and the depression which had begun in 1929 caused this figure to rise sharply to almost three million in 1933. Recovery from this high point was then painfully slow, with the figure only falling below two million in 1937. Furthermore, with unemployment came a loss of morale: unemployment benefit was so low it was impossible to buy clothes or household items or to pay for entertainment or trips to relieve the monotony and boredom. The unemployed were looked down on by those still in work, and felt humiliated. Unemployment benefit was cut in 1931 and applicants had to endure a humiliating means test. In some areas the cost of rent was not included in the benefit, resulting in homelessness and destitution. Soup kitchens were needed in many areas to feed the hungry. For the young, from school leavers of 14 to those in their early twenties, long-term unemployment meant never learning to work. As one bishop expressed it, 'unemployment is the factory of the unemployable'. Meanwhile the government consistently resisted any attempt to invest in public works to provide employment: austerity was the consistent policy until the outbreak of war.[11]

Temple's campaign for post-war reconstruction began when he was still Archbishop of York with a conference at Malvern in 1941. The campaign, run by the Industrial Christian Fellowship, would continue with Temple publishing a slim Penguin paperback, *Christianity and Social Order*, which went on to sell 139,000 copies and was read by many more because in the conditions of wartime these handy paperbacks could be slipped into a back pocket and read in spare moments, of which there were many for those in the armed services in wartime, and then passed on to others. Then a series of mass meetings were planned under the banner 'The Church Looks Forward'. This meeting in the Royal Albert Hall was the first of these, with others in Birmingham (November 1942), Leicester (February 1943), Edinburgh (June 1943), and ended with a youth rally back in London (October 1943). The speech glimpsed in the Pathé film, then, was a pivotal moment in something much larger. Temple was not just winning over an audience at a random mass meeting but spearheading a gathering movement for just and equitable social reconstruction to take place after the war. No wonder that Channon was worried.

It is also important to see how he was tying in this campaign with a government initiative, the Beveridge Report of 1942, a report by Sir William Beveridge on reforming and widening social insurance so as to abolish the 'five giants' of 'want, disease, ignorance, squalor and idleness'.[12] This was a ground-breaking set of detailed proposals to end hunger through state provision of proper benefits and pension, from the cradle to the grave. The report also prepared the ground for fighting disease through a national health service, to ending ignorance through state provision of education up to the age of 16, to abolishing the squalor of the slums through a campaign of national housebuilding, and to ending the idleness of unemployment through state investment in job creation.

It is important to note that Temple was a friend of Beveridge and was in contact with him when he was drawing up his own practical proposals in *Christianity and Social Order*. There was to be significant alignment between what they were both advocating.

Labour members of the wartime government had commissioned the report but the question remained as to whether there would be enough support across the country to put it into action. Public opinion needed to be won over, especially the middle classes whose taxes would have to pay for it all. This is where Temple's campaign came into the frame, because his audience was a significant section of those middle classes, those who came to church or who just thought of themselves as 'Church of England', and this is one of the reasons Temple could invite a government minister to join him on the platform to speak in support of what he was proposing.

The effectiveness of what Temple was doing is demonstrated by events over the next few years. Beginning with the passing of the Education Act of 1944 and continuing with the election of a Labour government in 1945, many of the social and economic objectives described by the Beveridge Report and advocated by Temple were eventually achieved. The government took control of the principal industrial resources such as coal and transport, and iron and steel, ensuring fair pay and decent working conditions. Widespread slum clearance and house building began, with rising employment and improvements in social security. The jewel in the crown was the creation of a national health service, providing comprehensive health care at the point of need rather than on the ability to pay. Taken as a whole, these measures amounted to the creation of the welfare state. There were, of course, other powerful forces behind these developments but Temple and those who supported him made a powerful contribution to their realization. He has been described as one of the architects of the welfare state,[13] and it is for this reason that Frances Knight, echoing other historians, has described him as 'the most significant person in the history of twentieth-century Anglicanism in the first half of that century'.[14] Frank

Field, the MP and ex-Labour minister, provides one illustration of why this is so. He writes that for him Temple's greatest achievement 'was to instil some of his own confidence into working-class voters, ensuring their resolve against returning after wartime to the life of the 1930s'.[15]

The extraordinary moment in the Royal Albert Hall in September 1942 and the person at the centre of it clearly raises some important questions, not least for those who want to learn how Christian leaders today can bring about transformative change in society. This book seeks to answer some of these questions by identifying what it was about Temple's life and thought that led him to exercising such significant leadership. In other words, it seeks to identify the elements at play in his life and thought that led him to making such an impact on church and society.

Some of the chapters look at Temple's ministry and the practical ways he provided leadership, the 'implementation part' of Blanchard's description of leadership above. There are obvious elements of this, such as the different roles he occupied and especially his ministry as Archbishop of York and then of Canterbury and as leader of the Church of England and wider Anglican Communion. But there are other facets to who he was, beginning with his early career as a lecturer in philosophy, continuing with his commitment to social reform especially through his support of workers' education, his speaking and writing as a Christian teacher and missioner, his ongoing ecumenical work to bring churches together and his speaking and writing as a spiritual guide. Temple had a multi-dimensional presence in church and national life over four decades and each dimension needs to be investigated.

Other chapters look at 'the vision part' of what Temple offered, the first part of Blanchard's description of leadership. These will be about the ways in which in his speaking and writing he provided a worldview with a sense of purpose and hope, briefly alluded to above but needing to be spelled out more fully and analysed for the kind of outlook he was advocating. This will include presenting its underlying philosophical and theological foundations, his views on church and nation and the relationship between them, and the Christian social principles and practical policy recommendations that he drew out of all that. All of this will highlight and expound the kind of leadership he provided not only for the Royal Albert Hall audience that Saturday afternoon but for the church and British society as a whole.

Finally, it is important to add that while the Pathé film clip appears to present an establishment figure speaking with great authority, the chapters that follow will add to and ultimately adjust this portrait in notable ways. A distinctive portrait of leadership will gradually emerge, but of what kind?

Notes

1 World Council of Churches, 'The Arusha Call to Discipleship: the World Council of Churches' Conference on World Mission and Evangelism, Arusha, Tanzania, 8–13 March 2018', *World Council of Churches*, www.oikoumene.org/resources/documents/the-arusha-call-to-discipleship, accessed 8 March 2022.

2 In Robert K. Greenleaf, *Servant Leadership*, New York: Paulist Press, 1977, 1991, 2002. His work and ideas are now promoted and developed by the Robert K. Greenleaf Centre for Servant Leadership (www.greenleaf.org).

3 London Business Forum, 'Ken Blanchard – Servant Leadership', *YouTube*, 19 May 2017, www.youtube.com/watch?v=ctZHSa4Qhd4, accessed 8 March 2022.

4 Peter Bregman, 'Ken Blanchard – Servant Leadership in Action – Bregman Leadership Podcast', *YouTube*, 4 March 2019, www.youtube.com/watch?v=PMx-gRZpldkY, accessed 8 March 2022.

5 Bregman, 'Ken Blanchard'. See Kenneth Blanchard and Spencer Johnson, *The One Minute Manager*, London: HarperCollins, 1994.

6 Joseph Galgalo, 'Service to God and Humanity: Modelling cathartic sacrifice as the leitmotiv of authentic Christian service', in C. Stückelberger, J. Galgalo and S. Kobia (eds), *Leadership with Integrity: Higher Education from Vocation to Funding*, Geneva: Globethics.net, 2021, pp. 26–7. Available from www.globethics.net/documents/10131/26882157/GE_Education_Ethics_8_isbn9782889313891.pdf/c12df3fo-d912-683a-599a-503288d10ba2?t=1626798082338.

7 Malcolm Grundy, 'The servant', in *Leadership and Oversight: New models for episcopal ministry*, London: Mowbray, 2011, p. 115. Jon Coutts highlights some ways in which this concept can be misused by churches wanting passive submission from their leaders: see *SCM Studyguide to Church Leadership*, London: SCM Press, 2019, pp. 4–6.

8 Jude Padfield, *Hopeful Influence: A Theology of Christian Leadership*, London: SCM Press, 2019, pp. 62–6.

9 British Pathé, 'The Church and Social Problems (1942)', *YouTube*, www.youtube.com/watch?v=tOTiLBDzYhM, accessed 8 March 2022. The meeting was on 26 September 1942.

10 Diary entry for 27 September 1942.

11 John Oliver, *The Church and Social Order: Social Thought in the Church of England 1918–1939*, London: A. R. Mowbray, 1968, pp. 153–5.

12 William Beveridge, 'Social Insurance and Allied Services', HM Stationery Office, 1942, available from news.bbc.co.uk/1/shared/bsp/hi/pdfs/19_07_05_beveridge.pdf.

13 D. L. Munby, in *God and the Rich Society*, describes *Christianity and Social Order* as 'one of the foundation piers of the Welfare State' (p. 157).

14 Simon Barnett, 'Why study William Temple with Frances Knight', *University of Nottingham*, 28 January 2015, https://mediaspace.nottingham.ac.uk/media/Why+Study+William+Temple+with+Frances+Knight/1_beved8tj, accessed 8 March 2022.

15 Stephen Spencer, *William Temple: A Calling to Prophecy*, London: SPCK, 2001, p. viii.

I

A call, but to what?

On what basis did William Temple provide leadership in church and nation? As we have seen, the British Pathé film clip gives the impression that he was a powerful prelate of the church, laying down moral law on the basis of the church's establishment within Christendom. Another film from Pathé, of his enthronement in Canterbury Cathedral in April 1942, reinforces this impression.[1] With his great bulk and expansive robes and mitre, Temple dominates the crowded scenes in the cathedral, moving with stately purpose and pronouncing a blessing from the top of the chancel steps with great solemnity. We are led to believe that here was a figure reaching the summit of ecclesiastical power and about to embark on a long and glorious reign as Primate of All England. Indeed, at the end of film the commentator with huge excitement announces that 'never before has an archbishop been enthroned in such solemn yet hopeful times. A great work of spiritual and social reconstruction lies ahead.' With even greater rhetorical emphasis the commentator continues, 'Behind the archbishop's call for a re-dedication of the nation and the church to the service of God is the feeling that here is the greatest opportunity the church has ever had of leading the world into a better way of life.' This great expectation apparently began to be fulfilled a few months later with the Albert Hall speech and the launch of 'The Church Looks Forward' campaign.

However, all was not as it seemed. The journey that Temple's life had taken and was taking had a different kind of character, not one of his seamlessly rising to the top but of a bumpier ride, with some surprising twists and turns and a very unexpected and distressing conclusion. To that journey, the warp to the weft of his leadership, we must turn.

Early life

A hero's life usually begins in humble circumstances with toil and struggle as the subject labours to climb out of obscurity and begin a journey to the heights of power and influence. Temple's journey was not like this at all.

He was born on 15 October 1881 into the British upper classes at a time when the British empire was at the height of its power across the world. His father Frederick Temple, already 60 years old, was a bishop, first of Exeter, then of London, finally becoming Archbishop of Canterbury when William was 16, and his mother came from aristocratic lineage. He was born into the rarefied and privileged environment of an episcopal palace in the Victorian era. This is vividly captured in a description of a typical day at Fulham Palace, the official residence of his father when Bishop of London. The palace was William's home during his formative years. He had one older brother, Frederick and, according to Temple's official biographer F. A. Iremonger,

> The day at Fulham began with prayers in the Palace Chapel. For this there was a well-established ceremonial. The boys waited in the vestry, which was separated from the chapel by a stone-flagged passage. The butler also waited, with the Bishop's surplice over his arm, and passed the time cleaning his finger-nails for the day with a pocket-knife. Mrs. Temple and other ladies would come hurrying down the passage, followed by the Bishop. He never stopped, but kissed each of his sons as he walked on; and the butler put his surplice over the Bishop's arms extended backwards, and on to his shoulders. The boys fell in beside their father, who put his arms around them, looking (as was remarked) like a large angel with wings as he entered the chapel. He turned into his stall, and William stepped over his mother's feet to take his place on her left. Going out [after the prayers], the boys chased after their father, who dropped his surplice just outside the door, without looking round, into the hands of the pursuing butler, and again put his arms over the shoulders of his sons.[2]

Iremonger adds that the impression left on Temple's mind by these daily prayers never faded. Nor might it! His father, when Archbishop of Canterbury (1897–1902), would go on to crown Edward VII as the successor to Queen Victoria in 1902, with brothers Frederick and William by his side as his attendants.[3]

This privileged beginning was very different to that of his father who had modest beginnings in Devon and who could only attend university in Oxford because he won a scholarship to pay his fees. He was in many ways a self-made man. William, on the other hand, received an education that instilled a strong intellectual self-confidence from the start. He had learned his Greek alphabet by the age of ten. As an 11- and 12-year-old he was already assessing the sermons he heard in church and recording in his diary that most of them were 'excellent'. He was already offering advice to any who would hear it. In one boyish letter to his older brother, written when he had just heard that his older brother 'is learning to play', he wrote that Frederick will probably find that the organ will suit him best, and he must not mind if his fingers are a good deal stiffer than his younger brother's; the drudgery will soon be over but he should be careful not to let music interfere with his work. For the young William, his music master recommends that he should not start on the organ till he has learned to play quite perfectly on the piano all the scales, major, minor and chromatic. After offering this probably not very welcome advice, Temple then capped it all by signing himself 'Your loving brother, the musician of Fulham Palace (and Church music selector) William Temple'.

The teenage William went to Rugby School, one of the most prestigious public schools of the time, and received a thorough academic education. He gained a grounding in the classics, philosophy, music and poetry. He was reading Kant and Mill by the age of 17. He imbibed the philosophical tradition of Thomas Arnold, who believed that the histories of Greece, Rome and Israel were three great steps forward on the path of the intellectual and moral development of humankind, and that modern Europe was the inheritor of all this: 'our life is in a manner a continuation of Greece, Rome and Israel', yet it 'exhibits a fuller development of the human race, a richer combination of the most remarkable elements'.[4] During the course of his life, Temple would see the collapse of this self-confidently imperial view of history.

His studies were encouraged and fired when he was at home. On one occasion he asked his father, 'Why do not philosophers rule the world, Father? Would it not be a good thing if they did?' There was an impressively quick and emphatic answer from the elderly bishop: 'They do rule it, silly, five hundred years after they are dead.'[5] His schooling also included a not-very-distinguished record on the rugby field (though his bulk made him useful in a scrum), and walking trips to the Lake District. He was already developing a remarkable proficiency in the use of language in speaking and writing. When he left the school his headmaster wrote in his final report that he thought 'anything' was possible for Temple in the future.

In the event, he won an exhibition to Balliol College, Oxford, where he studied Greek and Latin literature and philosophy. He came under the influence of the philosopher T. H. Green and his school. Green had been a philosophy tutor at the college in the 1870s and had also been heavily involved in work for social reform in the poor districts of Oxford. He and those who followed him in the college believed that they were not training young men to be professional philosophers but to be public servants, in government, church and law. Here was the first hint of a different kind of journey opening up to Temple, a journey from the entitlements of privilege towards the service of others. The Idealist philosophy they learned, based ultimately on the German philosopher G. W. F. Hegel, saw human society within a historical context: the nation was caught up in a process of purposive growth, and the role of public servants was to work for the increasing realization of a just and healthy society, one that was slowly emerging through its historical development.

When Temple arrived at Balliol, the Scottish philosopher Edward Caird was head of the college and was continuing to teach this morally serious outlook. He called on the undergraduates to fulfil the duties 'of the station in which we stand', so that this present world may have 'its worth deepened ... item by item, with all the elements that constitute it multiplied a hundred-fold in value, raised to a higher spiritual power'. Caird warned his listeners, though, that this ideal world would only be realized 'with persecutions'.[6] It is clear that Temple became caught up in this challenging yet progressive optimism and believed, like his peers, that he would have a significant role to play in serving the unfolding life of the nation.

He also developed a great love of literature. He absorbed Keats, Shelley, Coleridge and Spenser. But he wrote that Milton's longer poems bored him stiff, and Shakespeare, while outstanding, had a 'pagan magnificence'.[7] With the George Eliot of *Romola* he found himself entirely out of sympathy. Robert Browning, on the other hand, he found to be a giant. Temple was drawn not only to Browning's style of writing but also to his underlying view of the world. In one of Temple's earliest published essays, he described how he found Browning's writings fundamentally and thoroughly Christian: 'In both [Shakespeare and Browning] there is the joy of comedy, but in Browning only is there also the joy of work and worship.' 'To Browning', he also insists, 'the climax of history, the crown of philosophy, and the consummation of poetry is unquestionably the Incarnation'.[8] He confidently placed Browning with St John the Evangelist and Plato as being one of the three most formative influences on his own thought.[9]

He was awarded a first-class degree and went on to become a lecturer in philosophy at Queen's College, Oxford, where he taught courses on Plato's philosophy.[10] He harnessed his fluency with language in his teaching and had the gift of being able to communicate what he had learned with a calm and infectious enthusiasm. He had also developed a great, though rather high-pitched, roisterous laugh, one which seemed to shake the whole of his person and which endeared him to many, though it could infuriate others. And he developed a large waistline, having a lifelong passion for strawberry jam and strawberry ices. It was also his habit to finish the pudding while others smoked cigars. He later recounted how his white surplice, after being sent away to the cleaners, had been returned with a label saying, 'bell tent'.

A call

But the other journey, the journey into serving those who had none of the privileges he enjoyed, also began to take hold. What helped to bring this about?

First of all, those around him report an innate openness as a human being. His manner was always relaxed, friendly and simple, wholly unpretentious, never 'rattled', never confrontational and 'with no vestige of pomposity'.[11] He was, as Lancashire people would later say, without 'side' and was able to give the whole of his attention to whoever he was speaking to. This was a foundation for all that followed.

Another formative influence was probably his ongoing struggle with gout, a very painful recurrent illness that affected his feet and legs. The earliest attack occurred when he was just two years old and he suffered intermittently with it until his death. As well as causing him pain, it would have made him sensitive to the struggles with disease faced by others, not least by the urban poor in an era before the founding of the National Health Service.

A further prompt was certainly the influence of Edward Caird. The distinguished Glaswegian philosopher had been sharply critical of the huge contrast between the living conditions of the Victorian suburbs and the slum tenements of that industrial city. When he came to Oxford he encouraged students to spend vacations at one of the Oxford residential houses in the East End of London, such as Toynbee Hall and the Bermondsey Mission. This Temple did, and he later recounted how at his lodgings 'there was a tin bed, rather rickety, and I lay on it with anxiety, for I always carried weight in every assembly. There was a tin wash-basin and a chair with three legs, upon which I read Bosanquet's *Logic*.'[12] It was all a bit of an adventure, of course, and it is doubtful that the student houses did much for the people among whom they were placed. For Temple, though, it was an important step out of the confines of privilege.

Alongside this, and probably because of it, he became aware of a sense of calling. This was not so much a calling to ordination, as he had always wanted to be ordained and to follow in the footsteps of his father, as something more sharply focused and passionate. In a series of letters to close friends, reprinted in Iremonger's biography, Temple revealed the pattern of his thinking. The letters are full of the self-confidence already mentioned but they also reveal some deeper concerns that would drive him forward. To his close friend John Stocks, in September 1901 or 1902, he confided that

> I mean that the Church – and consequently the nation – is in a very critical state: I mean that it is doing very nearly as much harm as good – and perhaps more. And this because of its narrow spirit ... Our religion becomes more and more sensuous; preachers try to stir the emotions, not to direct the will. In short, anything more hostile to the New Testament than our modern English religion is hard to conceive.[13]

Temple overstates his case but tellingly goes on to describe the reasons for the harmful narrowness of his church. It arose from an inability to adopt 'the spirit of criticism' within the church. He meant by this a failure to rethink the Christian faith in the light of advances in scientific, philosophical and historical knowledge. *Essays and Reviews*, the controversial volume of essays of 1861, to which his father had contributed, had begun to apply critical ways of thinking to both the Bible and the creeds, but for Temple this needed to be continued in a more thoroughgoing way:

> Well, I believe that the only thing that can save us is a vigorous attack from within the Church on the existing conceptions of religion. While the Church is as it is, very few men of intellect *can* take [Holy] orders: and until they do things cannot be much better.[14]

Temple was trying to persuade John Stocks to be one of those who would offer themselves for ordination and take up the intellectual challenge. But in reality, he was wrestling with the reasons why he should enter the ordained ministry and why he was being called to commit himself to the intellectual reconstruction of the Christian faith.

But the malaise that Temple identified was not only intellectual, and so later in the same letter he wrote,

> As a matter of practical politics – what is our so-called Christianity doing? Men are still encouraged to get drunk than otherwise; the poor are not housed, nor the naked clothed nor the hungry fed ... the Church forgets that Christianity is not an attitude of mind, but a type of life: a man's spirit is known not by his opinion (creeds etc) but by his actions and general conduct.[15]

Temple, then, was not just questioning the way the Christian faith was currently being understood and taught but the whole way it was failing to respond to the social conditions of the time. Britain at that time was the richest nation in the world but a third of its population did not have enough to eat, had a life expectancy of a mere 30 years and lived in slum conditions that led to 13,000 deaths a year from measles and 7,500 deaths a year from diptheria. Seebohm Rowntree's shocking and influential report on poverty in the city of York had been published only three years before and Temple would have been aware of its findings. His letters show that he believed the church should have been confronting such social injustice.

In a letter to another friend in May 1901 he put this view in a historical context:

> The Church has been roused – by Wesley and others – to a new spiritual devotion: and to a new sense of beauty as an expression of this devotion by Newman: so we have got the devotion and its formal expression: the most important part remains – namely to put that behind all actions whatever, and identify religion with life.[16]

Temple was thinking of the epistle of James and applying its argument to his own day, that faith without good works is dead. In another letter to John Stocks in October 1902 he wrote that 'we have to teach S. James' doctrine' and that anyone who is not interested in '"good works" is in effect anti-Christ'. After this startling statement he went on to show the kind of view of Christ that he believed was now needed to underpin everything else:

> The Christ men believe in and worship is to a great extent a myth and an idol – very different from Him who lived and died 'to bear witness to the truth', and Whose Spirit lived and spoke in Socrates and Buddha and Mahomet [sic.] as it did also in Hosea and Luther and Browning. Men do not realize that Christ requires a good life and not church-going, and knowledge of God more than communicating.[17]

It was not only the current theology and practice of the Church of England that Temple was questioning, then, but the traditional under-standing of Christ found in most churches. He was wanting to abandon the idea that Christ can be found only in institutional Christianity and was advocating an inclusivist understanding of Christ's presence in the world: the Lord does not belong just within narrow ecclesiastical circles but to all humanity and to poor as much as rich. At the end of one letter, summing it all up, he wrote that

I know I am right in this, though I may exaggerate the evil: I don't think so however – and if I lived 700 years before Christ I should call it the word of the Lord. I don't know whether Amos actually saw things – probably not: but his vision is mine – 'I saw the Lord standing above the altar' (His own altar it was) 'and He said unto me, SMITE!' [18]

These youthful letters do not represent Temple's mature understanding of the Christian faith, for he would become more orthodox in his view of Christ as he got older. But they do reveal an emerging and passionate vocation, a vocation with four elements: a conviction about the need for a restatement of the Christian faith that was intellectually credible; an anger and protest at the harsh social conditions of the time; a commitment to reforming the Church so that it practised what it preached; and a belief in an ecumenical Christ who was not confined by human divisions but was the Lord of all and present with all. These letters reveal how his journey away from the entitlements of privilege and towards serving society as a whole was based on a deep sense of call and vocation.

This calling explains the boundless yet focused energy of Temple's subsequent career: it shows why he developed his extended interest in theological interpretation through an engagement with the philosophy of the day; it explains his long-standing commitment to social and educational reform, as strong at the end of his life as at the beginning; it explains his involvement with church reform, a cause that might otherwise seem at odds with his other interests; and it accounts for his commitment to ecumenical bridge-building, an aspect of his work that became increasingly important. These student letters, when read in the light of his subsequent career, reveal the basis for all that followed, being a passionate sense of vocation. This must be one of the secrets of his leadership, one of the key elements in its mix, one that needs to be clearly registered within the overall analysis of this book.

Ordination?

However, it was all very well for William Temple to believe he was called to serve others and bring about the transformation of church and society but how, in practice, was he going to do this? For someone who was endowed with so many gifts and who carried them with an easy confidence it may have seemed as if the path to power and influence would open up quickly and seamlessly. In fact this was far from the case, which makes his story interesting and instructive.

After completing his undergraduate studies, he became a lecturer in philosophy, as we have seen, based at Queen's College in Oxford. This allowed his studies to continue and it launched his teaching career, but the confined world of an Oxbridge college was never going to fulfil his sense of vocation. He needed to move forward in the wider world and decided to offer himself for ordination. This led to the first major upset of his life.

The catalyst for this upset was his own less-than-orthodox early understanding of the Christian faith. When he took up the philosophy lectureship at Queen's he spent some months on a sabbatical study leave in Germany. He wrote the following letter from Jena in 1905:

> I do honestly wish, though of course I don't do it, to 'confess Jesus Christ as Lord', and I believe that I am capable of, and definitely experience, what is called 'communion' with Him. I am inclined, I think honestly, to assent to the Virgin Birth, though I am pretty clear that it ought not to be in the creed, because it fastens attention on the wrong point. But it is hard to be really honest![19]

This was an unusual and uncomfortable state for Temple to find himself in. As one of life's great enthusiasts he was used to being very positive about all that interested him. But here he was caught by a cleft stick of convictions: on the one side his philosophical beliefs suggesting that the virgin birth and bodily resurrection of Christ should not be regarded as foundational to the Christian faith, and on the other side the belief he should offer himself to a kind of ministry which required his assent to such doctrines. He was used to being emphatic about his beliefs but now he did not know what to think. He took time to decide what to do, talking with friends and consulting with colleagues. But by January 1906, he reached the point where he thought he could proceed to ordination and he wrote to the Bishop of Oxford, Francis Paget, asking to be sponsored. He included some statements of what he believed but, dangerously, wrote, 'I am very conscious that my opinions are still subject to considerable change. In the statements I sent I stated definitely conclusions to which I am led by very slight preponderance of argument in some cases.'[20]

He was not prepared for Paget's response of 3 February 1906. The bishop, a high churchman who was not normally unsympathetic with attempts to marry Christian doctrine with modern ways of thinking, quoted this statement back to Temple and put a road block in his path:

> Weighing these words I have to say, with all respect, and with sorrow, and anxiety lest I may be judging amiss, that I could not take the responsibility of ordaining to the Ministry of the Church of England,

and sending forth as a teacher in its Name, one who, in regard to those two main points of history which I believe to be essential to, inextricable from our Creed, stands on such uncertain, precarious, unsteady ground.[21]

It must have taken some courage on Paget's part to say this to a son of an Archbishop of Canterbury who, in so many other ways, was brilliantly qualified for ordination. But say it he did and, perhaps for the first time in his life, Temple found that things were not going the way he expected. He wrote to his friend John Stocks that it was 'a most tremendous disappointment I confess'. The same letter also shows Temple writing with honesty that 'there are nasty elements in my disappointment – including the annoyance of a frustrated ambition to hear my sermons praised! ... But I had hoped to do useful work as a parson, and thought my gifts (!) peculiarly suited to that kind of work.'[22] He resigned himself to reforming the church 'from the outside' as an Oxford philosopher. This letter shows Temple growing in self-awareness.

During the following summer he wrote about the church in ways that recalled his undergraduate letters quoted above, his criticisms of it remaining undimmed:

> More and more I come to regard 'Churchiness' as a survival of the useless: it was necessary once; without the Dogmatism and ecclesiasticism of the early mediaeval church the whole of Christianity would have gone into smoke. But the walls built to protect now only confine and cramp, and should be pulled down.[23]

Temple added, ruefully, that 'it is better not to try a movement [of reform] outside the Church, but inside it. [But] If the Church turns one out [of its ministry] one must go on outside.' He would have to put to one side his assumption that his future lay through ordination.

Another door opens

But other things were happening in Temple's life while he was at Queen's. This was through one of the most formative relationships of his life, the friendship with Albert Mansbridge, the founder of the Workers' Education Association (WEA).

He met Mansbridge through his school and Balliol friend R. H. Tawney, the future historian and author of *Religion and the Rise of Capitalism*. Temple and Tawney had stayed together in the Oxford houses in the

East End of London where they were inducted into the harsh realities of life in the slums. Tawney stayed for long periods at Toynbee Hall and developed a close involvement in the newly established Labour Party. He persuaded Temple to attend the first national conference of the WEA in Oxford in 1905. The association was founded by the Co-operative Wholesale Society (the Co-op) and the idea was that it would be very different from previous university-led initiatives (in which the workers had only to turn up at classes provided for them). This time the workers and university teachers would be equal partners in engaging in education. The initiative and planning would come from the workers' side, the academic teaching from the university side. According to Tawney it was all to be based on the recognition in

> the working-class movement that if it is to solve its own problems, mobilise its own forces, and create a social order more in conformity with its own ideals, it must attend to the education of its members with the same deliberation and persistence which it has brought to the improvement of their economic position.[24]

Albert Mansbridge was the son of a carpenter in Gloucester and had to leave school at the age of 14 because his father could not afford school fees. He was self-taught and, after moving to London, was accepted into evening classes at King's College. He believed passionately in opening up education to ordinary people and founded a number of associations in Britain and around the world to enable this. For Temple, the young philosophy don from Oxford, Mansbridge was an inspiration, opening a door into the vivid world of the self-improving working classes in the hard years before the founding of the welfare state. When Temple met him he was an employee of the Co-op and it was through his vision, energy and perseverance that the WEA came into being and eventually succeeded. Through negotiation, persuasion and inspiration, Mansbridge was able to get representatives of the universities and the WEA to come together on a joint advisory committee to plan and supervise an educational programme for workers. His vision and his ability to reach across the bitter class divisions of Edwardian England deeply affected Temple, who later said, 'As a personal matter ... he invented *me*.'[25] This is a very revealing statement, showing a decisive step in Temple's journey, the journey into service that began when he was an undergraduate. Mansbridge touched the core of who Temple was.

Temple, in turn, was welcomed into the WEA by Mansbridge and its members and he placed himself at their disposal. He lectured around the country, speaking, for example, in Sheffield City Hall on 'the philosophic conception of liberty'. He took on committee work, being the co-secretary with Mansbridge of the tutorial classes committee. He wrote articles for its journal *The Highway* and, in 1908, was elected its first president, an honour he regarded as the greatest in his life. Temple was re-elected as president every year until 1924.

All of this was important in so many ways. Iremonger points out that except for the butler at Fulham and Lambeth and his 'scouts' at Balliol and Queen's, he had hardly spoken to anyone from the working classes till he joined the WEA. He had had no experience, for example, of the ordinary kind of home visiting undertaken by a parish priest. Nor had he yet lived in an industrial environment. Tawney later described the difference the WEA made to Temple:

> The 'We and They' complex, which is so marked even among the most virtuous members of the privileged classes, might have clung to him as a habit, even though he knew it to be damnable in principle. It could not survive continuous co-operation with colleagues whose educational interests he shared, but whose experience of life was quite different from his own.[26]

The contact with Mansbridge and the WEA was Temple's emancipation: it brought him into a wider, harsher but more vivid world where he rediscovered his own calling to the cause of social reform. It also formed the way he thought this reform should proceed, for his experience of the WEA showed him that the majority were not wanting to overturn society but to widen access to the material and cultural riches previously enjoyed by the few, a widening of their availability to all members of society for an equality of opportunity. As far as education was concerned, for example, reform should involve extending to the majority the kind of education he had received at Oxford. In a presidential address to the WEA at their Oxford summer school in 1912 Temple spelled this out:

> For it is the WEA which has understood more definitely than any other body I am aware of, that what it finds of supreme value in the great centres of education [such as the ancient universities] is the spirit of the place rather than the instruction: and those of us who have received, or have been in a position to receive, the best that Oxford can give, and those of us who have had just a taste of her treasures in the Summer School, will agree that Oxford does more for us than any lectures do. But while we say that, we need also to insist on a greater energy and efficiency, a greater and more living contact with the world of to-day in some, at least, of the centres of the old traditional type.[27]

Throughout his life Temple would work hard to facilitate this living contact across society, to break down barriers and build community though fellowship and service.

New opportunities

In the meantime, he continued with his lecturing and had short stays at the Bermondsey Medical Mission in the docklands of London, assisting the resident doctor with his medical and missionary work. He also became involved with the Student Christian Movement from 1907 onwards, attending their summer conferences. At one gathering, attended by 800 students from a wide range of churches, he heard Henry Scott Holland, the Dean of St Paul's, address the conference. He wrote that 'the thing that really lives with me is Scott Holland's extraordinary oration on the power of Christ to regenerate society here or anywhere else'. It seems that Scott Holland, who combined an inspiring radical political commitment with an orthodox Christian faith, had an important formative influence on Temple at this time. Iremonger suggests that Holland guided him to the conviction that 'the Catholic Faith does not consist of a number of separate articles or formulae, but is a coherent whole. It is one structure.' So, Holland's argument ran, if there were aspects of the faith that you knew by experience to be true, the 'intervening' ones could be accepted, even taken for granted, just because they belong to the integrity of the whole.[28] It seems that between 1906 and 1908 Temple's own Christian thinking moved in this direction, away from the philosopher's analytic approach to the theologian's integrative approach, accepting and then seeking to interpret the faith as a whole.

Charles Gore was also an influence. Gore was a leader of the Anglo-Catholic wing of the Church of England and the founder of a religious community, the Community of the Resurrection, in 1889. At this point in his life, he was bishop of the diocese of Birmingham. Temple described Gore as one 'from whom I have learnt more than from any other now living of the spirit of Christianity, and to whom more than any other (despite great differences) I owe my degree of apprehension of its truth'.[29] It seems likely that Gore helped Temple overcome his earlier doubts about the virgin birth and the bodily resurrection of Christ and allowed him to embrace an orthodox understanding of the creeds. Archbishop Michael Ramsey later also suggested that Temple owed his 'theological coherence' to Gore.[30] This influence is notable given the differences in their churchmanship, with Temple standing in the centre rather than within Anglo-Catholicism. They were also very different personalities.

A. E. Baker recounts the story of Gore and Temple walking away from a meeting at Church House in London. The meeting had had to be adjourned because Gore, not for the first time, had lost his temper. Temple was his usual genial, smiling self and Gore remarked bitterly, 'I have a vile temper. It is a terrible thing to have a bad temper.' But then, looking at his companion's smile, he added, 'But it is not so bad as having a good temper.'[31]

By the middle of 1908, Temple was again ready to approach a bishop about ordination. This time he wrote to Randall Davidson, the current archbishop of Canterbury, who had the right to ordain academics outside the diocesan structures. Temple went to see him and, afterwards, described Davidson as being 'the essence of kindness and sanity – without a glimmer of inspiration'. But this depressing impression was not corroborated by Davidson's actions: he decided that Temple should be ordained and undertook to square the circle with Bishop Paget of Oxford. There followed an unfailingly polite and painstaking correspondence between the two, during which Temple had to make another visit to Davidson.[32] Paget at first refused to give his blessing to the proposal. Davidson wrote again and this time informed Paget that he would ordain Temple. Rank, it seems, was being pulled. Paget at this point gave his unqualified blessing to the proposal.

Temple could at last sit the exams for ordination and he was made a deacon by Davidson in Canterbury Cathedral in December 1908, and a priest during the same month in 1909. It was the end of the beginning of his ordained ministry.

His ordination also launched his publishing career. In his deacon's year he prepared and delivered a set of addresses to the Student Christian Movement in London. They were published in 1910 in a volume aptly named (for him) *The Faith and Modern Thought*, his first book. In those lectures he spoke about the grounds for believing in God, the place of revelation in the believer's life, and the historic basis for Christianity. At the point in the argument where he describes the place of Christ in God's purposes, a question naturally arises about his views on the virgin birth and the bodily resurrection of Christ. These were the credal beliefs that had caused him some soul-searching and grief in 1905 and 1906: how does he handle them now?

The virgin birth was not mentioned: it would not be until he was a parish priest in London, in 1915 or 1916, that he would come to a definite belief in that, during a symphony concert at the Queen's Hall. But in the lectures the resurrection was given some prominence:

If we are to be on sure ground in taking [Christ] as the revelation of the Divine, it is necessary that the Divine Power should be seen clearly co-operating with Him, carrying Him through His ultimate self-surrender, and bringing Him out victorious. We need the Resurrection.[33]

The resurrection, therefore, was now central to Temple's thinking. But what of the bodily resurrection of Jesus? At this point his thinking was not quite so emphatic. Assuming a Platonic distinction between body and spirit, Temple wrote that after the resurrection

> ... what matters is that the Lord was alive. As far as I can see it does not matter very much what became of His Body. I do not doubt that His Body was in some way risen and glorified; but if anybody finds this incredible, that need not prevent him from believing in the reality of the Lord's Resurrection. That the Lord was alive seems to me certain.[34]

Paget would probably have found this position still too uncertain, precarious and unsteady. Temple had moved, but not far enough. The church, though, in the person of Archbishop Davidson, had also moved towards Temple, and the result had been his ordination. Temple was still only teaching what he himself could believe with honesty and integrity, but for the church it was now enough.

The trauma of being turned down by Paget resulted in Temple's inner growth in a number of ways. It gave him a rare experience of failure. It led him to further reflection on the Christian faith and to being open to the influence of Scott Holland, resulting in a more integrated understanding of that faith. It led, also, to a growth in self-awareness. It must have also increased his understanding and sympathy with others who had experienced failure (as a diocesan bishop he would later be very lenient with wayward clergy). But it did not result in him abandoning his passionate concern for restating the Christian faith in intellectually persuasive terms for the time. *The Faith and Modern Thought* shows that this ambition was still very much alive and, as we shall see, it would provide the motivating force behind his subsequent and influential teaching ministry. Meanwhile his contact with Albert Mansbridge and involvement with the WEA fundamentally affected him and pointed the way forward for Temple's own future work.

The years at Queen's, then, had offered both challenge and opportunity. Having heard a call and developed a passionate sense of vocation, and then having experienced the disappointment of being turned down for ordination, Temple showed humility in accepting this roadblock and pursuing other avenues especially in teaching. He also was open to and glad of the formative influence of Mansbridge and the WEA. Without such humility and openness it is hard to imagine his leadership developing in the way it did.

Notes

1 British Pathé, 'Archbishop Of Canterbury Enthroned (1942)', *YouTube*, 13 April 2014, www.youtube.com/watch?v=SOsSjVvGvRY, accessed 8 March 2022. See also the British Council film 'Message from Canterbury', made in 1943 and including Temple preaching from the pulpit of Canterbury Cathedral. Temple includes a powerful call for post-war reconstruction in the sermon: https://film.britishcouncil.org/resources/film-archive/message-from-canterbury.

2 F. A. Iremonger, *William Temple, Archbishop of Canterbury: His Life and Letters*, London: Oxford University Press, 1948, p. 5.

3 The affectionate way in which Frederick Temple regarded his sons is also shown in Peter Hinchliff, *Frederick Temple, Archbishop of Canterbury, A Life*, Oxford: Clarendon Press, 1998, pp. 162–5.

4 Quoted in Duncan Forbes, *The Liberal Anglican Idea of History*, Cambridge: Cambridge University Press, pp. 66–8.

5 Iremonger, *William Temple*, pp. 18–19.

6 Edward Caird, *Lay Sermons and Addresses delivered in the Hall of Balliol College*, Glasgow: Wentworth Press, pp. 70–1. For an overview of Green and Caird's religious thought, see Peter Hinchliff, 'Cut Loose from History: British Idealism and the Science of Religion', in *God and History: Aspects of British Theology 1875–1914*, Oxford: Clarendon Press, 1992.

7 In 'Robert Browning', an essay read out at Balliol, 1904, reprinted in William Temple, *Religious Experience*, Cambridge: James Clarke and Co., 1958, p. 33.

8 Temple, 'Robert Browning', p. 51.

9 William Temple, *Mens Creatrix*, London: Macmillan, 1917, p. vii.

10 See William Temple, *Plato and Christianity*, London: Macmillan, 1916.

11 Iremonger, *William Temple*, p. 499.

12 Iremonger, *William Temple*, p. 43.

13 Iremonger, *William Temple*, p. 98.

14 Iremonger, *William Temple*, p. 98.

15 Iremonger, *William Temple*, pp. 98–9.

16 Iremonger, *William Temple*, p. 100.

17 Iremonger, *William Temple*, pp. 102–3.

18 Iremonger, *William Temple*, p. 100.

19 Iremonger, *William Temple*, p. 106.

20 Iremonger, *William Temple*, p. 109.

21 Iremonger, *William Temple*, p. 109.

22 Iremonger, *William Temple*, p. 112.

23 Iremonger, *William Temple*, p. 114.

24 Iremonger, *William Temple*, p. 75.

25 Iremonger, *William Temple*, p. 77.

26 Iremonger, *William Temple*, p. 88.

27 Iremonger, *William Temple*, p. 83.

28 Iremonger, *William Temple*, pp. 125–6.

29 Iremonger, *William Temple*, p. 488.

30 James Carpenter, *Gore: A Study in Liberal Catholic Thought*, London: The Faith Press, 1960, p. 9 footnote 11.

31 A. E. Baker, *William Temple and His Message*, London: Penguin, 1946, p. 98. Paul Avis sums up the contrast between them in this memorable way: for Temple 'the glass was always half, and more than half, full (not half, and more than half, empty, as it typically was for Bishop Gore).' Avis, 'William Temple: Pioneer and Pillar of Christian Unity', *Ecclesiology*, 12 October 2020, brill.com/view/journals/ecso/16/3/article-p401_401.xml?language=en.

32 The letters are reprinted in Iremonger, *William Temple*, pp. 115–21.

33 William Temple, *The Faith and Modern Thought*, London: Macmillan, 1910, pp. 76–7.

34 Temple, *The Faith and Modern Thought*, pp. 79–80.

2

To break the mould or conform?

A question still needed to be answered: what was William Temple going to do with his life? He was ordained and passionately committed to campaigning on various fronts, to teaching and writing and to supporting the work of the WEA, but what was his daytime job going to be? The next decade of his life shows him taking up a curiously mixed set of jobs in response to this challenge. Once again, a narrative of smooth progress and ascent through the hierarchy of the church does not capture what was going on. We must look more closely and trace the contours of something more complex.

Distracted headmastering

Temple's upbringing and years at Oxford seemed to create two possible trajectories for his career. On the one hand, his privileged childhood, schooling and university education created one set of expectations among those around him and within his own mind. His moving from undergraduate life at Balliol to the lectureship at Queen's College conformed very well to such expectations. His intellectual interests in philosophy and literature and music were of a piece with them, as was his ordination as a deacon and priest within the Church of England. The expected course for such a talented and promising young man, following the revered example of his father, and previous archbishops such as Archibald Campbell Tait, would have been to become a headmaster of one of the prestigious public schools and then move on to being a bishop or other senior cleric within the established church.

But, on the other hand, Temple had discovered different ambitions within himself. He had become very critical of his church, accusing it of hypocrisy and regarding it as doing more harm than good within the nation. He had become offended and angered by the conditions in which ordinary people were living at that time and he wanted to do something about that. Finally, he had become critical of the way the Christian faith was being understood and taught and he believed that an intellectually rigorous reconstruction of belief was needed. Then, as we have just seen, Temple came into contact with the Workers' Education Association which gave him contact with independently minded working people but also showed him that his presence and contribution within that movement was wanted and valued. The possibility of a campaigning ministry had opened up to him, one that would sometimes bring him into conflict with the church establishment and he felt drawn towards this.

The struggle between these two trajectories was seen in the trauma of his being refused ordination by Paget. His upbringing and desire to follow his father had made him offer himself for ordination but his radical ambitions had made him rethink the Christian faith in an honest and rigorous way, and this had led him to state his beliefs in a way which Paget found too uncertain. When Paget refused to sponsor Temple we saw how deeply disappointed he was. Other young men might have reacted differently, seeing such a refusal as a release and an opportunity to follow other ambitions. Temple did not find it resolved anything: the conflict was within his own being.

Now, at the point in his life where he *had* been ordained and must decide which way to go, we can see the conflict reappearing. He learned that the governors of Repton School, a well-known public school near Burton-on-Trent, were to elect a new headmaster and that some thought that he should stand. Here was an opportunity to follow in his father's footsteps, not to Rugby School but to one very similar. His first response was to visit the school and weigh it all up. But, just before the election, he wrote to the outgoing head that he believed he should stay where he was in Oxford: 'I am sure I am meant to go on for a time as at present ... I must ask you not to bring my name before the Governors to-morrow.'[1] His friends were also advising him not to go to Repton but, if he was to move, to go to a parish in the East End of London, which would be a more radical move for him.

On his way to Australia, where he was to lecture to a number of Student Christian Unions, he heard that he had nevertheless been elected! He was now in a quandary. Those closest to him had advised him to stay where he was. His ambitions lay in a direction very different to running public schools. But the 'establishment path' was opening up to him and he felt its pull. He was given a deadline by which to reply. Twenty years later, speaking at a mission to Oxford University, he described how he came to the decision:

> having weighed up the question as carefully as I could – and we must always do that – and having come to no conclusion at all, I began at eight o'clock in the evening to say my prayers, and for three hours,

without a pause, I tried to concentrate all my desires on knowing clearly what was God's Will for me. I do not know how those three hours went; they did not seem very long; but when eleven o'clock struck I knew perfectly well what I had got to do, and that was to accept; and I have never had a shadow of doubt since that it was right.[2]

The impressive commitment with which Temple came to this decision indicates it was the right one. However, interestingly, the time at Repton was not a success. Even during the month when Temple took up the post he was writing to his brother that he doubted whether headmastering was really his line.[3] When he wrote to a friend explaining why he had accepted the post he did not say that the main reason was the running of a school or the desire to teach boys but, rather, the opportunity for furthering his views and hopes for English education through the Headmasters' Conference.[4] Such an ambition would take him out of the school rather than into it. And then, once he had arrived, everyone was expecting great changes in the running of the place. To the previous head he had written that the public schools 'seemed to me to reproduce our class-divisions in accentuated form, and that I should hope, after learning the ropes, to find ways of moving towards a system which would tend to diminish them'.[5] The teachers came to expect a minor revolution but nothing seemed to happen once he was in post. Sunday afternoon piano recitals were introduced, new hymns were sung at the chapel services and an attempt was made to introduce a house-tutor system, but the teachers opposed that idea and it was dropped. As term followed term it became apparent there was to be no revolution after all. Temple later explained that he had learned that institutions should be run on their own lines or else be scrapped – they could not be turned in new directions and run with the same power as before.[6] As time went on, Temple seemed to be away from the school more and more with speaking and preaching engagements elsewhere and writing essays for the volume *Foundations* (on which more below). Finally, by the time he left the school it was clear that the place had not been prospering under his headship. There was 'a fearful crop of failures' among the students, and Temple admitted that while he may have been good for the more mature boys he was 'not good with the general ruck'.[7] After just two years and three months in the job, the Archbishop of Canterbury, Davidson, asked him to be rector of St Margaret's Westminster, with an attached canonry at Westminster Abbey. Temple had little hesitation in accepting the post, though when it was discovered that a canon was required to have been a priest for at least six years he had to withdraw. He returned to Repton, but only for another year and a half.

In the light of all of this we could ask: why had Temple been led to Repton? One answer may be that he was purposely led into a cul-de-sac. The example of his father had been a powerful influence and had resulted in the son going to the same school (Rugby) and same college (Balliol). It had also placed headmastership in his path, for his father had been a distinguished headmaster of Rugby. William may have needed to discover that following the footsteps of his father was *not* the way forward for his career and that he needed to discover his own path. The undistinguished time at Repton will have shown him the need to be his own person.[8]

A roving rector

What, then, was his path? In a circular letter to the staff at Repton he described his reasons for leaving the school and taking up an appointment as Rector of St James' Church, Piccadilly, a well-endowed parish in the West End of London. The letter, inauspiciously, does not suggest that the reason for moving was the call to parish ministry but something else entirely:

> The reason that has chiefly weighed with me is this: during the last year I have been drawn more and more into the current of general Church politics and have felt wholly unable to resist; I have been made a member of three new Committees whose work is of central and urgent importance. But my work here has prevented my doing for those Committees the work which was really called for, while the interest of the problems with which they are concerned has drawn my attention some-what seriously away from school and its needs. I trust that the school has not yet suffered from this, but it would suffer before long. I have therefore felt bound to accept the offer of a position where I can respond to the claims made upon me without feeling that my primary duty is being neglected. Of the feelings to which this decision gives rise in myself I will not now attempt to speak.[9]

To accept a parish incumbency because it will provide a base from which to work outside the parish does not suggest Temple had found the role he was searching for. He was clearly more interested in national church affairs than in any more locally-based expression of ministry and this indicates that he would not be at St James' for very long.

Nor was he. Just over three years later he was moving to another post. And while he was at St James', he did not enter into parish ministry with any great enthusiasm. With the exception of his preaching, his biographer reports that he 'was not the stuff of which parish priests are made'.[10] He was not good at small talk with strangers, he had little experience of the mundane difficulties and worries of ordinary people and he did not enjoy home visiting around the parish. In this respect, St James' did not prove too demanding as there were relatively few homes in a mainly commercial area of London; added to this he had two curates and a parish worker who could carry out the 'routine' work of the parish. It was clear that being a parish priest was not his vocation and because Britain was now at war with Germany his kind of reasoned presentation of the Christian faith from the pulpit was not likely to make the impact it otherwise would. Temple's search for the role which would be the right fit for his gifts needed to continue.

His gout recurred at this time, as well. In a letter to a friend, he described how his doctor was encouraging him to lose weight and to hold his body

> in the right position. I believe in him because, after looking at me for a moment, he said 'Of course every time you take a lot of exercise, you are making your stoutness worse' – which is quite true. My fattening periods have always been those when I took most exercise.[11]

But he remained 'stout' for the rest of his life and his gout remained a recurrent and painful companion to the end.

Nevertheless, unsatisfactory as they were, the years at St James' were also very creative and formed the foundation of much that followed. Living at the heart of the capital and near the centre of national life, Temple could not avoid engaging with some of the difficult issues of the First World War. He could not avoid, for example, speaking on the morality of the war and the role of the churches within the nation. He was not a pacifist and believed that Britain had a duty to be involved in the war in Europe. But nor would he, unlike many clergy at the beginning of the war, act as a recruiting sergeant for the armed forces. Unlike his diocesan bishop in London, Arthur Winnington-Ingram, he did not preach 'war sermons' designed to generate a kind of jingoistic patriotism that would make young men join the armed forces. Instead, he provided thoughtful navigation on some of the key moral challenges.

One example is the way he responded to despair over the horror and waste at the front. Some were beginning to question how the God who allowed this to take place could also be a God of love. Temple gave voice to this in a 1916 sermon at St James': 'the blow fell, and many were much shaken in their belief in any God of love; and those who had never held any such belief asked how, in face of the events of these days, we could without hypocrisy maintain such a belief'.[12] There were two typical responses: one, found in many preachers, was simplistically to equate the coming of the war with the judgement of God and that the suffering and carnage was specially sent by God as punishment for the wrongdoings of Europe. The other was to abandon belief in God altogether. Temple did neither. In his sermon he showed how it was possible to hold together the belief that the war was caused by human actions rather than by God's intervention, with the view that there was nevertheless an element of divine punishment in what was happening. He described how he had heard people 'during this war speak about it as if God had deliberately caused the war in order to punish mankind for certain sins'. He reported that they usually named drunkenness or impurity or Sabbath-breaking as the sins in question. He continued,

> I venture to say that is sheer superstition. We can trace the actual causes of the war, and we know quite well that its causes were in human wills, and we are not at liberty to say that God intervened in the history of the world to inflict anguish and pain by means of the war as punishment for certain sins that have no relation to it. How could the war grow out of drunkenness? All the way through [the] Gospel of St. John we are taught that a judgement of God is not a deliberate act of His intervening in the world to make guilty people suffer, but an automatic product of His Presence and Revelation.[13]

So the war was not a deliberate judgement of God upon the world. Nevertheless, it was a judgement upon the sin of nations in an indirect way:

> The sin which led immediately to the outbreak of war we may believe to be mainly in one nation, but the root is to be found among all peoples, and not only among those who are fighting, but neutral peoples just as much. The punishment for that sin comes through the moral order which God has set up in the world, an order which reacts upon those who break it. So that if a man persists in doing what is contrary to the will of God, in doing evil which he has himself recognized as such, the consequences of his sin will at last overtake him. God has no pleasure in the infliction of that penalty, the penalty is rather a warning against indulging in the evil course at all. The pleasure of God is in men's salvation; men's salvation is His purpose.[14]

Through all the shattering carnage and seeming hopelessness it might still be possible, therefore, to believe in a loving creator who has given to the world a moral order, an order intended to lead to the salvation of all people. Human nature, in this order, has the freedom to accept or reject it, and the First World War, for Temple, was a consequence of a massive rejection of that order. But the possibility of conforming to the moral order and finding the grace of salvation was still open. In these few words, then, Temple was able to outline a realistic yet inspiring Christian ethical viewpoint that would lie at the heart of his leadership in the country in later years.

Temple described the war years as 'harder days than we had known' and he spoke of needing 'the strong authority of the Judge of men ... the Christ of the New Testament, the Christ whom we had forgotten, the Christ who rules whether we would have it or not'.[15] And for him the place where he found this Christ was, above all, John's Gospel. Beginning with the congregation at St James' and continuing with ordinands at Manchester, York and Canterbury, and with other gatherings of clergy and laity, he began to speak about and reflect on this gospel, meditating on its obscurities and finally publishing his *Readings in St John's Gospel* in 1939 and 1940 (see Chapter 10). The earliest form of his readings comes from the years at St James'.

He also edited a Church of England weekly newspaper, *The Challenge*, from July 1915 to the autumn of 1918. This was a paper dedicated to expressing 'the challenge offered by the cross of Christ to worldliness and indifference'. It claimed to be independent of all party matters in church and state, though others would describe it as having a liberal tone in its theology, in its general outlook and in its desire to see church reform bringing in a greater role for the laity in church affairs. He would write leaders while sitting in the board meetings of the paper, or in railway station waiting rooms, or in the early hours after addressing meetings around the country.

Temple advocated the right to conscientious objection through the pages of *The Challenge*. When considering the question of whether such objection to joining the armed forces was legitimate, he wrote that, 'The individual must, of course, follow his own conscience, which means simply his deliberate judgement with regard to the right course for him to follow.' And when there is conflict with the will of the state, 'what is to happen? First and foremost, there should be on each side absolute respect for the other. We must recognise the fallibility of the human conscience not only in the other man, but also in ourselves.'[16] Following on from this he became critical of many tribunals that adopted a contemptuous approach to those objecting to conscription.

The Challenge idealistically advocated total prohibition of alcohol for the duration of the war, but it also called for a living wage for every worker, for educational reform so that every child in the country would benefit, and for church reform. One member of the board described the paper as a somewhat amateurish affair, with none of its managing group knowing anything about the technique of journalism. But they 'plunged' along and Temple's editorship gave the paper a sense of direction and theological weight.

He was also heavily involved with the National Mission of 1916, an unsuccessful campaign of meetings and church services to attract the general population back to church. He continued to support the WEA and was involved with the YMCA, the British Association (as chairman of the education section) and much else. The roving and breathless character of his life at this time (and more or less of the rest of his life) is seen in a letter to his brother:

Here are my activities of the last fortnight. Oct. 8, Two sermons here. 9, Speech at Tottenham. 10, To Southwell. 11, To Nottingham: Sermon and Speech. 12, To Manchester: two sermons. 13, Three sermons in Manchester. Back to London. 14, Demonstration in Hyde Park. 15, Two sermons here. 16, Variety of Committees. 17, Three Committees. 18, To Ludlow: two sermons. 19, To Bridgnorth: two addresses – then to Hereford, and three addresses there. 20, To London: visited Nana for tea. 21, Quiet Day for teachers: 3 sermons. 2, Sermon here in morning: at Christ's Hospital (Horsham) in evening. 23, Two committees … So life is rather a strain![17]

These years also saw the death of his mother, who had kept home for him in Oxford, Repton and in London. She died, at the age of 69, early in the morning on Good Friday in 1915. Temple was due to lead the Three Hours Service that day and was determined that his parishioners should be allowed to keep the day without being distracted by what had just happened. So the news was kept within the house and, despite having just lost his closest companion, he led the service as planned. He later described himself as 'numbed' by the blow. His biographer describes the year that followed as the loneliest in his life.

During the following year, however, he was able to get to know Frances Anson, who worked at *The Challenge* offices. Temple's biographer says very little about his close personal relationships and we can only conjecture about this side of his life. When Iremonger reaches the point in the story where Temple and Frances Anson become engaged he seems more interested in the connections between her family and his family than in the actual relationship of the couple. All we are told is that Temple wrote to Mrs Anson asking for permission to marry her daughter and that they were engaged in May 1916. But Temple's own words to his brother after the engagement hint at rather more: 'I thought I should be excited, and of course I was before the final interview; but from that moment there has been simply a sense of floating on a quite calm sea of contentment and happiness – with the water deliciously warm so that one need never get out.'[18]

On the night before the marriage Temple sat late into the night finishing his book *Mens Creatrix*. He and Frances were married on 24 June 1916 in St James', with an address from the Archbishop of Canterbury, Davidson. On the honeymoon, Temple read aloud his favourite Browning poems to his new wife, but he also suffered a bad attack of hay fever (the cottage was opposite a hayfield in full flower). The holiday also included a visit to Repton School, where Temple preached, and to Alington School, where he also preached.

But his situation was not to remain as it was. What happened next in his career suggests that his radical ambitions were able to reassert themselves.

Campaigning for change

Temple was well aware that the National Mission of 1916 had largely failed in its objectives of re-converting the nation, and the reasons were not difficult to see: the war had shown the Church of England to be largely out of touch with the lives of the ordinary working people whose sons were now dying for their country in the trenches. If the gospel was to be heard the body proclaiming it would need to be reformed and many ancient abuses removed. There were remarkable anomalies in the way the church was run: a priest in one parish of 850 people received an income of over £6,000 a year while in a neighbouring parish another priest who ministered to 19,000 people received £400 a year, and other clergy received much less. A campaign was needed, to free the church from its identification with the anachronistic establishment of the past.

The Life and Liberty movement arose out of the recognition that if the church was to be reformed it needed self-government. Up to this point in the Church of England there had been no general synod or church assembly, no parochial church councils or electoral rolls, let alone deanery or diocesan synods. All changes in ecclesiastical law and practice had had to be passed by parliament and that institution was preoccupied with many other matters. But parliament would need to be persuaded to relinquish its control over the internal affairs of the church so that clergy and lay people could themselves take on the responsibility of running their own church. Life and Liberty was started by a small group of clergy who wished to generate enough support from within the church to persuade the bishops, and the national government, of the need to enable this kind of change. Furthermore many of the group believed that if this ultimately required disestablishment, so be it.

Temple, along with H. R. L. (Dick) Shepperd, was part of the group that drew up plans for the movement and he became an active member of its council (though he did not believe in disestablishment). The real challenge arose when the other members asked him to become its full-time worker. This would mean resigning the comfortable living at St James', leaving the career ladder of the church, leaving the centrally-placed rectory from which he had done so much and taking on a temporary position that might cease after only a couple of years. He would also only receive a third of the income he had been receiving. Furthermore, he had just married and his wife had just created a home for both of them in Piccadilly.

On the other hand, as we have seen, he was still searching for the role that would use his specific gifts to the full. He believed in the mission of the church to the nation and in the need for the church to reform itself if it was to carry out that mission. He also believed that the Life and Liberty movement was the vehicle to achieve this. And so, at last, in November 1917, at the age of 36, he allowed the radical calling that he had received as a young man to take the lead and draw him out of the safety and comfort of his current position into the bracing uncertainty of campaign leadership.

Henry Scott Holland wrote to Temple that 'you have gone over the top!' But he added, 'It does everybody good. God bless you!' Charles Gore approved. But Archbishop Randall Davidson, his long-term mentor, was less than enthusiastic. Such a move for someone like Temple was unorthodox, even freakish, and Davidson could not really sympathize with the passion behind Life and Liberty: why was there this need to reform the church? And so the person who had been a watchful guardian over Temple's career, making sure that the son followed in the footsteps of the great father, now felt rebuffed. Temple, in other words, had finally cut loose from his upbringing.

The break with Davidson came fully into the open when the bishops' Representative Church Council, chaired by Davidson, failed to take action on a report recommending the introduction of self-government for the church. Temple and the council of Life and Liberty were exasperated. The chaplains in the forces, who were in direct contact with the very people the church was needing to win back, were almost in despair that the church authorities were not moving things forward. Temple, on behalf of the movement, wrote a letter of protest to the press saying that the delay to church reform was imposing 'a grievous strain on the loyalty of many who believe passionately in the Church, not as she now is, but as she has the power to become'. With a rhetorical flourish he continued,

> We are clear that the Church just now has her greatest and possibly her last opportunity of vindicating her Catholic and national character. But this can only be achieved by a struggle fierce and sustained, by a purging thorough and sincere, and by a summons such as many hoped might be issued during these days of war to dare anything, that the Will of God might be done, as in Heaven, so on earth.[19]

Davidson wrote back to Temple that his own difficulties in leading the church were now 'greatly augmented' by Temple's letter, and that he felt it hindered the cause which he and Temple were both trying to advance. He disagreed with Temple that the time was now right to push legislation for the church through parliament. The war effort was consuming all of the government's time and energy and it could not now think of church reform. The letter to the press could well stiffen 'convertible people into unconvertibleness'. The whole matter was a 'distress' to the archbishop.[20]

Temple was learning the cost of going his own way. This division with Davidson would have been distressing. But he was not to be deflected and his work for Life and Liberty began in earnest at the start of 1918, continuing until June the following year. It involved travelling to different towns and cities, meeting with clergy and local civic and business leaders, speaking at mass meetings in the evenings and meetings of the Life and Liberty council itself. Through all of it, Temple spoke about and argued for self-government for the church. He urged everyone he met to join the movement so that the church leaders and especially the bishops would push for an act of parliament to bring it about. He threw himself into the work with his usual energy and enthusiasm and, in the first nine months of 1918 travelled to Manchester, Huddersfield, Great Yarmouth, Bradford, Walsall, Lichfield, Birmingham, Liverpool, Grimsby, Louth and Cambridge. He secured the support of vice chancellors, archdeacons, free church ministers, many parochial clergy and C. P. Scott, the editor of the *Manchester Guardian*. In early 1919 he travelled to France and Belgium to secure the support of the troops stationed there. He also continued to edit *The Challenge*. And, last but not least, Temple led a delegation of Life and Liberty members to meet the two archbishops (Davidson and Cosmo Lang of York) and urge them to support reform. The meeting itself involved 80 members of the movement facing the two archbishops in the dining room at Lambeth Palace. Davidson's ever cautious manner meant that feelings began to run high among some members of the delegation and one member blurted out, 'The trouble with your Graces is, you're both Scotsmen.' Embarrassment swept through the room but Davidson remained unperturbed. He was, in fact, impressed by the strength of the delegation and, at last, came round to supporting the case for reform.[21]

The bishops' Representative Church Council now had to approve the various proposals before they could be sent to parliament for inclusion in an 'Enabling' act. It met in February 1919. There was to be a new church assembly that would administer the church but there was a question: should women be allowed to sit on it? The Dean of Westminster thought they should not. Temple argued that they should: 'were women not full members of the laity and in many parishes were they not the mainstay of the devotional life of the church?' The advice of women on all the issues the assembly would consider was 'in the highest degree desirable'. In the vote the council agreed with Temple.

The other issue concerned the church 'franchise'. Who was to be allowed to vote for representatives on the new church assembly? Should it just be 'communicants', or those who had been confirmed, or all the baptized? Bishop Charles Gore and Lord Hugh Cecil and others were in favour of the confirmation franchise, on the grounds that full incorporation into the body of Christ came through being a communicant after being confirmed. Temple spoke in favour of the baptismal franchise: he argued, as ecumenical dialogues in the second half of the twentieth century would also later argue, that all baptized persons were members of the church and that if they were excluded from voting they would feel excluded altogether from membership. The Council again agreed with Temple and accepted the principle of the baptismal franchise. Gore was upset and later resigned as Bishop of Oxford over this, among other issues. Temple in turn was grieved at this difference of opinion with another of his mentors and friends but, overall, was elated that the Church of England as a whole had agreed on a scheme for self-government. Davidson would now introduce the Enabling Bill to parliament in the summer. By Christmas 1919, with a little more campaigning from Life and Liberty and some astute manoeuvring by Davidson, it had become an Act of Parliament.

Life and Liberty was successful, then, in its primary objective. What was Temple to do now? He had left his incumbency at St James' to devote himself to this work and now someone else was the rector at that church. He was back with the old problem of needing to find a job. Various offers had come his way, including the principalship of a church college in Agra in India and the mastership of University College, Durham, but Davidson had stopped him going to Agra, arguing that his contacts with the Labour Movement (whose party he had joined in 1918) and the WEA made it 'imperative' that he should stay in the home church so that it should reap the benefits of his unique experience. The Durham job, he was advised, would involve him going to 'a small field' and both Gore and Davidson advised against it. The chaplaincy at his old college in Oxford, Balliol, was becoming vacant and Temple was tempted by that, though it would involve rather more academic study than he was now used to. Finally, a canonry at Westminster became vacant: this would allow Temple to continue to have a role and voice in the national church and this attracted him. What that role should be, though, was not so clear. He accepted the offer from the Prime Minister and wrote to his wife that Westminster would give

> what I think I most need after these three years of rushing about – and that is the opportunity and even duty to 'worship the Lord in the beauty of holiness'. I want (need) to renew depth in religious life, and the peace which goes with it, if I am to have anything to interpret to the world at all… Anyhow, I hope and believe this will [also] give us more time together in some degree of peace than Oxford would have done – at least in term. But there is a lot to pray about, and I had better begin.[22]

While at Westminster, Temple continued to work for Life and Liberty, helping with the advocacy needed to get the Enabling Bill through parliament. But his main work became the preaching and teaching duties of a canon and the results are seen in a volume of published sermons, *Fellowship with God* (1920). Through many of the sermons Temple argues that the fundamental fact about human life is that God, in his love, has entered into fellowship with humanity through the incarnation, so that human life may, in answering love, enter into fellowship with him. The social dimension of this relationship, implicit in the word 'fellowship', was all-important for Temple and provides a connection with his developing views on society and the state. But he argues that this response is not to take place through the practical life alone, but 'in the perfect blend' of the practical life with the devotional life.[23] Up to now he had neglected the devotional life in his campaigning work with Life and Liberty. At Westminster, he optimistically hoped to give more time to the devotional side of his own response to God.

But he was not allowed to remain at Westminster long. He was soon made an offer he could not refuse and one which removed any agonizing choices and the possibility of wrong decisions about which way to go. Sixteen months after arriving at the Abbey he received a letter from Lloyd George, the Prime Minister, asking him to become the next Bishop of Manchester. He was slightly dazed by the invitation and asked for time to think it over. He telephoned the archbishop who told him to accept the offer immediately. Davidson, it later transpired, was behind the whole idea anyway. Gore told Temple simply to 'Go'. He wrote the following day accepting the Prime Minister's invitation.

So now, in the year he turned 40, Temple's wandering from post to post came to an end. He would now live in one place and fulfil the duties of one very demanding job for more than just one or two years: he would be at Manchester for eight years. He would go north, to the second most populous diocese in the Church of England and seek to lead its clergy and people in the work of Christ.

His rise to significant leadership during his thirties was, then, far from straightforward. Even for someone with so many gifts there was no straightforward path to follow. At different points in his early life, at one moment through rejection by his diocesan bishop, at another through failing as a headmaster and needing to move on as quickly as possible, Temple had to learn that it was not enough and indeed not even possible to follow in the footsteps of his father. He must search for his own way forward and at certain moments break with the expectations of his upbringing, above all when he took on the leadership of a campaign to reform the church, a role that fulfilled one of the elements of his original calling. This strange decade, in some ways out of keeping with the rest of his life, was nevertheless important and formative in its own way and helped to consolidate one of the constituent elements of the leadership he would later provide, his strength of will.

But before looking at his time in Manchester, we must turn to the content of his teaching in the books of this decade, for this was a parallel and equally important expression of the Christian leadership that was developing in him and through him in these years.

Notes

1 F. A. Iremonger, *William Temple, Archbishop of Canterbury: His Life and Letters*, London: Oxford University Press, 1948, p. 133.

2 Iremonger, *William Temple*, pp. 134–5.

3 Iremonger, *William Temple*, p. 128.

4 Iremonger, *William Temple*, p. 134.

5 Iremonger, *William Temple*, p. 147.

6 Iremonger, *William Temple*, p. 148.

7 Iremonger, *William Temple*, p. 128.

8 John Kent sees Temple's lack of success as a headmaster as illustrating the weakness of the argument he was using in the quotation above to prove the reality of divine guidance (Kent, *William Temple: Church, State and Society in Britain 1880–1950*, Cambridge, 1992, pp. 183–4). But, as I have argued, it is possible he

was led to accept the post at Repton so as to discover that his father's path was not to be his path.

9 Iremonger, *William Temple*, p. 151.

10 Iremonger, *William Temple*, p. 168.

11 Iremonger, *William Temple*, p. 170.

12 Iremonger, *William Temple*, p. 175.

13 Iremonger, *William Temple*, pp. 173–4.

14 Iremonger, *William Temple*, pp. 174–5.

15 Iremonger, *William Temple*, p. 175.

16 'Freedom of Conscience', *The Challenge*, 103 (14 April 1916). See also no. 183 (26 October 1917) and no. 188 (30 November 1917). The last article upholds the right of conscientious objectors to vote in elections.

17 Iremonger, *William Temple*, pp. 190–1.

18 Iremonger, *William Temple*, p. 199.

19 Iremonger, *William Temple*, pp. 244–6.

20 Iremonger, *William Temple*, pp. 247–8.

21 Iremonger, *William Temple*, pp. 256–7.

22 Iremonger, *William Temple*, p. 265.

23 William Temple, *Fellowship with God*, London: Macmillan, 1910, p. vi.

3

Searching for common ground

The years 1910 to 1920 saw William Temple not only move from post to post but also saw him begin to offer intellectual leadership through a teaching ministry of speaking and writing, so beginning to fulfil one of the ambitions of his early calling, of restating the Christian faith in an intellectually credible way. This began with the first of a series of slim volumes of addresses, *The Faith and Modern Thought* of 1910, continued with two contributions to a major volume of theological essays, *Foundations* of 1912, and reached a culmination with his first major work of philosophical theology, *Mens Creatrix* of 1917.

But what kind of teaching was he providing? There is a well-known distinction between the traditional 'banking' approach to education in which the role of the teacher is to pour knowledge and understanding into the open vessel of the student's mind, building up a body of new knowledge which is then tested for use in the world, and a collaborative approach in which the teacher's role is to help students draw on the knowledge and understanding already available to them in their own context. In one the teacher is a kind of dispenser who imports knowledge into the minds of those who do not have it, whereas in the other the teacher is a cultivator who encourages and supports students as they draw and build on what they already possess.[1]

With Temple this is not a question about the method of his teaching, because it is very clear that the only way he taught was through preaching, lecturing and publishing books, not through facilitating interactive discussion. As a visiting preacher or speaker he was not given the opportunity to facilitate discussion apart from sometimes answering questions at the end of a talk. This is really a question about the content of what he said and wrote and especially about whether he was seeking to import a whole framework of presuppositions, principles and applications into the minds of his listeners and readers, or whether what he said was an exercise in collaborating with the presuppositions and principles that they already held, in order to build on them. Was his teaching all about challenging their worldview or was it all about inhabiting and then transforming their worldview? Was he, in other words, adopting the approach of an apologist who searches for common ground with his or her audience in order to seek and find Christian teaching within that, or was he more of an evangelist coming to announce a different way of thinking, to challenge that worldview and impart a new body of knowledge and understanding? Both approaches have their place in Christian tradition: which was Temple's?

Making a case for belief in God

While a lecturer at Queen's College, Oxford, and in the year that he was made a deacon by Randall Davidson, we have already seen how Temple was invited to deliver a set of lectures to the Student Christian Movement in London. His audience were students and other young people wrestling with the challenges to faith posed by scientific discoveries and the rise of scepticism in many parts of society. The lectures were well attended and there was a demand that they should be published. This took place in 1910 with the title *The Faith and Modern Thought*. It became a best-selling volume, being reprinted several times and established Temple as an up-and-coming voice in the church. It is worth giving some space to its opening pages because they reveal clearly and concisely the type of reasoned, respectful and humble leadership he provided not only in this book but in his teaching ministry in general.

As already mentioned, the modern reader needs to be prepared for the way in which Temple comes from an era of non-inclusive language and that his use of language reflects this, and also that he has a habit of capitalizing the first letter of key concepts in his argument. But, on the other hand, he begins his argument in a seemingly postmodern way, not with logical reasoning as the starting point but from the human experience of a spiritual reality, in particular of the experience of dependence upon God. He presents an example of faith seeking understanding. He does this by building understanding from two converging directions, a type of argumentation we will see him use again later. He begins with human experience:

Now the first evidence to the religious man of the existence of God is his own religious experience. No one who has had even a moment of such experience can afterwards quite ignore it; it will perpetually challenge his attention. He may, of course, find great difficulty in combining the fact which he seemed then to reach with all the other established facts of science and everyday life. It remains there as a problem; and as evidence it always has this peculiar perplexity about it, that it is incommunicable.

If another man says, 'I have not the faintest idea what you mean when you talk about communion with God', how can we explain it to him?[2]

Temple then clarifies what he means by this kind of experience:

But may I say immediately that by religious experience I do not mean an ecstasy or an extraordinary thing that happens to a few people here and there, but simply that impulse, which comes upon most people at some time, to throw oneself back upon a Power greater than oneself, and the sense, the perfectly sure sense, that that Power has received one and is supporting one. Numbers of people have felt something of that sort. It is a sense of self-abandonment and yet of safety; and that seems to demand, as I have said, further support from outside; and that support must be of a rigidly scientific character: nothing else will do.[3]

Temple's aim is provide the necessary 'scientific' or, more accurately, philosophical support that brings understanding to this experience. He is not, then, trying to win an argument with a sceptic and make that person change their mind, but coming alongside the person who has a sense of God and offer logical ways of understanding and supporting it.

Temple then discusses a number of attempts to provide such support, such as the argument for God's existence from causation, which states that for any object or experience there must exist something that caused it, going back to a first cause. He does not find this convincing and instead looks for a principle that will explain not just individual experiences or events but 'the whole series together'.[4] He then offers one of his favourite examples of this principle, with a vivid illustration of its explanatory power:

Now there is in our own experience already one principle which does answer the question, 'Why?' in such a way as to raise no further questions; that is, the principle of Purpose. Let us take a very simple illustration. Across many of the hills in Cumberland [the Lake District] the way from one village to another is marked by white stones placed at short intervals. We may easily imagine a simple-minded person asking how they came there, or what natural law could account for their lying in that position; and the physical antecedents of the fact – the geological history of the stones and the physiological structure of the men who moved them – give no answer. As soon, however, as we hear that men placed them so, to guide wayfarers in the mist or in the night, our minds are satisfied.[5]

Temple then applies this principle in a general way:

> ... the moment we agree with anyone that a thing is good it never occurs to us to ask why it should exist. There is no problem of the existence of good. Purpose is a principle which we have already gauged in our own experience and which, where it is applicable, gives a final answer to the question Why; and there is no other principle known, at any rate to me, that does give a final answer to the question, Why.[6]

He then applies this to the question in hand:

> But surely it is scientific, when you already have a principle capable of explaining the fact, at least to investigate and see what can be done with that principle. It is not as though we had to invent the term 'Purpose' to explain the fact of the world, as the old scientists invented Caloric to explain the fact of heat. Purpose exists in our everyday experience. It supplies an answer to our question. It is then scientific to accept that answer provisionally as a hypothesis.
>
> I believe that the effort to understand this Purpose is not so hopeless as it looks at first. Scientific principle requires us at least to take seriously the hypothesis of a Purpose in the world, and, therefore, a real Will behind the world.[7]

He then goes back to his starting point, which was the spiritual experience of dependence, and shows how that experience is now explained and justified by this kind of principle:

> It appears from the investigation of science, from investigation of the method of scientific procedure itself, that there must be a Will in which the whole world is rooted and grounded; and that we and all other things proceed therefrom; because only so is there even a hope of attaining the intellectual satisfaction for which science is a quest.

Temple has much more to say but these quotations show his style of reasoned argumentation, carefully building a case, clearly and logically, showing his philosophical method. But they also show a brevity that leads the reader on, and how his argument is supplemented with some memorable images, such as way-marking stones of the Lake District, to illustrate and support his argument. There is a freshness about these lectures.

Also it is clear on which side of the educational divide Temple is to be found. He is coming alongside his audience and readers, seeking out common ground by identifying common spiritual experience and the difficult questions that go with it, and then seeking to build understanding and meaning from there, a teaching that grows through collaboration with their outlook rather than by challenging and replacing it. Whether or not his argument convinces readers today is a secondary question. This first lecture in his first book shows very well the kind of teacher that Temple was becoming.

Explaining Christ

But what about the dogmas of Christian belief, which are based on revelation rather than reason and therefore, it seems, needing to be received from beyond our own outlook. How does Temple approach and explain these? Is he consistent with the above? His first significant attempt at this was in a volume of essays written by a group of Oxford scholars and published in 1912 as *Foundations*.

This compilation was subtitled 'A statement of belief in terms of modern thought'. It was written as a response to modern gains in scientific knowledge, such as the acceptance of the theory of evolution and the rise of the critical study of ancient documents and especially of the Bible. It was the third volume from Oxford-based scholars that attempted to do this: the first had been the controversial *Essays and Reviews* in 1861 and the second *Lux Mundi* in 1889. The writers, who included the biblical scholar B. H. Streeter and the theologian Walter Moberly, set themselves the task of re-examining and, if need be, restating the foundations of their belief 'in the light of the knowledge and thought of the day'. This clearly shows the volume attempting to be collaborative in the way described above.[8]

Ronald Knox, a conservative theologian who was about to become a Roman Catholic, wittily summed up the outcomes of the volume as 'How much will Jones swallow?' In other words, Christian belief was restated so as not to go beyond what Jones, 'a modern cultivated man', may find acceptable. The problem, for Knox, was that the 'modern cultivated man' was increasingly not finding any religious belief acceptable, so such an approach was bound to leave increasingly little on the table. Temple wrote a long and illuminating letter back to Knox.[9] The nub of what he wrote was this: 'I am not a spiritual doctor trying to see how much Jones can swallow and keep down: I am more respectable than that; *I am Jones himself asking what there is to eat.*'[10] In other words, Temple was making no apology for identifying himself with the modern mind in all its questionings. Knox, like many others who were more obviously orthodox (whether Catholic or Evangelical), as Adrian Hastings pointed out, had emphatically rejected the package of modern culture.[11] Temple and his fellow essayists were committed to standing within that modern culture as they expounded the Christian faith, to find common ground with it.

How did he do this? His main contribution was a long essay on the divinity of Christ. It was his first published theological exposition, drawing on John's Gospel as well as Idealist philosophy (on which more below), written in a fresh and confident style. He began with some philosophical background by accepting criticism of a traditional way of viewing God's relationship with the world, known as Deism, and of more recent versions of it nicknamed 'the God of the gaps':

> A hundred and fifty years ago it was generally supposed that God had made the world and then left it to behave according to laws He had imposed, interfering now and then by way of miracle; God acted, in short, here and there, now and then. But gradually science explained this or the other 'intervention,' and it seemed that the sphere of the Divine activity was being curtailed. At last men came to regard all events as instances of 'natural law' – and there seemed to many no need for the hypothesis of God at all.[12]

Temple does not challenge this emerging view but, interestingly, accepts it. His next move, with the help of John's Gospel, is to find God and Christ *within* it:

> But in coming to this belief they had really come to believe in the world as a single system governed by a single principle – which is essentially what was meant by [the Gospel of John's doctrine of] the Logos. Religion is learning again to claim all creation as the sphere of God's operation; He works not here and there, or now and then, but everywhere and always. Science has not curtailed His sphere; it has restored us to that belief in His omnipresent activity which we should never have let go.[13]

So Temple is presenting the belief that the universe is governed by an inclusive principle, an 'omnipresent activity', a purpose in all things.[14] This links with his argument above, that the principle of *purpose* can encompass and explain the way things are. He then draws out the implication that 'if the explanation of the world is a Purpose, that Purpose must be rooted in a Will'.[15] So this is how God is connected with the universe: it is all the expression of his purposive will.

The key move of the essay is then to use this philosophically-based concept of 'will' for understanding the nature of Christ and especially how Christ was divine as well as human. It does this by arguing that while the 'subjective function' of Christ's will is human, the content of his will – its purpose – is the same as the Father's: 'What we see Christ doing and desiring, that we thereby know the Father does and desires. He is the man whose will is united with God's ...'[16] Temple helpfully explains this with the following analogy: 'When two people have the same thought or the same purpose, there is a real sense in which they are "of one mind' or "of one will"; yet they are not simply merged in one another.' So, while Christ is a distinct human being, not somehow merged with the Father, nevertheless 'in content of heart and will Christ is identically one with God'.[17]

All of this shows, first, that Temple is using the philosophical think-ing of his day as the starting point to understand a key doctrine of the Christian faith, the divinity of Christ. This again shows a collaborative approach to teaching that faith. But second it shows that his conclusions were clearly orthodox. Whereas Streeter, for example, went some way to embracing Albert Schweitzer's questioning of the bodily resurrection of Christ, Temple in his essay did not question the doctrine of the incarna-tion. For him Christ was God, and this was not so much a question as an answer to many questions: 'The wise question is not "Is Christ Divine?" but, "What is God like?" And the answer to that is "Christ".'[18] Temple's contribution was notable because of the route he used to get to this point, a route through the philosophy of his day.

However, this essay could only provide a brief sketch of his position. When pressed on the question of the relation of Christ to the Father, Temple could only state that, 'It is clear that no final answer can be given until philosophy has provided us with a final account of Personality, both Human and Divine.'[19] He would attempt to provide such an account five years later in his first major book.

Philosophical common ground

Mens Creatrix (Creative Mind) was this book, a heady brew of philos-ophy, theology, poetry and political thought. It had been planned in 1908 when he had been lecturing in philosophy at Oxford and had been written in odd moments at Repton and in London. More than half of it, he admitted, was dictated in spare half-hours at St James', Piccadilly. Temple modestly described its 370 pages as 'a stimulus, if it may be so, to some real philosopher to do more adequately what I am only able to sketch out'. Nevertheless, the book was a serious contribution to philo-sophical enquiry. It aimed to show how the kinds of questions raised by contemporary philosophy, especially the philosophies of knowledge, art and ethics, can be answered by religion, which is described as the culmination of science, art and morality, and in particular by the incarnation of Christ. In the prologue he described the book in the following dramatic way:

> We shall watch the Creative Mind of Man as it builds its Palace of Knowledge, its Palace of Art, its Palace of Civilisation, its Palace of Spiritual Life. And we shall find that each edifice is incomplete in a manner that threatens its security. Then we shall see that the Creative Mind of God, in whose image Man was made, has offered the Revelation of Itself to be the foundation of all that the Human Mind can wish to build. Here is the security we seek; here, and nowhere else. 'Other foundation can no man lay than that which is laid, which is Jesus Christ.'[20]

The book was going to attempt, then, to bring human culture and knowledge into dialogue with Christian revelation, the latter offering answers to questions raised by the former. It was to offer an account of a reasoned exchange between the two, finding a unity of 'Mind'. Temple was quite clear, however, that reason alone would not prove the case he was trying to make: 'Yet even at the last the security is of Faith and not of Knowledge; it is not won by intellectual grasp but by personal loyalty; and its test is not in logic only, but in life.'[21] The actual experience of the Christian life, in other words, was the only sure route to knowing the truth of Christianity. Despite its grand ambition, then, the book was not going to attempt to force the reader to accept its conclusions through unarguable logic. Even though it was basing its case on a common ground of shared philosophical foundations ultimately it would only be issuing an invitation, to take up the Christian life, to try it and see. This reinforces and extends the collaborative approach of the earlier writings we have just examined.

But there is another way in which Temple's argument seeks to establish common ground with his readers and the wider society of which he was part. This is not so much about the way he made his case as the subject matter of that case. It has to do with the way in which he understood the nature of the reality they all shared. It is a way of thinking that underlies much of his writing, but *Mens Creatrix* provides a good example in a section about the nature of *value* and, in particular, about the way that value comes about. This section illustrates how Temple saw human affairs as having a key role in the constitution of reality itself.

He first calls to mind a beautiful object such as a painting or a piece of music, and then comments:

For it seems impossible to deny that when a beautiful object is appreciated, it gains in quality itself. Whether or not a thing can fitly be called beautiful if no one can see it, I do not know; but I am quite clear that, if no one can see it, it does not matter whether it is beautiful or not. Its value begins when it is appreciated. Good must mean good for somebody; apart from consciousness, value is non-existent.[22]

Value, then, comes about through the process of a mind appreciating an object and finding it valuable. Before this process takes place, value does not exist. Now it is important to recall that every human being that engages in such a process is also caught up in human affairs and ultimately in the developments of history: the appreciation of the picture is part of a museum visit, which is part of someone's life, and that life is part of a wider stream of social and historical development. Value, then, is implicitly tied to the unfolding of this stream of life. This means that the future can affect the past, for the value of the picture or piece of music may grow as the person and the wider community treasures it more and more. So Temple writes that 'the value of the Past is not irrevocably fixed; it remains to be determined by the Future'.[23] In other words social and historical development is being given a fundamental role in the realization of value (a key feature of his thought as a whole: see Chapter 6).

Moreover, Temple understood value to be ontologically basic: 'Value is the element in real things which both causes them to be and makes them what they are, and is thus fitly called Substance.'[24] Value, for this outlook, is not only realized through human experience and history but is also the ultimate reality of the world, that which both causes everything *to be* and which causes everything *to be what it is*. Taken together with the above, these commitments show that for Temple value comes about through human history and, in doing so, actually causes history to be what it is. Furthermore, there is an implication that value is drawing the past and the present into itself: the world is becoming increasingly more valuable and this through the agency of human history.

In a related way, Temple describes how the realization of value comes about through the life of the human community as a whole, the life of society:

... the object when appreciated becomes something which it was not until then. But if so, and if there are various Values which cannot be all realised for the same consciousness, then the variety of intelligences is necessary for the full actualisation of the value of the world. The complete truth, therefore, if we include Value, is only grasped by the whole society of intelligences, and can never be fully grasped by one alone.[25]

This is why the book seeks to show how the natural sciences, the arts (including drama and poetry) and morality were activities that could be seen as exhibiting different facets of 'Value' or 'Mind', an all-encompassing reality that showed there was an underlying unity behind these different activities. For Temple the reality of Mind had come about through an organic and unfolding process of evolution and, within that, through human history. The earliest and most primitive forms of life were not sentient, they were not thinking beings. Only towards the end of the evolutionary process, when humanity came into being, did Mind emerge.

In this way Temple shows how he was building his exposition on the findings of recent evolutionary theory. More significantly the structure of his argument shows how he was drawing on the philosophy of British Idealism. This was a school of thought found in the work of T. H. Green (1836–82), Bernard Bosanquet (1848–1923) and F. H. Bradley (1846–1924) among others, which drew on the ideas of the German philosopher G. W. F. Hegel from the early nineteenth century. Temple absorbed this tradition from Edward Caird, the Master of Balliol College where Temple studied as an undergraduate. (Caird became the dedicatee of Temple's magnum opus of 1934, *Nature, Man and God*.) Caird was the author of the standard introduction (at that time) to Hegel's philosophy and Temple's theory of value bears some resemblance to the presentation of Hegel's logic in that volume, except that Caird talks of *knowledge* rather than *value*. He writes, 'the Hegelian Logic ... treats at once of the method and of the matter of knowledge, of the process by which truth is discovered, and of the truth itself in its most universal aspects'.[26] So the gaining of knowledge by a person affects knowledge itself and, in particular, it increases its scope, its matter and its reality. In this way human consciousness is given a role in the constitution of reality, a role similar to value in Temple's ontological theory.

In *Mens Creatrix*, in a more general way Temple argues that Mind was responsible for the achievements of human culture, not least the cultures of Greece, Rome and Palestine (as the famous headmaster and commentator Thomas Arnold had argued in the early Victorian era: see Chapter 6). Temple believed that Mind was the goal towards which evolution had been moving and was the force drawing evolution to this goal. The full disclosure of Mind would therefore provide the key to reality, though philosophy itself was unable to find this disclosure.

At this point in the argument Temple had now prepared the ground for his presentation of that full disclosure, who was Christ the incarnation of Mind:

The whole process of that revelation which has been going on through nature, through history and through prophets, comes to complete fulfilment in the Incarnation ... Only in the life of Christ is this manifestation given. What we see in Him is what we should see in the history of the universe if we could apprehend that history in its completeness.[27]

And for Temple, the Fourth Gospel came closest to expressing this mystery when it declared that 'The Word was made flesh and we beheld His glory.'

In these kinds of ways, then, we see how Temple believed that the content of the Christian faith and especially the doctrine of the incarnation was not something that radically challenged and dismantled human culture and knowledge but was part and parcel of that culture and knowledge, sharing much common ground with it and fulfilling it from within. Its truth was one of inclusion rather than exclusion, of being *for* rather than *against*.

But can this attempt to establish common ground be declared a complete success? The philosopher Dorothy Emmet commented that, in spite of its clarity of style and exposition, *Mens Creatrix*

is a curiously disjointed book. It bears the marks of having been dictated in odd half-hours ... It passes quickly from one large topic to another: from idealist logic to discussions of art, tragedy, ethics, international and social politics, and Christian theology, without the ground gained at each stage being established sufficiently firmly to bear much searching criticism.[28]

Even more seriously, the discussion of evil, which occupies the longest chapter in the book, was not as convincing as it needed to be. The existence of evil in the world was clearly a problem for Temple's argument. How could the evolution of the world be the purposeful unfolding of Mind when there was clearly so much that was so terribly wrong, not least the carnage taking place on the battlefields of the First World War when the book was published. Temple recognized the problem of evil and grappled deeply with it. He argued that the existence of evil served a greater purpose: with human suffering, for example, there was often a positive good that could come out it:

Pain, coupled with fortitude in its endurance, especially when this is inspired by love, and meeting the full sympathy which at first lightens it and at last destroys it by removal of its grounds, is sometimes the condition of what is best in human life.[29]

He admitted that this could not be seen with all cases of human suffering in the world. The biblical scholar and theologian J. W. Rogerson, in a more recent and sympathetic discussion of Temple's philosophical thought, asked, what of the suffering of the concentration camps (yet to take place when *Mens Creatrix* was published), a suffering arising out of an evil that was so appalling it could never be justified by any future outcome? Temple could only write that

> All we can claim is that we have found a principle on which, where we can trace its operation, suffering becomes a necessary element in the full goodness of the world; that in some cases this principle can actually be traced; that in others its action must be assumed if we are to maintain the rationality of the world.[30]

Rogerson says, though, that he could never

> have encouraged the inmates of Auschwitz or Buchenwald with the thought that *their* suffering was a necessary part of purposeful reality and that good was bound to come from it – indeed, that the world would ultimately be a poorer place without the opportunities which concentration camps provided for overcoming evil with good.[31]

He and other recent commentators, in the face of evil, prefer *not* to maintain the rationality of the world: it cannot be as unified and purposeful as *Mens Creatrix* argued. Indeed Temple himself, as we shall see later, came finally to acknowledge the irrationality of the world.

Mens Creatrix, then, did not find the secure common ground that Temple was seeking for his presentation of Christian teaching. As he had suspected (when writing the preface) he had not, after all, been able to rise to the challenge of presenting an adequate philosophical structure. Consequently his thinking and teaching needed to continue to develop before it would rise to the challenge of the calling he had received as a young man. Nevertheless *Mens Creatrix* is important because it reveals the way in which he aimed to present the Christian faith, one of serious and reasonable collaboration with the outlook of his listeners. In his letter to Ronald Knox he had stated, after all, that 'I am Jones', a contemporary person of learning seeking truth, and this conditioned his whole approach. As we follow him into the next phase of his life and ministry, now as a bishop, it will be important to see how his teaching ministry developed in response to the shifting intellectual climate of his time.

Notes

1 See, for example, Paulo Friere's *Pedagogy of the Oppressed*, English trans., London: Sheed and Ward, 1972.

2 William Temple, *The Faith and Modern Thought*, London: Macmillan, 1910, p. 4.

3 Temple, *The Faith and Modern Thought*, pp. 7–8.

4 Temple, *The Faith and Modern Thought*, p. 15.

5 Temple, *The Faith and Modern Thought*, p. 16.

6 Temple, *The Faith and Modern Thought*, pp. 16–17.

7 Temple, *The Faith and Modern Thought*, pp. 17–18.

8 For a discussion of *Foundations* as a whole, see Peter Hinchliff, *God and History*, pp. 232–44. Hinchliff emphasizes the variety of theological opinion found in its different essays.

9 Reprinted in F. A. Iremonger, *William Temple, Archbishop of Canterbury: His Life and Letters*, London: Oxford University Press, 1948, pp. 161–6.

10 Iremonger, *William Temple*, p. 162.

11 Adrian Hastings, *A History of English Christianity 1920–2000*, London: SCM Press, 2001, p. 232.

12 William Temple, 'The Divinity of Christ' in *Foundations: A statement of Christian belief in terms of modern thought*, London: Macmillan, 1912, p. 243.

13 Temple, 'The Divinity of Christ'.

14 Temple, 'The Divinity of Christ', p. 245.

15 Temple, 'The Divinity of Christ', p. 244.

16 Temple, 'The Divinity of Christ', p. 248.

17 Temple, 'The Divinity of Christ', p. 250.

18 Temple, 'The Divinity of Christ', p. 259.

19 Temple, 'The Divinity of Christ', p. 248.

20 Temple, *Mens Creatrix*, London: Macmillan, 1917, p. 4.

21 Temple, *Mens Creatrix*, p. 4.

22 Temple, *Mens Creatrix*, p. 84.

23 Temple, *Mens Creatrix*, p. 172.

24 Temple, *Mens Creatrix*, p. 15.

25 Temple, *Mens Creatrix*, p. 84.

26 Edward Caird, *Hegel*, London: Wm Blackwood, 1883, p. 186.

27 Temple, *Mens Creatrix*, pp. 317–18.

28 Iremonger, *William Temple*, p. 523.

29 Temple, *Mens Creatrix*, p. 278.

30 Temple, *Mens Creatrix*, p. 281.

31 J. W. Rogerson, 'William Temple as Philosopher and Theologian', *Theology*, September 1981, London: SPCK, pp. 330–3.

4

First steps in servant leadership

When William Temple arrived in Manchester, he was now a diocesan bishop, he was a significant force in national church affairs and a respected writer and editor. He was now in a position to carry forward the passionate ambitions that had called him to ordination in 1908. But how was he going to do this? His first ambition, a theological one, was to restate the Christian faith in a way that was intellectually credible, but was this going to be through cutting across contemporary ways of thinking or working within them? His second ambition, a social reforming one, had arisen out of anger at the desperate social conditions of the time and a determination to change them, but was this going to be through calling for radical change or working through gradual reform? His third ambition, an ecclesiastical one, was to help reform the Church of England so that it practised what it preached, and already we have seen him begin to fulfil this through campaigning for self-government for the church, but was this the start of something more thoroughgoing? Finally, he had wanted to convey how Christ was not confined by human divisions but was the unifying Lord of all, an ecumenical ambition, but was this to be through overtly challenging the churches to unify or through working for unity from within? Overall, then, Temple faced a choice between being the kind of leader who stood out in front of others, challenging and unsettling the status quo and pointing the way forward through force of character as well as words, a directive leader in the tradition of Martin Luther, John Wesley and Florence Nightingale. Or was he to be the kind of leader who worked from within a community, working in partnership with others to move it forward at the right moment, a collaborative leader in the tradition of Thomas Cranmer, Thomas Bray and Mary Sumner? The Pathé film of Temple speaking to a packed Royal Albert Hall with radical proposals gives the impression that he was of the first kind, but was this actually the case?

Re-forming a diocese

During his years in Manchester, and when he was Archbishop of York in the 1930s, Temple had a vast range of interests and commitments, but the four ambitions mentioned above clearly and impressively emerge as major themes of his work. The following chapters will consider each of them, asking what kind of leadership is seen in the way he fulfilled them. Of the four the ecclesiastical ambition needs to be the first to be examined, for the lion's share of his time in Lancashire as Bishop of Manchester was given over to church concerns and, in particular, with leading the clergy and people of that diocese. And here, if he was to reform the church so that it practised the faith that it preached, he faced a daunting challenge. As things stood it was impossible for the bishop to know and pastorally care for all the clergy and parishes of his diocese. It was huge, extending from the city of Manchester in the south to Lancaster in the north and including Blackburn, Burnley, Preston and Blackpool. It included densely populated industrial conurbations, rural towns and villages, moorland and fells and seaside resorts such as Morecambe and Blackpool. Above all it had a population of 3.5 million and over 600 parishes (in 1847 the population had been 1.1 million). It had become too large for the diocesan bishop to be able to visit all the parishes and relate to all the clergy. The Archbishop of York, Cosmo Lang, was clear what he thought was needed:

> There is the momentous question of the division of the Diocese which will require both great energy and great care, and you would have to put to the test your views about the division of dioceses which you expressed to the National Assembly [Temple had argued in favour of the division of the larger dioceses]. Further, it is only right to say that there are few places in England where Churchmanship and Conservatism go more closely together than Manchester, and I have long felt that there was need of someone who would make a more effective appeal to the new power of Labour than has been made in the past; but I am sure that this will have to be combined with some wise and tactful considerateness for traditions which go very deep into the life and history of the Church in Manchester.[1]

Would Temple pick up Lang's challenge and see through the division of the diocese? He would find resistance, not least from the legacy of his predecessor, Edmund Arbuthnott Knox, who had epitomized both the conservatism and Protestantism of Anglicanism in Lancashire. There was a widespread description of church life in the diocese as 'Lancashire low' and the Oxford movement, which had sought to spread High Church thinking and practices within the Church of England, had made little impression in the county. Knox supported and reinforced this Protestantism. He opposed ritualism in worship and on one famous occasion, when he found a new wooden processional cross standing in the chancel at St Catherine's Church, Burnley, he took it down, broke it and threw it out into the churchyard![2] At the annual Blackpool Mission, clergy from the diocese would preach on the beach at Blackpool over the August bank holiday week. Stands would be set up where these missioners, whom Knox had invited, would preach. However, he had the habit of roaming around the stands and listening to the closing words of an address. If the subject matter was not approved by him the missioner would be told that his services were no longer required and that he 'could leave by the next train'.[3] Knox was also the author of *Sacrifice or Sacrament* (1914), a defence of the Protestant doctrine of the Lord's Supper against the Catholic influence of the Tractarian movement. He attacked the liberal school of biblical criticism and would later oppose the revision of the Book of Common Prayer in parliament in 1928 and 1929. (His son, Ronald Knox, already quoted in the previous chapter, shared his father's opposition to liberal theology: in 1917 he was received into the Roman Catholic Church.)

Edmund Knox's conservatism was seen in his opposition to the dividing of the diocese and in his resistance to the pressure for division. He was an accomplished administrator who presided over every diocesan organization. Temple's biographer describes Knox as an autocrat who kept in his own hands the strings of every diocesan organization. The people of the diocese 'accepted the regimentation imposed upon it by a bishop whose enthusiasm and efficiency were held to justify the rigour of his rule'.[4] This approach allowed the diocese to function as an institution but his successors, if ever they lacked the same energy and enthusiasm for administration, would not be able to maintain it. And, crucially, individual pastoral support of all the clergy and parishes had not been possible under such a regime.

Temple came to the diocese determined to be a different kind of bishop from the outset. He wrote to his brother that

> When I have learned the ropes I shall be able to settle which committees, etc. I mean to attend. Just now I must go to all of them to see what they do and how they do it. Knox attended them all and largely ran them. But that I won't do. Probably I shall be thought lazy, but there are plenty of other things to do.[5]

The question is whether he followed through on this and whether in practice he was a different kind of bishop.

Temple was consecrated bishop in York Minster on 25 January 1921 and enthroned in Manchester Cathedral on 15 February. He was accompanied from Manchester town hall to the cathedral by the Lord Mayor and mayors of 30 boroughs across Lancashire. The judges of the Assize courts were also in the procession, together with attendants called javelinmen! The suffragan bishops of Burnley and Whalley were also present and in the ceremony in the cathedral, the dean, on behalf of all the clergy, pledged 'loyal obedience and comradely support'. Temple replied by asking the people of the diocese to pray for him that he might 'never let go of the unseen hand of the Lord Jesus and may live in daily fellowship with Him. It is so that you will most of all help me to help you.'[6]

The first few months of his episcopacy, in his own words, was 'a wild kind of turmoil'. In the first six weeks he visited 24 churches 'with Confirmations apparently incessant'. But, 'it is jolly to be in a place where so much happens and one is really up against the things that matter. It is in that way far the most invigorating job that I have had.'[7]

The first question was whether the diocese would be divided. The Manchester Diocesan conference had already recommended that this should happen. It had considered one or two different schemes for doing this, including the creation of two new dioceses, with one based on Lancaster and including the southerly part of Carlisle Diocese and the other on Preston or East Lancashire. After Temple had arrived it became known that Carlisle would *not* surrender part of its domain. The conference then decided, in June 1922, on the simple division of Manchester Diocese into two, with Blackburn as the new See town.

This was the first time that Blackburn had been mentioned in the debates. Up to this point the likely contenders had been Burnley, Lancaster and Preston. There was 'no little contention' in the diocese about the choice. Of all the towns, Preston was geographically the most central, it was the county town for the county council and one of the most ancient boroughs in England, but Blackburn was chosen. G. A. Williams, in a history of the diocese of Blackburn, thinks that the choice of Blackburn was due to the influence of Temple himself on the diocesan conference. Williams reconstructs Temple's thinking in the following very plausible way:

> The consideration which motivated William Temple was that Blackburn was not far removed from the centre of the new diocese, and there was a railway connecting it with the east and west areas of the county. The very large and predominantly Roman Catholic population of Preston

was a further consideration. But the chief argument in Temple's mind was the suitability of Blackburn Parish Church to be the new cathedral.

Williams then describes some of the reasons for its suitability:

It was a fairly large church, not yet a hundred years old, situated in a large churchyard which would allow for possible expansion. This same area of land about the church could also allow for the development of a Close in which the administrative offices of the diocese could be established. Furthermore, it was built on sloping terrain, being on the bank of the River Blakewater. In order to provide a level platform on which the church could be built, when it was erected in 1820–6, a spacious crypt had been provided underneath the church. It is quite probable that no future use of this area had been considered at the time of construction, but Temple could see all kinds of useful purposes to which it could be put. Again, it would be inevitable that the church would have to be extended if it were to fulfil its function as the mother church of a diocese which would be by no means small. Before this could be done, the platform on which the extensions were to be built would have first to be extended, and this would provide, beneath the church, an area in which there could be constructed a conference hall large enough to accommodate the Diocesan Conference, as well as a place where the members could eat, and other apartments to enable the cathedral to be an educational and social centre, as well as a home of the arts. From this point on Temple saw to it that no further consideration was given to any of the other aspirant towns to be the See town. Blackburn it was to be.[8]

Not everyone agreed. Williams recounts how Lord Shuttleworth of Gawthorpe, who had served on Queen Victoria's Privy Council, thought the new diocese should be based at Lancaster, with the priory church as the cathedral. He thought that the traditional county town should also be the See town. Temple had to go and drink tea with him and tell him that whatever he thought, Blackburn Parish Church was to be the new cathedral. From that day on, Lord Shuttleworth never mentioned Temple's name and gave up his patronage of one of the parishes in the diocese.[9]

This first phase of his time as bishop shows Temple taking the initiative over a contentious issue, the division of the diocese. It shows how he believed fundamentally that a bishop should know and pastorally support every parish and every clergy person in their diocese, so a diocese needed to be small enough to make this possible. This in turn shows how he valued meaningful human interaction over his predecessor's directive approach to leadership. Second, in the face of opposition (over which town was to become the home of the cathedral), Temple did not change his mind but built a case based on the practicalities of the situation (of turning a parish church into a cathedral), as Williams shows. Therefore, a second feature of his leadership was a strong element of pragmatism.

It took two years for parliament to pass the necessary bill and for it to receive royal assent. The next challenge was financial. How would Temple get the people of the diocese to give enough money to turn this vision into a reality? A Bishopric of Blackburn fund was set up to raise enough money to create the capital needed to pay a new bishop £3,000 a year and to buy a residence. Iremonger reports that £80,000 was needed and that Temple consulted widely about how to raise the money. He addressed many public meetings up and down the diocese explaining what was happening and calling for support. A fund was launched at a meeting in Blackburn in 1925. A Mrs Elma Yerborough, the daughter of the local brewer Daniel Thwaite, gave the first donation, a generous £3,000. Temple himself sold some of his own shares and made a donation of £1,000, but the richer lay people of the diocese were slow to come forward with other donations. At another launch the following year in Manchester, King George V, in his capacity as Duke of Lancaster, sent word that he would donate one hundred guineas (£105). Bishop Knox was present at the launch and now, generously, spoke in favour of the division. Other donations raised the total amount given to £24,700.[10] There was still a long way to go but Temple did not give up. After further consultation it was decided that each deanery would be asked to raise £3,000, making a total of £62,000, and that literature should be despatched to each church to encourage them in their efforts.

Churches began to respond, especially when envelopes were printed so that people could donate even the smallest sums. This flexible and inclusive approach meant that by Easter 1926 the full £80,000 had been raised, with a third coming from the Deanery of Blackburn. Williams reports that it was a phenomenal achievement: 'No other diocese in the country had raised so much money with such rapidity for the creation of a new diocese.'[11] Temple's patient and responsive approach, built upon his valuing of meaningful human relationship and his pragmatism over the practicalities, had now borne fruit.

The Ecclesiastical Commissioners in London were now able to certify that enough money had been raised to house and pay the bishop and so the new diocese could be legally created, with Blackburn Parish Church as its new cathedral. This was done by the issuing of an Order in Council on 12 November 1926, the date on which the diocese came into being.

The final step was the appointment and enthronement of a new bishop. Percy Herbert, the suffragan bishop of Kingston in Southwark diocese, was appointed by the Prime Minister. Like Temple he had been educated at Rugby School and then went to Trinity College, Cambridge. For his curacy he returned to Rugby and then later became the incumbent of St George's, Camberwell in London. He was consecrated a bishop at the age of 37 and moved to Blackburn at the age of 41. He was formally elected bishop on 27 January 1927 and enthroned on 27 February by Temple and the Bishop of Liverpool. The new bishop knocked on the cathedral door using a mallet whose stone head had been found in a stream at the ancient Whalley Abbey (near Blackburn) and the shaft of the mallet was made from one of the oldest yew trees in the abbey churchyard. The *Blackburn Times* reported the event under the headline 'Flint Mallet Dints Church Door'.

The arrival of Bishop Herbert was the successful culmination of Temple's efforts over the previous few years to establish the new diocese. In what was meant to be an episcopally-led church the bishop could now, in both Manchester and Blackburn, get to know all the clergy and visit all the parishes of his diocese over a four or five year period. The bishop could become a pastorally supportive shepherd and servant of his flock. Temple, then, through his efforts to reform the church in Lancashire, was beginning to reveal his approach to episcopal leadership, one of putting interactive human relationship front and centre, combined with a strong element of pragmatism and a good degree of patience.

Pastoral ministry

Reforming structures was one thing but actually supporting clergy and parishes in real life was another. Temple would only be able to be called a reforming bishop if he changed hearts and minds as well as structures. How well did he do this with those committed to his charge? His biographer gives us a series of pictures with which to build an answer.

To begin with, the challenges were formidable. Even after the division he was still left with overseeing the second largest diocese in England. The work involved many mundane duties. There was the constant worry of finding enough funds to pay the clergy. But by the time the diocese was divided he was able to ensure that every clergyman was paid at least £300 a year and that most were paid more than £400. The gap between the poorest and richest clergy was slowly narrowing but there was still a huge difference between these sums and the £3,000 or more that bishops and some incumbents were paid. Furthermore this would be an ongoing challenge for Manchester diocese after the division as many of the wealthier parishes were in the north and now in the new Blackburn diocese.

Temple appointed suffragan bishops to assist with his ministry, choosing the name of Middleton for a new suffragan bishopric because of the ancient origins of its parish church. But there was no area system for the bishops and they roamed over all the diocese in an inefficient kind of way. Temple did not call his suffragans for regular meetings, though he did seek their advice on some matters. He made them chair of some of the diocesan councils and boards but he never consulted them about parochial appointments. The contrast with Knox, then, was not a total one. In these respects, Temple still directed rather than collaborated in the way in which he led the diocese.

However, this needs to be offset by the way he led the governing boards of the diocese. The secretary of the all-important board of finance has left the following illuminating account of Temple's style of chairing the board, one which while very positive also shows some critical evaluation of his approach:

Temple always found time to keep himself fully informed, and he never took the chair at a meeting for which I was responsible without first going through the agenda and getting a grip of all the questions to be considered ... [he] saw to it that responsible laymen and clergymen were in charge of affairs. By giving them his complete confidence, he secured wholehearted and competent service. In presiding over diocesan committees, Dr Temple's method was to give full latitude of expression from all sections, and discussion was never stifled. Some may have said that he suffered fools too gladly, but the freedom he allowed was rarely exploited and seldom did a meeting go over the prescribed time. He had a quick intuition and sensed unerringly the moment when the matter in hand could be put to the vote. Whatever minor defects his method had, it possessed the supreme advantage of giving the feeling of free and unfettered discussion, and in Lancashire this meant much. He himself spoke little at meetings except to guide discussion and at the end to give a masterly summing up.[12]

The ability to summarize protracted and complex discussions became something of a hallmark of Temple's leadership in a range of arenas. Sometimes, indeed, there was amazement from others that he could find form and meaning in fractious debates, as we will see in later chapters. But overall, this approach demonstrates a significant ability to place himself at the service of the body he was leading, rather than expect that body to serve his own wishes.

But what of his informal interactions with the people of the diocese? He entered enthusiastically into the culture of church life in Lancashire, thoroughly enjoying the Whitsunday walks, when Sunday school children and adults would process through towns and cities, the girls wearing white and carrying baskets of flowers, the boys carrying an array of banners, to the accompaniment of brass bands. He also actively supported the missionary society rallies, as well as the Mothers' Union and Girls' Friendly Society.

Importantly, part of Temple's re-forming of the diocese was to raise the place of women in its life. He had supported women's ministry for some time, such as in 1916 when he wrote that 'Personally I want ... to see women ordained to the priesthood. But still more do I want to see both real advance towards the re-union of Christendom, and the general emancipation of women ...' He had to wait until 1928 before he saw all women (and men) over the age of 21 gain the right to vote. But as Bishop of Manchester between 1921 and 1928 he was able to advance women's ministry in that diocese through instituting reforms in the way women were employed, including instituting a pension scheme for full-time workers and improving their conditions of work and pay, reforms that had been long overdue. In 1925, a diocesan training house for deaconesses was established and the liturgy for making deaconesses was used for the first time in the diocese.[13] When he left the diocese, the diocesan women workers wrote to him to express appreciation for the 'sympathetic and fair treatment' that deaconesses and lay workers had received from him and for his showing 'equal respect and consideration for women's work as for men's'.[14] This work continued at York when he was archbishop.[15] They also wrote how he had 'done great service in raising the whole conception of the Ministry of Women throughout the Church in England'.[16]

Other reforms included establishing a retreat centre. Whalley Abbey, a great pre-Reformation abbey that had been dissolved by the crown and rebuilt as a squire's home after the Reformation, came on the market. Temple was determined that the church should repossess it as a retreat centre and appointed a committee to negotiate with the owner. The final price agreed was just under £18,000, which seemed excessive to some in the diocese. However, after it was opened it became a valued house for retreats and conferences. The diocese of Blackburn, in which it was located, purchased it in 1928.

One of the most memorable aspects of Temple's time at Manchester were the Blackpool missions. These, as we have seen, had been started by Bishop Knox, who believed the church should follow the people and who, on this principle, took a band of clergy missioners to the town which had become a popular holiday resort for thousands of Lancashire mill workers. Preaching platforms were set up along the full extent of the beach, from South Shore to Fleetwood. Temple kept up the tradition of the bishop going to Blackpool, but not to check up on the clergy missioners. Instead he decided to speak, at midday, in the parish church during the week, on St John's Gospel in the first year, and on the book of Revelation in the second. One of the other clergy described their misgivings when he learned what Temple was planning to do:

> Lunch-hour talks! In church! During August Bank Holiday week! In Blackpool! On The Revelation! Most of us felt that he was batting on a sticky wicket, and despite extensive postering not more than 40 or 50 people turned up. The next day there were over 200, and for the remaining days the church was packed, a queue outside stretching almost down to the Front, waiting to get in – a wonderful example of his judgment and an amazing testimony to his power of exposition![17]

The missioners stayed at a local school, Rossall, and would spend the evenings in each other's company in the senior common room, which was below the headmaster's study. It is said that Temple's roisterous and high-pitched laughter was able to penetrate the floor above 'where the headmaster would have liked to be busy'. Another missioner described how impressed they were with Temple:

> His perfectly ordered and amazingly clever mind is a constant source of astonishment … At Rossall he is most friendly – just like a big brother to every man. His notoriously hearty laugh is a tonic, but all the time you feel he is reading you through and through, behind those veiled eyes. On Sunday night, after four crowded services, at each of which he had given a masterly address, I went into his room to find him busy editing the *Pilgrim* [a monthly journal on politics and religion]. He was still at it at eleven o'clock! In spite of the exceedingly strenuous week, he found time to read two volumes of French history and made notes of the same, and all this time he was suffering intense pain from a very bad attack of gout.[18]

Temple clearly enjoyed the weeks at Blackpool. During the one in 1925 he wrote to his wife:

> It has been a delicious day from morning to night. I had an easy time, as I was only speaking twice this morning (Central Pier and Tower) and had no fixtures after lunch … I took a small and most delightful

Confirmation at S. Stephen's – of the 5 dancing girls at the Winter Gardens, who are shortly going to New York. Then my address in S. John's ...[19]

He also visited other northern parts of his diocese before it was divided. He wrote the following letter to his wife from Carnforth vicarage on the edge of the Lake District:

... 2 delightful services yesterday – 13 [confirmation] candidates at Yealand and 63 at Warton (the mother parish of Carnforth), and 2 delightful Vicars. I shall have officiated in 8 churches in this Deanery, as well as 4 in Lancaster and one in Garstang, when I get home on Wednesday. I hope you are getting some peace and rest. I can hardly be said to be achieving that, but it is a rest in itself to be in the country; and a service in a country church is very refreshing.[20]

All of these vignettes are revealing, from Temple's initiative in setting up a retreat centre at Whalley to the way he contributed to the Blackpool mission. They show that he did not simply respond to what was set before him, as the report above on the way he chaired meetings might suggest, but that he brought his own gifts and perspective to the diocese, not to impose them but to offer them as something others could pick up if they chose. Lancashire mill workers clearly did pick up on his gifts of biblical exposition over the August bank holiday week in Blackpool. His approach to leadership was, then, one of offering a purposeful and educative service.

His disposition to serve is seen in his own lifestyle. Money was tight for the Temples in Manchester because the previous bishop, Knox, received his pension of £1,400 a year (a massive £63,000 in today's money) out of Temple's income, which reduced it considerably. The bishop's house needed to be maintained and run and there was little cash to spare. For nearly four years, Temple, with simple humility, did all his travelling on trains and trams and only hired a taxi when it was absolutely necessary. A committee was finally set up to raise the funds for buying a car. Money was soon raised and Temple chose a modest Austin 12. He also set about learning to drive and became a painstaking, though never a good, driver. He could only see clearly out of his left eye and complained that he had to 'look round his nose' in order to reverse. Nor could he claim any knowledge of what lay under the bonnet.[21]

Not everyone, though, warmed to Temple. According to Sir Walter Moberly, the Vice-Chancellor of Manchester University, Temple was found by some to be a little too impersonal and intellectual for real warmth or intimacy and his preaching sometimes went over the heads of the congregation he was addressing, such as when he preached to a congregation of schoolchildren on recent changes in the theory of education.[22] Many in the city of Manchester did not, apparently, take him to heart in quite the way some of his predecessors had been taken to heart. And so, despite his profound teaching ministry, he would not, ultimately, be remembered by many at this stage of his career as a people's bishop.

Temple, for his part, had one criticism of the people of Lancashire: 'Our people love to be doing things. They are a little impatient of any effort from which they do not see some amount of real result.' He was thinking especially of the business people of the county and of the way they combined great practical ability with a sentimental kind of Christianity. He would have preferred them to spend more time in thinking about and determining the right kind of conduct, especially in their treatment of their workers, who in many of the mills were still being treated harshly.[23] In other words he found himself agreeing with Archbishop Lang's description of the 'Conservatism' of the people of the diocese, quoted at the start of this chapter, which would need to be handled with a good degree of 'considerateness'. He had not really been able to do that.

Overall, then, Temple had gone a long way to reforming the church, especially through the successful division of the diocese, which was a significant achievement. But there was another kind of reform that was needed, of hearts and minds, and a different kind of bishop would have gone further with this in the congregations of the diocese. Through the division of the diocese Temple had made it possible for human relationship to be at the heart of the bishop's ministry, having created a more manageable diocese, as we have seen, but he was not the one to build significantly on that foundation through warm interaction with the people in the pews. On the other hand, his approach to leadership was more collaborative than directive, especially when compared with his predecessor, serving the ongoing life of the diocese in a purposeful and educative way, and including the virtues of pragmatism and patience when things needed to get done. Temple also had a winning humility, though in some respects he was not as personally collaborative as he could have been. Finally, while his ministry did not touch the hearts of people it did touch the minds of many, especially of the clergy, and he did empower female lay workers and deaconesses in ways which were widely appreciated.

The years at Manchester show Temple finding his feet as a bishop. While his leadership had its limitations we see him embody a purposeful and informed service of the people of his diocese, a servant leadership he would take forward to his later roles.

The next role became clear in July 1928 when, with the retirement of

Randall Davidson as Archbishop of Canterbury and the translation of Cosmo Lang from York to Canterbury, Temple was invited to become the next Archbishop of York. He was now to be freed from the burden of running a large and busy diocese and given the opportunity to provide leadership on the national stage. He was enthroned as Archbishop of York on 10 January 1929, at the relatively young age of 48, beginning the longest and in many ways most fruitful time in his ministry, one centred above all on a pastoral ministry of teaching. Before looking at what happened it is important to see how this teaching ministry grew and developed in his earlier life.

Notes

1 F. A. Iremonger, *William Temple, Archbishop of Canterbury: His Life and Letters*, London: Oxford University Press, 1948, p. 286.
2 G. A. Williams, *Viewed from the Water Tank*, Preston: Palatine Books, 1993, p. 27.
3 Iremonger, *William Temple*, p. 313.
4 Iremonger, *William Temple*, p. 287.
5 Iremonger, *William Temple*, p. 287.
6 Iremonger, *William Temple*, p. 291.
7 Iremonger, *William Temple*, p. 296.
8 Williams, *Viewed from the Water Tank*, p. 51.
9 Williams, *Viewed from the Water Tank*, pp. 42–3.
10 Williams, *Viewed from the Water Tank*, pp. 51–4.
11 Williams, *Viewed from the Water Tank*, p. 54.
12 Iremonger, *William Temple*, pp. 302–3.
13 Iremonger, *William Temple*, pp. 305–7.
14 Iremonger, *William Temple*, p. 307.
15 Iremonger, *William Temple*, p. 452.
16 Iremonger, *William Temple*, p. 307.
17 Iremonger, *William Temple*, p. 314.
18 Iremonger, *William Temple*, pp. 314–15.
19 Iremonger, *William Temple*, p. 317.
20 Iremonger, *William Temple*, p. 317.
21 Iremonger, *William Temple*, p. 309.
22 Iremonger, *William Temple*, p. 318.
23 Iremonger, *William Temple*, pp. 326–7.

5

Towards pastoral and spiritual leadership

Temple was not only a teacher of philosophical theology but over the course of his life became a hugely respected spiritual teacher, above all through one of the most popular works of devotion of the mid-twentieth century, his *Readings in St John's Gospel* of 1939–40. What lay behind this dimension of his leadership? Some of his earlier writings show a growing attention to divine and human love as being at the heart of all things and with this theme, especially when compared with his philosophical writings, we see Temple finding a more pastoral and compassionate tone.

It is important to acknowledge that Temple recognized the centrality of love from the start. It appears in his first book, *The Faith and Modern Thought* of 1910, in a passage which dwells on a great paradox, that God is 'omnipotent' and 'yet we are free'. Temple is deeply committed to both of these realities, yet how can he be? He answers that this 'remains an unintelligible paradox, until we remember that the change in man's will that is accomplished when love is won from his heart by the love of another is at once his own act and the act of the other.'[1] In *Issues of Faith* of 1917 he helpfully unpacks this:

> There is only one way in which our lives can be controlled by any power without our feeling that our freedom has been interfered with, and that is when others gain our love and devotion. When we do something in order to give pleasure to one whom we love, our action of course is determined by that other's pleasure, and yet there is no conduct in which we feel to be so freely expressing ourselves as this. Here, and here alone as far as human experience shows, you find the way in which our conduct may be controlled without our freedom being overridden.[2]

In *The Faith and Modern Thought*, Temple then uses this paradox of love to explain the heart of our relationship with God:

> So it is in all our experience of God; we are not driven on by some external force as a mechanical body is set in motion by an external force; but love is won from our hearts by the love of God. We cannot resist giving

it, when we see the love of God; but what makes it impossible for us to resist is just our human nature; nothing else. We are free precisely in our inability to refuse our love. It is the expression of our own nature; it is not something imposed on us from without; it is the natural expression of what we are.[3]

But what difference does this experience of God's love make in the life of the Christian? How does it find personal and spiritual expression? In answering this question, we see Temple begin to find his voice as a pastoral and spiritual guide.

Reflective sermons

At Westminster Abbey he preached on a regular basis and his sermons were collected together and published as *Fellowship with God* in 1920. In them we find Temple reflecting on the Christian life in sensitive and encouraging ways. Through many of the sermons he urges that the fundamental fact about human life is that God, in his love, has entered into fellowship with humanity through the incarnation, so that human life may, in answering love, enter into fellowship with him. The social dimension of this relationship, implicit in the word fellowship, was all-important for Temple and, incidentally, provides a connection with his developing views on society and the state (see Chapter 6). In many places Temple argues that this response is not to take place through the practical life alone but 'in the perfect blend' of the practical life with the devotional life.[4] And it is the way in which he presents the devotional life which shows the new tone.

This is found in a sermon on the Holy Spirit, in a warmly encouraging presentation of the place and importance of the Holy Spirit in the Christian life.[5] He begins with a sympathetic portrait of human nature:

Deep in every one of us is that spark of the divine fire, which is scarcely ever – perhaps Never – extinguished in this earthly life. Through all our sins and all our frivolities it still burns on. Even if we have spent our days in selfish pleasures and our years in worldly ambitions ... the Holy Ghost Himself within us, helping the infirmities of our prayers with groanings that cannot be uttered, and always making for us the perfect intercession which is according to the will of God.[6]

We are, in fact, able to be caught up in the life of the Trinity itself:

God within us is answering to God without us and above us, to God as He issues His law from heaven, to God as He teaches His children through the human lips of Jesus. Like answers to like; deep answers to deep; God makes answer to Himself.[7]

This then allows Temple to offer spiritual guidance to his readers:

How then shall we seek the aid of the Comforter? Let me answer the question with another. Do you often pray to God the Holy Ghost? And if you do, what thought have you of Him to whom you pray? We pray to the Almighty Father, to whom we and all things owe our being. We pray to God our suffering Saviour, by whose passion we are redeemed. So far our thoughts are definite; when we turn to the Holy Spirit they are often vague. But our prayers will be enriched and made more potent if we add to them prayers to the Holy Spirit with an understanding of what we do.

Temple then offers the following broad and inclusive portrait of the Spirit:

Let us then pray to the Mighty Spirit who guides the processes of natural creation, the courses of the stars, the procession of the seasons, the development of species; who strives ceaselessly in human history to express in and through men that love which is the nature of God who made them; who works especially in the Church, the school of Christ's disciples, inspiring, correcting, reforming, supplying; who was given without measure to Jesus of Nazareth, so that in Him we see what the Spirit would make of us: and as we pray let us remember that this Mighty Spirit dwells within ourselves, soul of our souls, our own truest self, always, despite our chattering and our sinning, 'to God's great service dedicate'.[8]

This leads to the following energizing exhortation:

So when we say, 'Come, Holy Ghost, our souls inspire,' we are not only calling One to enter us from without; we are calling One forth from within our inmost hearts, that our words may be His utterance and our deeds His actions. Cease not to pray to God in Heaven; cease not to pray to God in Christ; but pray also to the God within your breast, the 'Almighty ever-present Deity,' to the voice which urges you to right and warns you of wrong, and impresses the austere, imperious claims of beauty or of truth. Pray so, and God within your soul shall answer;

you will find His power there ready to issue forth in words divine which your lips will speak, in godlike actions done through you. You shall learn what St Paul meant when he said, 'I live; yet not I, but Christ liveth in me.' For through all your weakness and meanness there will break the irresistible power of Almighty God – the Holy Ghost, the Comforter.[9]

In another sermon, Temple helpfully makes clear the way in which this agency of the Holy Spirit picks up and continues what Jesus was doing during his earthly ministry.[10] He does this through a meditation on the ascension of Christ, normally a story that preachers struggle to explain but here is brilliantly expounded:

The Ascension of Christ is His liberation from all restrictions of time and space. It does not represent His removal from the earth, but His constant presence everywhere on earth.

During His earthly ministry He could only be in one place at a time. If He was in Jerusalem He was not in Capernaum; if He was in Capernaum He was not in Jerusalem. But now He is united with God, He is present wherever God is present; and that is everywhere. Because He is in Heaven, He is everywhere on earth; because He is ascended, He is here now. In the Person of the Holy Spirit He dwells in His Church, and issues forth from the deepest depths of the souls of His disciples, to bear witness to His sovereignty.

The Ascended Christ is the source of the Holy Spirit as we know Him. Christ has departed from the physical companionship of men; but He has not left us comfortless; He has sent the Comforter, the Spirit of Truth and Love.[11]

Temple then offers a range of ways in which the Holy Spirit can be present and at work in our lives, which is also the presence and work of our personal relationship with Christ:

The power of the Holy Spirit is revealed to us chiefly in the call of God to our souls; in the voice of conscience, pointing our duty; in the yearning for a fullness of life that is now beyond our reach; in the imperious claim that truth and beauty make upon the student and the artist; in the realisation of fellowship with the Eternal to which we have sometimes risen in prayer and meditation and worship and communion; in the strength beyond our own that has been given us in difficulty or trouble; in the growth and purification of character as we have persevered in duty and discipleship. To put it shortly, our experience of the Spirit is experience of a personal relationship.[12]

An extended essay

Christus Veritas (Christ the Truth) of 1924 represents a return to the kind of philosophical theology associated with his early career as a philosopher. But it also contains a warm exposition of the place of divine and human love in the scheme of things, showing Temple's pastorally minded teaching ministry integrated into and enriching his philosophical theology.

This volume was Temple's second major essay in philosophical theology, written while he was Bishop of Manchester but, like *Mens Creatrix*, having its roots in his studies at Oxford. It began with the premise that governed Temple's whole view of the world, that Christ and the Christian faith was true for all people, and it restated this doctrine in some of the categories of the Idealist philosophy he had learned at Oxford. Temple claimed the book was different from *Mens Creatrix*, which had been concerned with making a philosophical case for the underlying truths of Christianity. This second volume was more theological in its interests, expounding the nature of religious experience, the relationship between history and eternity, the nature of God, worship, the atonement and the Trinity and, above all, the significance and work of Christ. This shows a shift from basing his argument purely on reason to basing it on religious experience interpreted by reason, moving away from any sense of trying to win an argument with the sceptic. In this way there is a greater humility about what is being attempted.

Temple stated that the book was an expansion of a footnote that appeared in *Mens Creatrix*[13] which argued that the incarnation of God in the life, death and resurrection of Jesus of Nazareth perfectly represents, and fashions, the entire course of world history, from the earliest beginnings at the start of evolution through to the final stages of human history. The incarnation influences the outcome of terrestrial history, in other words, and it provides the key to unlocking the meaning both of the world and of the peoples that live within it. *Christus Veritas*, then, is an outline of how this is so, 'an exposition of the Christian idea of God, life and the world, or, in other words, a Christo-centric metaphysics'.[14]

How the incarnation represents and fashions terrestrial history is uncovered in the course of the book. The foundation of the argument, an optimistic one also argued in *Mens Creatrix* (see above), is that value, or as Temple preferred to write, Value, is the ultimate reality in the world. The value that anything is given by another being, whether it is an object or a person or a situation or a group of things, actually constitutes its existence: 'Value is the element in real things which both causes them to be and makes them what they are, and is thus fitly called Substance.'[15] So everything that exists does so because it has been valued by others: the relational valuing of something by another being itself constitutes the reality of the thing itself. This means that everything that exists expresses, to a greater or lesser extent, an element of absolute value. Biological evolution and human history, then, are viewed as part of one relational process, and this process is seen as leading to the emergence of the supreme and absolute value which bequeaths ultimate reality to everything. The world is an integrated whole, constituted by an unfolding process of valuing relationships, with each phase leading to the next more valuable phase, until the achievement of 'a commonwealth of values', which Temple describes as a human fellowship which realizes in community the values of truth, beauty and goodness, brought about by absolute value.

This opened the way for Temple to introduce the concept of love and to move to a more theological mode of writing. For him 'love' is another word for 'value', and this shows how love is bound to enter into the process of reality to bring about more and more love, because that is its very nature. Value as love will want to enter into the deepest possible fellowship with all those who emerge from the evolutionary process. In other words, it needs to become incarnate as a human being to call and invite all people into personal fellowship with itself.

In this way, Temple prepared the ground for his presentation of Christ. Christ is not just a human being but is absolute value, or Love itself, expressing itself in human terms. And he is a love who sacrifices himself in order to bring about the final glorious realization of ultimate value, a value that is the crowning goal of evolution. Christ's life, death and resurrection, then, is the key to understanding the purpose and meaning of reality and, within that, of the terrestrial world.

In an important passage in *Christus Veritas* he summed up many of these claims:

> Christian experience is witness, not to a Man uniquely inspired, but to God living a human life.
>
> Now this is exactly the culmination of that stratification which is the structure of Reality; far therefore from being incredible, it is to be expected, it is antecedently probable. Even had there been no evil in the world to be overcome, no sin to be abolished and forgiven, still the Incarnation would be the natural inauguration of the final stage of evolution. In this sense the Incarnation is perfectly intelligible; that is to say, we can see that its occurrence is all of a piece with the scheme of Reality as traced elsewhere.[16]

Temple's Christology was therefore full-blooded: 'We may say, then, without any hesitation that Christ is not a man exalted to perfect participation in the Divine Nature or Life; He is God, manifest under the conditions of humanity.'[17]

Taken as a whole, *Christus Veritas* was an ambitious and sustained attempt to interpret and represent the doctrine of the incarnation in modern terms. Whether it was a successful attempt depends on the strength of its argument about value. This argument suggested that all aspects of reality could be explained by the value they contained and that this value could be seen to be progressively realized through evolution and history. But, as with the argument in *Mens Creatrix*, the fact and magnitude of evil in the world can undermine such optimism. Can the concept of value be understood as perfectly representing the world when so much of that world is needlessly cruel, harsh and without meaning, as Rogerson argued above? (see p. 52). Temple himself had recently witnessed one of the most destructive and wasteful wars in history: was that also part of absolute value?

Nevertheless, as already stated, the argument of *Christus Veritas* is based on Temple's own experience of faith as well as on logic, and this feeds into its pages, such as in its rich and suggestive expositions of divine and human love. The worth of these pages does not depend on the success of his overall philosophical argument but stand as impressive testimonies in their own right. They occur in some well-crafted discussions of theological questions that show Temple expounding a range of doctrines beyond that of the incarnation. One notable example is his discussion of the atonement,[18] in which he criticizes an over-reliance on the analogy of the law court to explain what happened on the cross, preferring instead the idea of a personal restoration between God and the penitent believer. From the outset, Temple is very clear that if we are to understand Christ's atonement we should not begin with a need for it to satisfy God's wrath, but with Christ's sacrifice as an expression of God's love:

> The great doctrine of the Atonement has suffered more, perhaps, than any fundamental doctrine of the Christian faith from the pendulum-swing of human thought as it sways from one reaction to another. Let us then make a few points clear at the outset. No doctrine can be Christian which starts from a conception of God as moved by any motive alien from holy love. If it is suggested by any doctrine of the Atonement that the wrath of God had quenched or even obscured His love before the atoning sacrifice was offered by Jesus Christ, that doctrine is less than Christian. The starting-point in the New Testament is never the wrath of God but always His love. 'God commendeth His own love

toward us, in that, while we were yet sinners, Christ died for us.' 'God so loved the world that He gave His only-begotten Son.' (Romans 5.8, St John 33.16)[19]

Temple also uses the notion of love to explain helpfully the petition in the Lord's Prayer 'forgive us our sins as we forgive others', which seems to suggest that God will only forgive us on condition that we forgive others, so undermining the grace of God. In the following it should be noted that when Temple writes of 'men' and 'brothers' he is referring to humanity as a whole:

> God's forgiveness of men and men's forgiveness of their brothers are bound up in each other; and it is not difficult to see how this comes to pass. God's forgiveness is restoration to intimate fellowship with God; but fellowship with God is fellowship with self-forgetful and self-giving Love, of which forgiveness is a necessary outcome. If we do not forgive, we are not in fellowship with God. The repentance, which is the condition of God's free forgiveness, is a turning away from our selfish outlook and the adoption of God's outlook, from which forgiveness necessarily proceeds. God's forgiveness of us and our forgiveness of our brothers are not related as cause and effect but rather as the obverse and reverse of one spiritual fact. They are in their own nature indissolubly united. It is not by an arbitrary decree that they are associated together; they are one thing.

Temple then grounds all of this in the analogy of parental love:

> And here especially we have to remember that we are children before our Father. How can the Father take into affectionate intimacy with Himself two children who refuse to be on friendly terms with one another? He can only forgive us, as we forgive our brothers.[20]

Then, in the closing pages of the book, which summarize his theological argument, he shows how this self-forgetful and self-giving Love is to be found at the heart of God's own life, the life of the Trinity:[21]

> God is Love; therefore He seeks Himself in an Other; this seeking is the eternal generation of the Son, who is Himself the Other that is sought; the Son as the Divine Self-utterance is the agent of creation so that in Him all the universe is implicit; within the universe the Creator-Son lives a human Life and dies and rises again, so declaring to the universe the nature of its Creator.[22]

It is this love which reaches out and gradually incorporates his people, recalling 1 John 4.19, 'we love because he first loved us':

> ... thus He calls forth from finite spirits the love which is theirs because He made them, though by self-will they had obscured it; so the creature becomes worthy of the Creator; and the same love which the Son reveals to men and elicits from them everlastingly unites the Son to the Father; this is the Holy Spirit.[23]

Then, bringing the discussion down to earth, Temple qualifies these grand statements with the recognition that as human beings our vision of God is only very limited and, in the end, all we do is receive and pass on the love that he offers:

> We are His children, and cannot fully understand Him; but He is our Father and we know Him enough to love Him. As we love Him we learn, for His sake and in His power, to love men. So loving, we become partakers of the Divine Nature, sharers in that divine activity whereby God is God.
>   Thus nothing falls outside the circle of the Divine Love.[24]

Here, then, is a statement of the paradox of divine sovereignty and human freedom that Temple first described in *The Faith and Modern Thought* in 1910, but now expressed in the language of spiritual guidance and encouragement.

Teaching on prayer

Further insight into Temple's development as a spiritual guide is provided by a slim volume he published two years after *Christus Veritas*, one of a series of books on the personal dimension of Christian faith commissioned by the Bishop of London. This book, *Personal Religion and the Life of Fellowship* of 1926, shows him combining big metaphysical themes with some more intimate pastoral teaching. It is his teaching on the connection between prayer and love that is especially revealing and would become characteristic of much of his later speaking and writing, showing his gradual shift from academic lecturer to pastorally-minded teacher.

In the following, Temple is offering an answer to the question 'why pray?' He does not offer an instrumentalist answer, that prayer gets things done (though he does not rule out prayer making a difference:

'there are activities of God which are released (so to speak) by prayer').[25] Rather, his answer goes deeper: we pray because of who we are in our hearts and minds. As he unpacks this, he also encourages those who think their prayers are thin and worthless to keep praying:

> Only this shall be said: Prayer is an expression of love. Where there is no love, there cannot be any prayer. Sometimes the love may be very feeble, and only just strong enough to give rise to a real prayer; yet, if we make that prayer, it will strengthen the love it springs from, as an expression of an emotion tends to strengthen that emotion. And so a better prayer becomes possible.[26]

In fact, prayer is not a task to be performed but something inherent to the Christian life:

> Prayer and love deepen each other. If we are Christians in any living sense, our love is sure to find expression in prayer, and so to become deeper. Prayer, therefore, and especially mutual intercession, is one great means of increasing the volume of love in the world.[27]

Then with further encouragement Temple describes how those who pray in this way are connecting powerfully with the being of God and with his Spirit:

> But God is love; and the love from which prayer springs is the Holy Ghost at work in our hearts. The Christian can never think of love as a mere sentiment or state of feeling; it is a power; it is the supreme power of the world. That it should be generally realised as this is the first condition of human welfare. And one way to this is prayer, which expresses and so increases the love that is to prevail over all other forces.[28]

Temple is here making one of the most characteristic moves in his theology, which is to lead the reader away from a narrowly individualistic view of the topic and towards a socially located one. It is easy to think of prayer as a relationship between the isolated individual and their God, but for Temple this will not do:

> ... we are God's children; the welfare of ourselves and of all others depends on our recognition of this fact. That recognition must show itself in two directions – towards our Father, God, and towards our brother-men [and sister-women]; the natural way to express these two things at once is to pray to God for them. So we both express and increasingly realise our fellow-membership in the family of God.[29]

This has the following practical implication:

> In that form of prayer, then, which is called Petition we do not come as isolated individuals each to his own God. We come as members of a family to the Father of a family; we pray for them as for ourselves, and we ask from the Father of all nothing for ourselves which we do not also ask for others.[30]

Then, provocatively, Temple offers the following vivid example of the social dimension of prayer, expressed in the idioms of his time:

> In the [First World] war we could rightly pray for victory only so far as we sincerely believed that this was good for the Germans. At any time in those dreadful years an Englishman and a German could have knelt side by side saying the Lord's Prayer; and they would have meant exactly the same thing. This is always true of Christian prayer.[31]

This social dimension of prayer reaches 'its culmination in the Eucharist. There, above all, we are to find our unity with Christ, and with one another in Him.'[32] Temple describes how all the symbolism of the service

> ... insists on this. There we kneel side by side in virtue of our common discipleship. Differences of rank, wealth, learning, intelligence, nationality, race, all disappear; 'we, being many, are one bread.' We receive the food which has, by its consecration, become for us the Body of the Lord, that it may build us up into that Body, so that as different limbs, but one Body, we may be obedient to His will and carry out His purpose.[33]

Finally, Temple sums up what he thinks is going on in worship with what becomes one of his favourite words in his later writings, 'fellowship' (which can also be rendered as 'solidarity'). This, for him, encapsulates our relationship with God and with one another. It has already been highlighted in the title of the book, *Personal Religion and the Life of Fellowship*, and now, at a central point in its pages, it is given a key summative role that closely associates it with another of his favourite words, love:

> Fellowship, then, is at the heart of Christian worship. Each of us must lay bare his own heart before God; each must offer his own prayer, which is love in utterance and desire; each must come to receive into himself the gift of the divine life of love. But each must come as one member of

the family of God, rejoicing in the presence of all His children before the one Father, 'who made and loveth all'.[34]

In all these passages Temple the spiritual guide and pastoral teacher here finds a clear, warm and often uplifting voice that will find fuller and richer expression during his years as Archbishop of York. But first, prompted by the connection he makes between prayer and society, we need to look at the development of his political thought, another key component of his growing leadership in church and society.

Notes

1 William Temple, *The Faith and Modern Thought*, London: Macmillan, 1910, p. 150.
2 William Temple, *Issues of Faith*, New York: Macmillan, 1917; London: Macmillan, 1918, p. 5.
3 Temple, *The Faith and Modern Thought*, pp. 151–2.
4 William Temple, *Fellowship with God*, London: Macmillan, 1920, p. vi.
5 Temple, 'The Comforter', Sermon VII in *Fellowship with God*, pp. 81–92 (Westminster Abbey, 2 May 1920).
6 Temple, 'The Comforter', pp. 89–90.
7 Temple, 'The Comforter', p. 90.
8 Temple, 'The Comforter', pp. 90–1.
9 Temple, 'The Comforter', pp. 91–2.
10 Temple, Sermon IX, 'The Exalted Christ and the Coming of the Spirit' in *Fellowship with God*, pp. 106–17 (Westminster Abbey, 16 May 1920; London: Macmillan, 1920).
11 Temple, 'The Exalted Christ', pp. 108–9.
12 Temple, 'The Exalted Christ', pp. 110–11.
13 On p. 318: 'And even then it is to be remembered that we have not the World-History without the Incarnation as one expression of the Divine Will and the Life of the Incarnate as another; for that Life is a part of History, though it reveals the principle of the whole, and it is through its occurrence in the midst of History that History is fashioned into an exposition of the principle there revealed. We have here a series which is part of another series and is yet perfectly representative of it. (Cf. the Supplementary Essay in Royce's *The World and the Individual*)'.
14 William Temple, *Christus Veritas*, London: Macmillan, 1924, p. ix.
15 Temple, *Christus Veritas*, p. 15.
16 Temple, *Christus Veritas*, p. 139.
17 Temple, *Christus Veritas*, pp. 138–9.
18 Temple, *Christus Veritas*, pp. 255–65.
19 Temple, *Christus Veritas*, p. 257.
20 Temple, *Christus Veritas*, pp. 264–5.
21 Temple, *Christus Veritas*, from chapter XV, 'Love Divine: The Blessed Trinity', pp. 278–85.
22 Temple, *Christus Veritas*, p. 283.

23 Temple, *Christus Veritas*, p. 283.

24 Temple, *Christus Veritas*, p. 284.

25 William Temple, *Personal Religion and the Life of Fellowship*, London and New York: Longmans, Green and Co., 1926, p. 40.

26 Temple, *Personal Religion and the Life of Fellowship*, pp. 39–40.

27 Temple, *Personal Religion and the Life of Fellowship*, p. 40.

28 Temple, *Personal Religion and the Life of Fellowship*, p. 40.

29 Temple, *Personal Religion and the Life of Fellowship*, pp. 40–1.

30 Temple, *Personal Religion and the Life of Fellowship*, p. 41.

31 Temple, *Personal Religion and the Life of Fellowship*, p. 41.

32 Temple, *Personal Religion and the Life of Fellowship*, p. 48.

33 Temple, *Personal Religion and the Life of Fellowship*, p. 48.

34 Temple, *Personal Religion and the Life of Fellowship*, p. 49, quoting Samuel Taylor Coleridge in 'The Rime of the Ancient Mariner': 'He prayeth best, who loveth best All things both great and small; For the dear God who loveth us, *He made and loveth all.*' This quote also suggests that Temple's earlier tying together of prayer and love comes from this source.

6

Changing views of human history

William Temple's leadership was based on more than his pastoral and spiritual teaching, though these were central to who he was. Through the 1920s and 1930s, he rose to national leadership in the church and ultimately in society at large. Significant leadership is always underpinned by insight and vision, insight into the way things are and a vision of how they can be different and better. What was Temple's insight and vision? In particular, what particular insight did he have into the nature of human affairs through the ups and downs of human history and in the present? Second, what was his vision of how society could be different and better? This chapter addresses the first of these questions.

Answering this question is not easy because Temple said different things at different times. This was one area in which there was important change and development in his thinking over the course of his life. We need to spend time seeing where he started and with those thinkers who formed his early views, and then trace the steps that he took towards his mature outlook, the one that underpinned his active ministry as an archbishop. It should be added that his early views on the meaning of human history are of their time and will seem dated and even naïve.

Early historicism

Starting with those who influenced Temple as a young philosophy lecturer, there is no doubt that the British Idealists were a key influence upon his thought, as we have already seen. Late nineteenth-century philosophers such as T. H. Green, Edward Caird and Bernard Bosanquet have been described as providing 'the real clue' to his overall position.[1] This is especially the case for his views on society, the state and the wider development of human history of which they are part. At the heart of this influence is an outlook sometimes called historicism, the view that human history, understood as an all-encompassing process of human change and development, set within the wider context of evolution and of cosmological change, discloses what is ultimate about human existence. In other words, historicism denies that there is any aspect of human existence not conditioned by history: we are ultimately evolving beings and there is no unchangeable core of human existence or indeed of the world itself. Such an outlook opposes the traditional understanding of a supra-temporal or eternal realm standing over earthly change, one that discloses what is ultimate.

The origins of this position, for the British Idealists as well as for Temple, lie in the German School of philosophy of the late eighteenth and early nineteenth centuries. 'Against the scientific empiricism of the French and the English [philosophy of the time]', as Isaiah Berlin stated, 'the Germans put forward the metaphysical historicism of Herder and Hegel.'[2] Such historicism is seen in the way that history became the central concept of Hegel's philosophy. According to Hannah Arendt,

> The great impact of the notion of history upon the consciousness of the modern age came relatively late, not before the last third of the eighteenth century, finding with relative quickness its climactic consummation in Hegel's philosophy. The central concept of Hegelian metaphysics is history. This alone places it in the sharpest possible opposition to all previous metaphysics, which, since Plato, had looked for truth and the revelation of eternal being everywhere except in the realm of human affairs.[3]

An example of this use of the notion of history is found in Hegel's *Lectures on the Philosophy of World History*. Writing of 'the historical principle' behind the life of a nation, he described its importance in the following terms:

> Each historical principle, in its concrete form, expresses every aspect of the nation's consciousness and will, and indeed of its entire reality; it is the common denominator of its religion, its political constitution, its ethical life, its system of justice, its customs, its learning, art, and technical skill, and the whole direction of its industry.[4]

The historical dimension of a nation's life expresses the nation's fundamental reality. This is a statement that clearly embodies historicism, for the process of historical development is deemed to disclose what is ultimately true and real. It is this kind of statement that demonstrates why Hegel, as Hannah Arendt asserted, was the philosopher who classically articulated philosophical historicism.

Temple's rootedness in this kind of outlook is seen in the way in his early writings he defines certain phenomena. We have already seen how he understands the value of any object or event to derive from its appreciation by human consciousness: 'Its value begins when it is appreciated. Good must mean good for somebody; apart from consciousness, value is non-existent.'[5] So every human consciousness that engages in such a process is also contributing to the developments of history. The appreciation of a picture, for example, will be part of a visit to a museum which is part of someone's wider life affected by their place in society and its ongoing life and development. As we have already observed, social and historical development is being given a fundamental role in the realization of value.

A different example comes from when Temple crossed the Atlantic to give the Bishop Paddock lectures at General Theological Seminary in New York in 1915, published as *Church and Nation*. Among a number of subjects these lectures show the high importance of human history in Temple's thinking at this point in his life. He posed the question 'what is the central principle of God's guidance of his people, so far as it may be deduced from the tiny fragment of history that we really know?'[6] The phrase 'his people' does not just refer to the people of Israel but to European peoples in general on both sides of the Atlantic. He was asking what is the basic pattern that can be discerned in the course of their history as revealed by its study. His answer is that

> Its principle in the fragment of history that we know has been that isolated excellences should be brought to perfection first; and after something like perfection has been reached in the separate departments taken singly, the combination of them is brought about, in order that the richer and fuller life may be perfected, in which all of them find a place.[7]

It is 'the attainment of perfection' that governs the course of history, beginning with separate perfections which then come together to create a general or complete perfection. This sweeping and highly problematic claim demonstrates historicism, in that the historical development of different 'perfections' is deemed to lead to the absolute reality of perfection. However the statement is very abstract. Further light is shed by the way Temple correlated this theory with specific historical events. He pointed to the three cultures of Palestine, Greece and Rome and then described their formative influence on European culture: 'the history of Europe is to an enormous extent the history of the inter-action of these three forces as they mingle and combine'.[8] So, by implication, modern European life is the combination of the different qualities of Palestine, Greece and Rome and is therefore the realization of something new and even better:

... a new type of personality, not known to history before, and exemplified by your own United States and by the British Empire; the conception of sovereign States linked together in a single life, and exercising therein a joint sovereignty in dealing with those who lie outside the federation, is something of which history bears no record.[9]

This sweeping view, with its colonialist implications, is one that Temple would quickly abandon, as we shall see. For now it is important to note that the new 'corporate personality' makes no reference to a reality beyond history, such as eternity or the divine. Rather, it is out of human history itself that it comes about, another example of historicism.

The influence of the Hegelian view of history in these lectures can also be detected at two points in the appendix 'On Providence in History'. The first is where he wrote that 'the most outstanding facts in history known to us ... plainly reveal the providential guidance of its course'.[10] This association of providence with historical events is found in Hegel, who wrote that 'world history exhibits nothing other than the plan of providence'.[11] Second, more strikingly, is the focus by Temple on specific political leaders and their historical significance, in particular the careers of Alexander the Great and Napoleon. For Napoleon 'appears at a critical moment, is active precisely as long as he can serve what we now see to have been the cause of progress, and is then removed'.[12] Notice how progress is personified and then described as making use of such people. Both Alexander and Napoleon were subjects of Hegel's reflections, who called them 'world-historical individuals' (he also included Julius Caesar in this category). As Temple was later to suggest of Napoleon, Hegel saw the cause of progress 'using' these figures. In what became a famous image, that of the 'cunning of reason', 'Reason is represented ... as "using" the passions of men to fulfil her own purposes. Particular men and their purposes fall in the battle, but the universal purpose carries on safe above it.'[13] In this appendix Temple is again found to be standing in a tradition going back to the German philosopher.

It is also possible to trace the channel through which this influence was relayed. This was the group of Anglicans associated with Thomas Arnold, who was headmaster of Rugby School between 1828 and 1841, the school that Temple would subsequently attend. There were six in the group, including Julius Hare and Connop Thirlwall, the translators of B. G. Niebuhr's *History of Rome*. Hare, in the 1848 edition of *Guesses at Truth*, asked 'what is the true idea of the history of the world?' His answer, which anticipates Temple's 'central principle' quoted above, was as follows:

The philosophical idea of the world will be, that it is to exhibit the gradual unfolding of all the faculties of man's intellectual and moral being – those which he has in common with the brutes may be brought to perfection at once in him as they are in them – under every shade of circumstance and in every variety of combination.[14]

Hare is implying that the course of human history will lead to a coming together of perfections of human faculties which have already been attained on their own. Such an idea received explicit expression in Arnold's writings who, furthermore, used the same historical examples that Temple would use. Duncan Forbes helpfully summarizes Arnold's position:

> Universal history ... is fundamentally rhythmical. Each period of civilisation is also a period or epoch of universal history. For Arnold, the history of Greece, the history of Rome, and the history of modern Europe constitute three such periods of civilisation, three steps forward on the path of man's intellectual and moral development ... Roman law, Greek intellect, Christian ethics, he conceives as perfect in themselves. There is progress only if these fall into good racial ground. Morally, therefore, though 'our life is in a manner a continuation of Greece, Rome and Israel', yet it 'exhibits a fuller development of the human race, a richer combination of the most remarkable elements' because the perfection achieved by Greece, Rome and Israel in their various fields of endeavour mingled with the virtues of the German nations, and the result was a step forward.[15]

Even though Temple substituted the United States and the British Empire for the German nations in his *Church and Nation* lectures, and even though the idea of a coordinated international federation is not present in Arnold's outlook, the similarities between the two are clear. Furthermore, Temple's use of the term 'personality' to describe the character of corporate bodies is also found in Arnold, who argued that the study of modern history is the study of 'national personality'.[16] The influence of Arnold on Temple is also attested by Temple's biographer, who describes the influence of Arnold on other aspects of Temple's life.[17]

Recognizing paradox

However, when Temple came to publish *Mens Creatrix* in 1917, a year after *Church and Nation*, he began to shift his position. First, he deleted his references to the United States and the British Empire and substituted

'Christendom', a reference less easily undermined by the harsh reality of the First World War in which nationalism was fuelling the slaughter on the battlefields of Europe. Second, he began to acknowledge the existence of another divine reality that was different from human history yet in a relationship with it. We see both of these changes in the following:

> We may expect then that the course of history will continue in the future, as in the past, to consist in the conversion of nations, the building of the Christian State, and the incorporation of the Christian States within the fellowship of the Church, until at last Christendom and Humanity are interchangeable terms. Then, as the Divine life of which the Church is the channel leavens all things, the Holy City will be realised, descending from God, the New Jerusalem which is the moral and social life of mankind made perfect in the love of God.[18]

This outlook still sees human history as a continuous progression towards a kind of perfection, one that will include the whole of humanity within its scope, yet that perfection is brought about from above, as it were, by divine intervention. This demonstrates signs of an important shift away from historicism in his outlook.

More signs are seen in *Christus Veritas* of 1924. When discussing actual human history Temple again presents his notion of there being an increasing perfection coming through corporate bodies in the world. This time he speaks of the British Commonwealth rather than the British Empire but then adds, significantly, that 'it may be predicted with some assurance that this will not happen unless other conditions are fulfilled, to which at present men pay little attention in forming their political opinions'.[19] He now feels that his analysis must 'go down to the elements', including negative forces described as ignorance and competition at work in human history as well as positive forces such as cooperation.[20]

This long overdue recognition that human affairs are far from what they should be leads Temple to acknowledge that complete meaning cannot be found from within their ebb and flow: there is much that is 'incomplete'.[21] Instead, meaning must be found from a point of view outside and above the process, whence the process can be regarded as a single whole:

> In other words, history is fully intelligible only in the light of eternity. But, on the other hand, eternity must be conceived as requiring the actual historic process as part of its own content; for otherwise we render history unmeaning by the very means through which it is thought to secure its significance.[22]

Temple is here beginning to move beyond both historicism and Platonism in an interesting way, to something of a paradoxical understanding of the relationship between history and eternity:

> If history exists merely in the movement of its process it is unmeaning; if, on the other hand, it is the temporal presentation of a self-subsisting eternal Reality, it is unmeaning. As we must regard history in the light of eternity, so we must conceive eternity in the light of history. History and eternity must be conceived as to interpret each other.[23]

At this point in the discussion Temple uses a favourite analogy from the theatre to explain what he means. He has already used it in *Mens Creatrix* and he uses it again in a later and more extended discussion of the same topic from his Gifford Lectures, published in 1934 as *Nature, Man and God*. We go now to this discussion in which he is lecturing after the economic collapse of the late 1920s and in a Europe whose outlook is increasingly bleak. There is now an increasing urgency to make sense of human history in ways that do not ignore the waywardness of human affairs.

In the seventeenth lecture on 'The Meaning of History', Temple helpfully offers two analogies, different yet complementary, the first of which is from the theatre, to understand the relationship between history and eternity. Both will depend on the imagination making a reasonable leap from the detail of the analogy to something which, ultimately, is beyond human comprehension. He describes how the analogies will help make sense of the relationship between 'the complete and all-controlling supremacy of the Eternal' and 'the ultimate importance of History and its moral choices', among other things. He introduces the first analogy, which is the relationship between the writer of a play ('the dramatist') and the characters and plot of the play itself. He begins by focusing on the second of these and the way they acquire an independence from their creator:

> Dramatists have declared that when once they have set their several characters in motion, they have no further control over the conduct of those characters. Indeed in so far as a dramatist creates after the fashion of those poets who apprehend their own thought in the act of express-ing it, it must be so.[24]

In other words, in great drama the characters shape and form the way they interact with each other and they shape and form the direction of the play as a whole. This is where the analogy corresponds with real life. The dramatist, though, retains an absolute control, even to the extent of cutting short the composition and destroying it. His thought, active in self-expression, is immanent in the play; the play is made by it, and apart from it no episode in the play takes place; further, the vitality of every episode comes from the relation of that episode to this thought. Yet the dramatist himself is absolutely transcendent in respect of the play. Upon him it depends whether there shall be a play at all. The play depends upon him for its existence; he does not in that sense depend upon the play at all.[25]

Yet in a deep way he *does* depend on it:

But because his vocation is to be a dramatist, he fulfils his nature by writing plays; if he did not write them he would be untrue to himself. The self-expressing thought through which the play comes into existence is part of the principle of his being. Consequently the play itself, and its content, is of vital consequence to him.[26]

For Temple, then, the dramatist in these respects is like God the creator of all, one who is complete within himself but who creates the world out of the abundant generosity of his love and who comes to care 'vitally' about those he creates, beings who live out their own lives in their own ways within the ebb and flow of human history. Yet, ultimately, they depend entirely on him.

Temple then introduces his second analogy, again using the non-inclusive language of his time, an analogy which gives greater scope to the freedom of those whom God creates. He begins with the role of a parent:

We now turn to another form of human creativity, which we have the highest religious sanction for regarding as an analogue of the divine. The father in a human family is to his children at once the source of their existence and a present Providence. Because ... of his love for them, prompting him to give up what he values most if so he can serve their welfare, their doings are of vital concern to him. He gave them being; to a great extent he shapes their circumstances; perhaps his influence over them is so great that they will never knowingly act against his wishes.[27]

Then, very briefly, he describes the freedom of those he has helped create:

yet they are free to respect his wishes or not; if they do so, it is because it appears to them good to do so; when he controls them, he does not coerce them, because his control is effective through their wills and not either apart from or against their wills.[28]

The children, then, are free to live their lives in whatever way they choose, in real life and not just in the text of a play. If they do what their father wants they do so out of their own free will.

Finally, Temple then describes the limits of the analogies, showing that they are analogies and not similes:

> The analogy of the dramatist breaks down because his creations are not substantially alive; the analogy of the human father breaks down because the father himself is only another finite spirit, subject to successiveness in the same way as his children. But if we can think the two analogies together we find ourselves adumbrating a conception which seems to meet some at least of our requirements.[29]

So do these analogies succeed in holding together the sovereignty of God and the reality of human freedom, so maintaining the paradox? They do if, as Temple believes, the ultimate meaning of history 'is found in the development of an ever wider fellowship of ever richer personalities. The goal of History, in short, is the Commonwealth of Value.'[30] This would clearly uphold the sovereignty of God's purposes and therefore of his own sovereignty. But to many this will seem too idealistic about the future of humankind, especially given what unfolded in Europe during these years and during the Second World War. They will prefer the opposite point of view, which Temple acknowledges, the possibility that 'History is indeed

> a tale
> Told by an idiot, full of sound and fury,
> Signifying nothing. (*Macbeth* Act 5)'[31]

This would undermine the sovereignty of God's purposes. But, almost as an afterthought, at the end of the chapter, Temple suggests another way of looking at these things, one which is able to recognize that at the present moment the course of history and, similarly, the course of our personal lives, may well lack meaning and purpose, with things being bad and getting worse. Temple suggests the analogy of the play can accommodate this, because within the action of each act it is hard and sometimes impossible to see where the play is going. The best dramas have the capacity to surprise and even shock the viewer with their twists and turns of plot line, as villains become heroes and heroes become villains, and sometimes we can be left thinking that all hope has been lost. Yet, Temple argues, 'From the standpoint of the end, necessity governs the whole; from any earlier standpoint, there is contingency and indeterminacy.'[32] In great dramas, in other words, the viewer can find themselves completely at sea during the course of the play but yet when the curtain comes down at the end the unity of the whole is revealed: each character and episode has contributed to the totality in a deeply life-affirming way. And this is why we keep going to the theatre or cinema, because of their powerful combination of freedom and necessity.

So, in a similar kind of way, 'We are living out such a drama – the drama of which the plot is the creation of finite spirits by divine love, and the fashioning of their initially selfish individualities into the Commonwealth of Value.'[33] As mentioned, this may seem too idealistic to some, who prefer Macbeth's view. Yet when it is recalled that for the Christian faith 'God is love' and that love has the greatest of paradoxes at its heart, that the more it is given away the greater it becomes, so that however bad the course of events turn out to be the power of God's love is not undone, Temple's proposal becomes plausible and even persuasive, based on his two evocative analogies, showing how the one who is a sovereign creator can also be one who bequeaths real freedom to those he creates, a freedom which they can abuse and reject but which is not undone by that abuse and rejection, only strengthened.

Increasing realism

Temple had more to say about the meaning of human affairs and human history as Britain prepared for war in 1939. This was within a broader context of a remarkable shift in his overall perspective (which will be mentioned at other points in this book as well).

As the 1930s drew to a close, Temple began to adjust what he taught in an unexpected and impressive way. The rise of the Nazis, together with division in the German Protestant churches over what attitude to adopt towards them, created confusion and uncertainty in much of the European and British theological community. As a senior churchman, in contact with international church leaders and theologians through the ecumenical movement, he was profoundly affected.

To trace this shift, we should start with Temple's chairmanship of the Archbishops' doctrine commission. This had been appointed by Archbishop Davidson in 1922 to agree the core elements of Christian doctrine upon which the different parties within the Church of England could agree. Twenty-five people were appointed to the commission, broadly representing the Protestant, Catholic and Liberal traditions within the church. Temple was appointed chairman in 1925 and called the group together annually, with small working parties meeting twice annually. It was a long-term process, for the report was not finally published until

1938 when the world was very different from how it had been in 1922. Temple acknowledged this in his chairman's introduction, where he described great changes in secular science, philosophy, political thought and theology, where 'the work of such writers as Karl Barth in Europe and Reinhold Niebuhr in America has set many problems in a new perspective.'[34] But while in its sections on the church and the sacraments the report showed the influence of Catholic thought on the mainstream of Anglicanism and the way in which the old divisions between traditions were beginning to be broken down, as a whole it was a self-confessedly cautious document. Given the times in which the commission was meeting the report was remarkable for what it did not say more than for what it did. The Church of England in its official capacity, at this late stage in the unfolding European tragedy of the 1930s, showed itself unwilling or unable to respond theologically to what was happening all around it.

But Temple, in his introduction to the report, did respond in a significant way. He suggested that there now needed to be a shift of emphasis, from a theology of incarnation (which had been characteristic of the last 50 years in Anglican theology, including of his own work) to a theology of redemption. By 'theology of the incarnation' he meant the kind of outlook that sought the presence and work of Christ in the world as it currently stood: God was present in the world and all that was necessary was to open our eyes and trace his presence all around. But a theology of redemption

> tends rather to sound the prophetic note; it is more ready to admit that much in this evil world is irrational and strictly unintelligible; and it looks to the coming of the Kingdom as a necessary preliminary to the full comprehension of much that now is.

So, 'If the security of the nineteenth century, already shattered in Europe, finally crumbles away in our own country, we shall be pressed more and more towards a theology of Redemption.'[35]

It is clear from this that Temple was now beginning to believe that much in this world is indeed irrational and strictly unintelligible. This is confirmed in a letter to Dom Gregory Dix in 1939 in which he described how his own early writings had fallen into the 'incarnational' category and were now unable able to address the world of the 1930s:

> So far as [my work in the field of theology] has had an influence, I think it was due to the fact that I was a philosopher, by profession at least, before I seriously turned to theology, and I was able to build bridges across which people could travel, from the outlook common

in universities and such places from 1910 to 1920 or even 1930, to a Christo-centric view of the world. That is what *Mens Creatrix* and *Christus Veritas* are all about. I don't think it was a blind alley, because I do think it led to Christ. The trouble with it now is not where it leads to, but where it starts from; and this is a point at which nowadays an increasing number do not stand, though some still do.[36]

As war approached a different starting point became necessary. As A. R. Vidler would later put it, Temple now recognized that he had been a theologian for Christmas rather than for Passiontide, of the God of Emmanuel, the God-with-us in the world; but now there was a need for a theology of the Passion, of the God who saves us from the world.[37] In the introduction to the doctrine report he suggested that if the commission began its work again it should concentrate on the themes of redemption, justification and conversion and that the church as a whole should turn from an emphasis on pastoral ministry alone to one which is 'as much evangelistic as pastoral'.[38]

These thoughts were developed in one of the most revealing articles that Temple ever wrote, an article in the journal *Theology* simply entitled 'Theology to-day'. It was written as a response to a growing rift between the theologians of his own generation and younger theologians such as E. L. Mascall, V. A. Demant and Dom Gregory Dix. The latter rejected the whole attempt to marry theology with Idealist philosophy and were wanting to base a new Anglican theology on the neo-Thomism of continental philosophical theologians like Jacques Maritain. In the article, Temple looked back on his own theological journey, recalling his debt to the Idealist philosophy of Edward Caird, Bernard Bosanquet and Josiah Royce, described in earlier chapters. He recognized that now something else was needed. He recalled his own statement in *Christus Veritas* that what was needed was a 'Christo-centric' metaphysics and stated that this would not be a practicable task in anything less than many generations. With candour and humility he wrote that

> our task with this world is not to explain it but to convert it. Its needs can be met, not by the discovery of its own immanent principle in signal manifestation through Jesus Christ, but only by the shattering impact upon its self-sufficiency and arrogance of the Son of God crucified, risen and ascended, pouring forth that explosive and disruptive energy which is the Holy Ghost. He is the source of fellowship and all true fellowship comes from Him. But in order to fashion true fellowship in such a world as this, and out of such men and women as we are, He must first break up sham fellowships with which we have been deluding ourselves.[39]

The whole tone of this statement is quite different from his earlier writings. It is speaking of a divine judgement upon the current order of things in a way which Temple never used to do. It shows the influence of the Christian Realism of Niebuhr, whom Temple knew and respected, as well as possibly Barth (though Temple denied any direct influence).[40] It shows the development of a more overtly prophetic standpoint, with the way to the future now seen as lying through a cleansing break-up of the ways of the world. No more is he attempting to describe the meaning of human history. We should also note, however, the continuities with his earlier thought: there is still an overriding concern with the coming of a better future, though now he sees it coming in a different way. Also there is still a concern with the social nature of that future, being one of 'fellowship', though now this fellowship is seen not to come through human progress but through God's intervention in history.

Temple looked back at the treatment of the problem of evil in his earlier books, a treatment which we have already seen is problematic (see above, pp. 51–2). He now believed that 'formally' it covered the ground but, again with humility, he recognized that in the current circumstances the approach, the tone, the emphasis, all seemed to be wrong:

> War – nothing less – overshadows life. We have to maintain our faith in God under the shadow and shock of war. Facile generalisations are an affront. We must start from the fearful tension between the doctrine of the Love of God and the actual facts of daily experience. When we have eliminated war, it will be time to discuss whether its monstrous evil can then be seen as a 'constituent element of the absolute good' (*Christus Veritas*, p. 254). Till then we had better get on with the job of eliminating it by the power of the Gospel, which we must present, not as the clue to a universal synthesis, but as the source of world-transformation.[41]

These are poignant statements from someone who could have easily rested on his laurels and not questioned his three major works of philosophical theology. But now he was prepared to acknowledge that his treatment of the problem of evil was inadequate and, with that, to question the foundations of his Christo-centric metaphysics. He now recognized that evil could not be justified in the current order of things. And he believed that propping up his own theological reputation was less important than bridging the increasing divide in the theological community.

But, again, continuity must also be noted. The overriding concern, here as before, was the future and especially the moving of this world towards God's new world. And so, with that in mind, Temple saw two main tasks for theological reflection. The first was the 'thinking out afresh what are the standards of life to which a society must aim at conforming if it is to be in any sense a Christian society'.[42] This was a social and ethical question and it showed how theology was called to be practical, to offer guidance on the problems of daily living. The second task was to 'recover our apprehension of the Gospel', a gospel of redemption, 'a deliverance from the system of things – "the world" – which deserves the destruction which is coming upon it ... We proclaim, not general progress, but salvation to them that believe.'[43] Temple ended his article with a memorable call to dig the foundations deeper than before, and 'to light beacons in the darkness rather than to illuminate the world'.[44]

To encourage all this to happen within the Church of England he called a number of meetings with the younger theologians, not only with the neo-Thomists but also with others who had been influenced by Karl Barth's rejection of natural theology and his construction of a dogmatic theology based on revelation. There were two meetings in 1940 and another in 1944. The younger and the older groups did not agree on fundamentals, and when the scheme to unite the churches of south India was dividing those of the Catholic tradition from the rest, the divisions became altogether more fraught. But Temple was greatly stimulated by the discussion and debate and allowed the new ideas to influence and form his own thinking. The others came away impressed above all by what one of them described as 'the fact of his holiness'.[45]

The implications of all this for his understanding of human affairs and human history were again spelled out in a short article of February 1944, 'What Christians stand for in the Secular World', a supplement to the *Christian News Letter*. Here, in a vivid way, he wrote that Christianity still

> enables us to 'make sense' of the world, not meaning that we can show that it is sense, but with the more literal and radical meaning of making into sense what, till it is transformed, is largely nonsense – a disordered chaos waiting to be reduced to order as the Spirit of God gives it shape.[46]

This chapter has described dramatic development in Temple's views on the meaning of history, from the broad, confident and over-simplified generalizations of his early publications rooted in the historicism of the British Idealists, to the sophisticated discussion of a paradoxical relationship between history and eternity in his mature years when he was an archbishop, and then to these late shifts away from any attempt to find meaning in a world which he now found to be 'irrational and strictly unintelligible'. As a whole we find a figure who is prepared to keep searching and reflecting on the way things are, one who did not rest on the laurels of his major publications but who kept digging for the truth. His humility appears in the way he was prepared to critique and in some respects put to one side his earlier work in philosophical theology. The disposition of a student is seen in the way he was eager to engage with and learn from theologians of a younger generation in order to discern the real meaning or meaninglessness of human affairs and the world at large. All of this shows his preparedness and commitment to put himself at the service of others for the forging of a truthful vision of the way things are.

Notes

1 J. W. Rogerson, 'William Temple as Philosopher and Theologian', in *Theology*, London: SPCK, September 1981, p. 324.

2 Isaiah Berlin, *Karl Marx*, London: Oxford University Press, 1939, p. 15.

3 Hannah Arendt, 'The Concept of History: Ancient and Modern' in *Between Past and Future*, Harmondsworth: Penguin, 1977, p. 68.

4 G. W. F. Hegel, *Lectures on the Philosophy of World History* (trans. H. B. Nisbet), Cambridge: Cambridge University Press, 1975, p. 138.

5 William Temple, *Mens Creatrix. An Essay*, London: Macmillan, 1917, p. 84.

6 William Temple, *Church and Nation*, London: Macmillan, 1915, p. 144.

7 Temple, *Church and Nation*, pp. 147–8.

8 Temple, *Church and Nation*, p. 152.

9 Temple, *Church and Nation*, p. 155.

10 Temple, *Church and Nation*, p. 201.

11 G. W. F. Hegel, *Die Vernunft in der Geschichte*, quoted in Charles Taylor, *Hegel*, Cambridge: Cambridge University Press, 1975, p. 389.

12 Temple, *Church and Nation*, p. 203.

13 Taylor, *Hegel*, p. 392.

14 Duncan Forbes, *The Liberal Anglican Idea of History*, Cambridge: Cambridge University Press, 1952, p. 64.

15 Forbes, *Liberal Anglican Idea*, pp. 66–8. Quoting from Arnold's *Miscellaneous Works* and *Introductory Lectures on Modern History*.

16 Forbes, *Liberal Anglican Idea*, pp. 68, quoting Arnold's *Introductory Lectures on Modern History*, p. 44.

17 F. A. Iremonger, *William Temple, Archbishop of Canterbury: His Life and Letters*, Oxford: Oxford University Press, 1948, pp. 92–3.

18 Temple, *Mens Creatrix*, p. 332.

19 William Temple, *Christus Veritas: An Essay*, London: Macmillan, 1924, p. 78.

20 Temple, *Christus Veritas*, p. 78.

21 Temple, *Christus Veritas*, p. 89.

22 Temple, *Christus Veritas*, p. 89.

23 Temple, *Christus Veritas*, pp. 89–90.

24 William Temple, *Nature, Man and God. Gifford Lectures*, London: Macmillan, 1934, p. 441.

25 Temple, *Nature, Man and God*, pp. 441–2.

26 Temple, *Nature, Man and God*, p. 442.

27 Temple, *Nature, Man and God*, p. 442.

28 Temple, *Nature, Man and God*, p. 442.

29 Temple, *Nature, Man and God*, pp. 442–3.

30 Temple, *Nature, Man and God*, p. 448.

31 Temple, *Nature, Man and God*, p. 450.

32 Temple, *Nature, Man and God*, p. 451.

33 Temple, *Nature, Man and God*, p. 451.

34 William Temple, 'Chairman's Introduction' in *Doctrine in the Church of England, The Report of the Commission on Christian Doctrine Appointed by the Archbishops of Canterbury and York in 1922*, London: SPCK, 1938 p. 6.

35 Temple, 'Chairman's Introduction', p. 17.

36 Iremonger, *William Temple*, p. 606.

37 A. R. Vidler, 'The Limitations of William Temple', *Theology*, London: SPCK, January 1976, p. 262.

38 Temple, 'Chairman's Introduction', p. 17.

39 William Temple, 'Theology to-day', *Theology*, Vol. 123, no. 4, July/August 2020, p. 257.

40 For an illuminating discussion of Niebuhr's influence on Temple see Alan Suggate, 'William Temple and the Challenge of Reinhold Niebuhr'. John Kent, however, argued that Suggate and others overplayed the extent to which Temple, under Niebuhr's influence, moved from the optimism of his early theology to a neo-orthodox pessimism about the world in the late 1930s. There was some movement in this direction but the belief in the possibility of making the world a better place remained strong, as the next chapter will show. See Kent, *William Temple*, pp. 166–7.

41 Temple, 'Theology to-day', p. 257.

42 Temple, 'Theology to-day', p. 258.

43 Temple, 'Theology to-day', p. 258.

44 Temple, 'Theology to-day', p. 259.

45 Iremonger, *William Temple*, p. 610.

46 William Temple, 'What Christians stand for in the Secular World', *Christian News Letter*, February 1944. Reprinted in *Religious Experience*, pp. 243–4.

7

Finding a social vision for the future

The last chapter considered Temple's changing understanding of the past, of human history. But what about his vision for the future, of a different and renewed society, the vision that galvanized the audience at the Royal Albert Hall in September 1942? What kind of leadership did he offer in and through this?

If we are to understand what he proposed we must begin with his early views on the nature of society, liberty and the state. These provide the starting point from which his mature views developed, views influenced by the desperate events of European history in the early twentieth century. These led him to develop and deepen those views, especially around the role of the state.

Early collectivism

Hegelian historicism is associated with state collectivism, the view that the nation state emerges through history, surmounting individuals and societies and bringing about social freedom and fulfilment. As Hegel wrote, 'The state is the embodiment of concrete freedom. In this concrete freedom, personal individuality and its particular interests, as found in the family and the civic community, have their complete development.'[1] The individual is most fully free, then, when he or she is bound up with the state, rather than when he or she is separated from state direction and coercion (as in J. S. Mill's *On Liberty*). Bernard Bosanquet supported this point of view: the state is 'a necessary factor in civilised life'.[2] Moral duty, in this context, is a case of following the conventions of society and the state. Another of the British Idealists, F. H. Bradley, wrote, 'we must say that a man's life with its moral duties is in the main filled up by his station in that system of wholes which the state is, and that this, partly by its laws and institutions, and still more by its spirit, gives him the life which he does live and ought to live'.[3]

Once again it is possible to see the influence of this tradition on Temple and especially on his thinking about society and the state. It is seen in the discussion of the nature of liberty in *Mens Creatrix*. Temple's definition of liberty or freedom took its cue from the idea of society, through the state, being primary or sovereign over the individual. He wrote,

> liberty in the State is found when the citizens combine together in a common purpose which they are agreed in maintaining against any impulse, not only in others but also in themselves, which would thwart that purpose. In both individual and society *liberty is control of the parts by the whole which they constitute.*[4]

So liberty is defined by the idea of a common purpose guiding and even controlling the individual. In other words, the situation of being controlled by the sovereign (the sovereign being constituted by oneself and all others in a common purpose) is that of freedom. So when the state orders everyone to pay their taxes for the upkeep of society, for example, this leads to the realization of freedom. Such an order is not a curtailment of the freedom that we would otherwise be enjoying but is itself the way in which we are given freedom to enjoy. Temple would later argue that taxes allow the state to provide education, housing, health care, pensions and many other benefits that allow its citizens to live lives of purpose, fellowship and real freedom. When citizens are reluctant to pay taxes, the state forces them to do so, for the sake of society as a whole and therefore for their sake. In these kind of ways, Temple falls into line with the collectivist tradition of Hegel and the British Idealists in which freedom is bequeathed to the citizen by the state:

> Liberty as we have defined it is bound up with Obedience. The principle requires both that the authority, governing the parts of the soul or the several citizens in the State, should be vested in the whole soul or the whole body of the citizens, and also that the directions issued by this authority should be accepted and obeyed.[5]

All of this is the reason why Temple attached another word to 'freedom' in order to emphasize this point: 'The true aim alike of State and individual is that condition which may be called either free order or ordered freedom'.[6]

A stronger example of state collectivism comes from one of his earliest published writings, *The Education of Citizens* of 1905, written when he was 24. In this pamphlet he gives the state a pre-eminent role in defining the rights of people, in opposition to the view that such rights exist quite apart from whatever the state decides. In one passage there is the following outburst:

We want no impassioned appeals to the Rights of Man, or other purely fictitious dogmas; man has no rights except the right to do his duty, and to be made fit to do it and it is only his presumed determination to do his duty by the State that makes him a subject of such rights as these ... [A man's] whole being is comprised in the fact that he is a member of the State.[7]

This startling statement bears some resemblance to Hegel's association of rights with duty in his *Philosophy of Rights*: 'a man has rights in so far as he has duties, and duties in so far as he has rights ... A slave can have no duties; only a free man has them.'[8]

This outlook also affects Temple's view of the nature of moral duty. In one of his earliest books, *The Nature of Personality* of 1911, he writes that,

> ... we thus find that morality consists in the subordination of our own Purpose and sub-conscious aims to the Purpose of society of which we are members ... we must always take the moral convictions, which have grown up out of the experience of the race, as our guide.[9]

This strong statement is adopting a deontological position in ethics in which duty is determined by pre-existing rules, which are the convictions of the race, rather than teleologically by the consequences of the various options in a choice. As an example, Temple cites the common practice of the English to spend Christmas Day with their families, a practice that has now become a conviction that everyone should spend Christmas Day with their families wherever possible.

This view of practical moral duty again shows the underlying historicism of Temple's early thought, because 'the convictions of the race' have tended to grow and develop over time. Practices and convictions around how Christmas should be observed, for example, have evolved since Victorian times. They have become the conventions of history. So it is not a trans-historical or 'natural' order that should guide the agent in his or her decision making, but the experience of a people formed by historical development. Temple's closeness to Bradley should also be noted, for Bradley, as we saw, suggested that moral duty was a case of living according to one's station in life. Such a station, whether of a doctor or a factory worker or mother or teacher, has been formed by the sweep of history and by the handed-down convictions and conventions of those who make up society.

From dominating state to welfare state

But in *Mens Creatrix* there is also evidence that Temple was beginning to shift his view of the state. After affirming that liberty is linked with obedience he places a kind of restraining order on the state:

> The State must also remember that it exists by no other right or title than that of all associations of men; it is bound therefore to recognize 'Personality' equal in essence to its own in all associations or corporate bodies within itself, whether they be religious, educational, economic or of any other type.

The state, then, should not ride roughshod over the independent life of the many intermediate communities that make up the rich and varied life of society. Instead, 'It must aim at their "freedom" as it aims at the freedom of individuals, only claiming, in this case as in that, to be the supreme source of order in virtue of its including all other associations within itself.'[10] The notion that the state exists in order to serve society is beginning to make an appearance in his writings.

In a footnote, Temple declares that this point is 'of capital importance' and references John Neville Figgis' *Churches in the Modern State*. This is significant because Figgis was a strong opponent of state collectivism, seeing the rise of the absolute state directly linked to 'the horror of that very economic and industrial oppression which is the distinctive gift of modern capitalism to history'. Drawing on Hobbes, Figgis labelled the state as 'the great Leviathan', blaming Hobbes for its ascendency in political theory.[11] It is clear that Figgis was helping Temple to shift away from his earlier views (though Temple would not follow Figgis in his call to restrict the reach of Christian law just to Christians themselves, rather than to society as a whole, responding to the religious heterogeneity of the modern state[12]).

Figgis' influence on Temple is confirmed by Temple's Scott Holland lectures of 1928, *Christianity and the State*, in which he draws on Figgis and in the preface acknowledges his debt to *Churches in the Modern State*. It is one of a small number of books to which he has 'chiefly had recourse'.[13]

In the lectures, Hegel and his English disciples, including T. H. Green, are now criticized for their identification of society and the state: 'Hegel himself had bewilderingly treated the national State as a kind of incarnation of the Absolute; all his general philosophy should have led him to find this (if anywhere in our possible experience) in the organized fellowship of mankind.' Temple had hoped the League of Nations would lead the world in this direction. 'His English disciples did not follow him in his virtual deification of the State, but they were not far behind.' Temple later spells out the problem with all this: 'Under the influence of an *a priori* theory which identifies them, men have attributed to the State what in fact Society was achieving not only without, but even despite, the action of the State.'[14] So now, drawing on the work of G. Unwin and R. M. McIver, he argues that '(1) Society is more than the State, and has a life which is largely independent of the State; (2) social progress largely consists of the expression and development of that independence.' The state, then, is being put firmly in its place, though he still recognizes that '(3) the State is distinguished from other "social cohesions" by the fact that it alone is entitled to use force in order to secure obedience to its commands.'[15]

This happens more emphatically when Temple looks back to the First World War and describes the conflict as 'a struggle between the idea of the State as essentially Power – Power over its own community and against other communities – and of the State as the organ of community, maintaining its solidarity by law designed to safeguard the interests of the community'. Against this 'Power-State', most clearly embodied by pre-First World War Austria and Prussia, Temple now argues for a 'Welfare-State' and here, in fact, casually coins a term that will later become hugely influential.[16] This distinction would be drawn again in later publications, such as *Citizen and Churchman* of 1941,[17] and was adopted by other academics such as the economist Sir Alfred Zimmern. After the Second World War, of course, it came to be used widely as a description of the general package of reforms and initiatives put in place by the Labour Government of 1945–51. In these lectures Temple unwittingly played a highly significant role in the evolving political life of the nation.

So the state 'is an organ of community'.[18] Later he drives this home with the statement that 'The doctrine of State-absolutism ... cannot be Christian, for it ignores or defies the sole absolute sovereignty of God.'[19] He later adds that 'the modern respect for "conscientious objection" to what the State requires, whether that be military service or some other action which the conscience of an individual may condemn, is a great sign of progress.'[20]

Then, in a series of short articles whose publication is unverified, Temple develops this outlook even more. In 'The Real Meaning of the War', he now unambiguously identifies state absolutism with the doctrine of the Nazis, and contrasts this with a Christian view of the role of the state:

The issue at stake in the war is between two different conceptions of the nature of Man. Is every man and woman a child of God destined for eternal fellowship with Him? Or is the individual no more than a citizen of an earthly state, an episode in the ever-flowing stream of life? If the former is true, the State must recognise in every citizen something superior to itself; in other words we get the conception of the 'Welfare State', according to which state exists for the sake of its citizens, both collectively and individually. But if the other doctrine of man is true, then each individual exists for the State, which is itself the object of his final allegiance and the prosperity of which is the measure of right and wrong – the conception of the 'Power-State'.[21]

This shows how far Temple has moved in his view of the state. We shall return to this quotation below but for now it helps us chart this development.

In one place Temple even explicitly distances himself from his early view. In a letter to a publisher who wanted to republish *The Education of Citizens* he makes the following revealing comment on its teaching:

> I should now want to give a different emphasis at many points, but I would mention only one. The doctrine that the State is the logical *prius* of the individual is true in its own place and in certain relationships, but it is supremely dangerous unless it is balanced and even outweighed by the recollection that each individual is a child of God and has a status and dignity independent of any earthly society.[22]

Distilling social principles

If the state was no longer to direct the future course of society, where was direction and hope to be found?

As we have seen, Temple stepped back from trying to uncover the meaning of human affairs and human history. But he did not lose hope in the possibility of a better future for the world. As he reflected on the ways in which human history interacted with God's eternal kingdom, albeit a paradoxical relationship, he continued to encourage others to see how they could be caught up in the dynamic realization of a better future, one which might seem far off but which was already being born all around them: 'For human History is nothing other than ourselves; and we make its meaning by living out its process in the power, already available to us, of the Eternal Life which is at once the source of that meaning and its culmination.'[23] It was an empowering theory which, as the philosopher

Dorothy Emmet attested, made those who heard Temple speak catch a sense of hope, an ethical religious faith infusing his whole ministry.[24]

But we have also seen that Temple was not a blind optimist. He knew that making progress would not be easy. In *Christus Veritas* he made the following sobering statement:

> of any emancipation from selfishness itself, or any attainment of perfect fellowship in self-surrender to the absolute good, our historic progress hitherto gives no promise whatsoever.[25]

In his mature years, perhaps under the influence of Reinhold Niebuhr, he came to emphasize the persistent sinfulness of humanity, a strain of realism in his thinking. In his best-selling book *Christianity and Social Order* of 1942, he described in one memorable passage how we are all implicated in original sin from the moment we are born:

> When we open our eyes as babies we see the world stretching out around us, we are in the middle of it; all proportions and perspectives in what we see are determined by the relation – distance, height, and so forth – of the various visible objects to ourselves. This will remain true of our bodily vision as long as we live. I am the centre of the world I see; where the horizon is depends on where I stand ... So each of us takes his place in the centre of his own world. But I am not the centre of the world, or the standard of reference between good and bad: I am not, and God is.[26]

He goes on to state that only by giving the whole of our devotion to Christ can we be saved from this inherent sinfulness.[27]

Historical development would not, on its own, lead to the goals he believed in, and for the time being, as he neatly points out a little later, 'The art of government in fact is the art of so ordering life that self-interest prompts what justice demands.'[28] Some other way was also needed, a way which would put people in touch with true knowledge, beauty and fellowship. For Temple this was the way of faith in Christ and trust in the eternal love of God:

> Man needs education; but still more he needs conversion. Man needs political progress and social reform; but still more he needs redemption; man needs peace and security, but still more he needs eternal life.[29]

Any vision for the future, then, was going to need to draw on both dimensions of this rallying call: action to address injustice and also turning to receive the saving light of eternity.

The way in which Temple did this was not through painting a portrait of a utopia but through a more prosaic process of working from primary to secondary social principles to be applied in every situation, and then to some specific practical policy recommendations. He developed his social principles in the 1920s, for the first time in the journal *The Pilgrim*[30] and continued to do so in the 1930s and above all in *Christianity and Social Order* of 1942. He added the practical policy recommendations in that volume, to great effect. The primary social principles were a succinct distillation of his understanding of God's will for the future development of society. They were, first, that God has a purpose that runs through and beyond human history,[31] this one drawing on the rich discussions described in the chapter above. The second, deeply rooted in his Christian faith as well as the impact of the times in which he lived, was that humankind has inherent 'dignity', with an ultimate destiny while being caught up in the 'tragedy' of original sin.[32]

Temple then deduced certain secondary 'social principles' from these, 'principles on which we can begin to act in every possible situation'.[33] He was not wanting to offer technical solutions. He used the analogy of building a bridge: his social principles were of the type that would expect the bridge to be safe for all users and environmentally appropriate, but not about the technical engineering questions, for which you needed someone with the relevant expertise, like an engineer. They were not, then, blueprints of what society should be in the future, blueprints that he was imposing on wider society, but more like a set of values coming out of the primary principles that were to be embodied at every turn.[34]

The first and key principle Temple named 'liberty' or, in *Christianity and Social Order* 'freedom', and he defined it in a particular way, the respect for personality in all people: 'if each man and woman is a child of God, whom God loves and for whom Christ died, then there is in each a worth absolutely independent of all usefulness to society. The person is primary, not the society.' Temple immediately clarified what this meant for their relationship with the state: 'the State exists for the citizen, not the citizen for the State'. This means society must be so organized that people can freely express their own personalities through deliberate choice: 'it is the responsible exercise of deliberate choice which most fully expresses personality and best deserves the great name of freedom'.[35]

Temple did not follow J. S. Mill in believing that freedom was the simple absence of coercion, Isaiah Berlin's 'negative freedom', to be free *from* interference. But did he therefore swing across to Berlin's 'positive freedom' with its collectivist implications? For Temple it remained true that freedom depended on society and, in particular, the state fulfilling a positive role in the lives of its citizens, especially through education, in equipping them for a purposeful and creative life in which they would play their part in moving society forward: as he put it, there must be 'the best possible training' so that people would be empowered to make deliberate choices, the freedom *for* living a purposeful life. And it was this kind of thinking that had led Temple to develop the concept of the welfare state. But we have already seen how he moved away from collectivist thinking, coming to believe that the state needed to serve its citizens rather than stand over them.

Rowan Williams, in a 2008 lecture at St James' Church, Piccadilly, tellingly drew out the implications of this outlook:

> Now that is a very searching and a fruitful definition of what a welfare state might mean. The state exists for the sake of its citizens, but there is a deeper dimension to that than simply saying that the state has the duty to *provide* for its citizens; it is more that the state recognises in the citizen 'something superior to itself'. That is not an immediately transparent formula, but I take it to mean something like this: the state deals with human beings in their fullness, in their capacity for creativity, self-motivation and self-management. That is, the state deals with human beings in their *freedom*, not just in their *need*.[36]

Williams then drew out the political implications of this outlook:

> And if the state recognises in human beings that dimension of creativity, of capacity for self-management and self-motivation, the state, as Temple believes it ought to be, will recognise in each person a unique contribution to a corporate enterprise. And by the time you have granted that, you have already somewhat dismantled the notion of the state itself as a monolith. You have already begun to see the state as a broker of different kinds of creativity: the state as *negotiating* with its citizens, not as a single block.[37]

Temple himself suggests this kind of brokering/negotiating role in his description of the second social principle. This principle arises out of the social dimension of liberty: 'No man is fitted for an isolated life; every one has needs which he cannot supply for himself; but he needs not only what his neighbours contribute to the equipment of his life but their actual selves as the complement of his own. Man is naturally and incurably social.'[38]

So the second social principle is 'fellowship' or, to use a contemporary idiom suggested by Chris Baker, 'solidarity'.[39] As Temple explains, 'Liberty is actual in the various cultural and commercial and local associations that men form. In each of these a man can feel that he counts for something and that others depend on him as he on them.'[40]

Fellowship or solidarity, then, is expressed through the intermediate groups of family life, school, college, trade union, professional association, city, county, nation, church. This is where the brokerage/negotiation of the state comes into play: the state has a key role to 'foster all such groupings, giving them freedom to guide their own activities provided these fall within the general order of the communal life and do not injure the freedom of other similar associations'.[41]

Temple's welfare state was not to be a centralized, paternalistic and bureaucratic institution imposing a monochrome uniformity across the life of its subservient citizens, something its later critics accused it of becoming, but to be a community of communities, holding the ring but not controlling the outcome of the game, providing a framework for a rich ecology of intermediate groupings that are the primary arenas of people's mutual empowerment, solidarity and freedom.

But does this mean Temple was opening the way to assertive forms of dynastic, tribal or ethnic localisms? His third social principle guarded against this: 'The combination of Freedom and Fellowship as principles of social life issues in the obligation of Service.'[42] In other words, individuals and groups are not to seek their own welfare first but to serve the general welfare of all people. The welfare of their own groupings, including of their own family, is subservient to that. He argues that we should use wider loyalties to check the narrower:

> ... we can and should check these keener loyalties [to family, locality, business, trade union ...] by recognising the prior claim of the wider [nation and humankind]. So a man rightly does his best for the welfare of his own family, but must never serve his family in ways that injure the nation. A man rightly does his best for his country, but must never serve his country in ways that injure mankind.[43]

Local communities, the state and the nation are therefore each to serve what is greater than them. Assertive tribalism or ethnic exclusivism or nationalism have no place in Temple's outlook: the needs of all and, he would certainly add today, the ecological needs of the planet, come before those of nation states and the intermediate communities within them. This can be put in a slightly different and an increasingly popular form of language, that the interests of the common good will come first, at all levels of society.

In the 1920s, he had also included a fourth principle, self-sacrifice, but he came to recognize that this could only be adopted by those who had a deliberate Christian commitment and so he omitted it from *Christianity and Social Order*.

The way that Temple expounds the three social principles provides a rich conception of human society which, while rejecting the negative liberty of Mill and Berlin, cannot be equated with its opposites of state collectivism (responsible for the dependency of welfarism), or with an ethnic or tribal nationalism (responsible for conflict and warfare). Temple offered a distinct position which emphasized the role of local communities in creating the freedom and solidarity of peoples' lives, what might be described as a state-supported communitarianism, one that has more in common with John Neville Figgis than with John Stuart Mill or Karl Marx.

As an afterword it is important to note that these three social principles do not include equality. Temple's school friend and life-long colleague R. H. Tawney became a passionate advocate of the principle of equality, understood as the demand that the gap between rich and poor should be narrowed and that all citizens should come to own comparable quantities of wealth. The state, Tawney believed, should undertake a redistribution of wealth, through taxation and benefits, to bring this about. Temple shared much in common with Tawney, including a long-term commitment to the improvement of educational opportunities for the working population. Temple was also, according to Tawney,

> a natural equalitarian. He thought that the most important fact about human beings is that they are human – which meant to him the children of God – and that temper, while confirmed by his convictions, was in him so natural and instinctive, so obviously not an acquired attitude but a fountain of affection and geniality welling up from within, as to create in others the sense of brotherhood which it assumed.[44]

However, Temple did not agree with Tawney about equality. He believed that everyone had an equality of worth before God, as Tawney shows, but he did not see that this implied everyone should occupy the same kind of position in society and be treated in the same kind of way. In a charge to the clergy of Manchester diocese in 1925 he argued that

> in fact it appears to be the case that great emphasis on Liberty will always put Equality in the shade, and great emphasis on Equality will always make Liberty impossible. For men are born with different capacities and different gifts, and if you insist upon the principle that everyone must be free to develop his own life [as Temple does], the result will be an emphasis on Liberty, but there will be no Equality;

whereas if you begin with an insistence that all are to be counted alike, however different their gifts and powers, then of necessity you will put great restraint upon many of the citizens and possibly on all.[45]

The equality that he believed in, an ultimate equality of worth, was perfectly compatible with the idea that 'some should command and some should obey'.[46] As far as the ordering of society was concerned, then, liberty rather than equality was to be the primary principle.

This was reinforced in *Christianity and Social Order* but in a way that also shows Temple's deep commitment to equality of opportunity, especially through education:

apart from faith in God there is really nothing to be said for the notion of human equality. Men do not seem to be equal in any respect, if we judge by available evidence. But if all are children of one Father, then all are equal heirs of a status in comparison with which the apparent differences of quality and capacity are unimportant; in the deepest and most important of all – their relationship to God – all are equal. [So] Why should some of God's children have full opportunity to develop their capacities in freely-chosen occupations, while others are confined to a stunted form of existence, enslaved to types of labour which represent no personal choice but the sole opportunity offered?[47]

This anger led Temple to reiterate his call for widespread and deep educational reform when the war was over, as we see below. Overall, then, while Temple and Tawney disagreed about equality they profoundly agreed on the need for educational reform.[48]

Engaging with practicalities

For Temple, the third step in moving from vision to practice was to be the application of his social principles to the current state of British society, seeing how far that society fell short, and then formulating a number of practical objectives which Christians 'are entitled to call upon the Government to set before itself ... and pursue them as steadily and rapidly as opportunity permits'.[49]

Temple brought passion to this task, as we have already seen, arising out of his anger at the terrible polarization of British society between the wars. Mass unemployment had led to hunger and squalor, especially during the great depression of the 1930s. Without a welfare state the poorest sections of society were at the mercy of the economic cycle.

The Jarrow Crusade, a march of unemployed shipyard workers from the north-east of England to the Prime Minister's residence in Downing Street, was an attempt to highlight the plight of millions of people in the industrial heartlands of the country. The marchers walked from Jarrow to Downing Street over several days and through wind and rain, with a petition for the Prime Minister. When they arrived at Downing Street, they were told that Stanley Baldwin was too busy to see them.

Temple's view of English society had been unequivocal all his life:

> We see on the one side a considerable number of people enjoying a great many of the good things of life with singularly little regard to the needs of others, and we see on the other side a vast amount of real want and destitution, and also a great amount of vice which is largely due to poverty. That is a state of affairs with which the Christian cannot rest content.[50]

He did not rest content! His response in the early years of the Second World War was to formulate some practical objectives and then frame some specific policy recommendations for the government and the nation, recommendations with some teeth to them. The practical objectives were outlined in the conclusion to *Christianity and Social Order*, under the title 'The Task Before Us'. These included the requirement that education should be for all 'till years of maturity', that every worker should have a voice in the conduct of their business or industry, that everyone in work should have two days rest in seven and if an employee, an annual holiday with pay.[51]

The specific policy recommendations, on the other hand, were presented in an appendix, 'A Suggested Programme', and it was these which engaged with the specific needs of the moment. It is revealing that Temple developed them out of discussion with colleagues such as William Beveridge, the economists Alice Lascelles and John Maynard Keynes (the economist of post-war reconstruction), Stafford Cripps (the future post-war Chancellor of the Exchequer),[52] and his friend R. H. Tawney. Beveridge was especially important because he would show that the state could and should do what Temple was proposing. They had known each other since university days and had then both belonged to a group that had tried to reform Oxford University, as well as both being supporters of the WEA.[53] As noted, he was the author of the historic government report of 1942, *Social Insurance and Allied Services*, also known as the Beveridge Report, published a few months after *Christianity and Social Order*, which laid out proposals to be enacted at the end of the war for eradicating the five great giants of 'want, disease, ignorance, squalor and idleness'.[54] Beveridge had been working on his proposals in 1941 at the same time that Temple was writing his book, and Temple's policy recommendations in many ways anticipate what Beveridge would propose. These recommendations, as Malcolm Brown has written, were 'provisional, from careful negotiation'.[55] They have sometimes been labelled as 'middle axioms' because they stand between general principles and actual legislation, though Temple himself did not generally use that label.[56]

They are worth quoting in order to see the level of detail that Temple includes:

- decent housing should be built near where workers worked;
- family allowances should be paid to mothers for each child after the first two;
- wages should be sufficient for a family of four;
- milk and one good meal a day should be provided at school;
- education should be the primary occupation of everyone up to the age of 18;
- the state should eradicate unemployment through public works, as and when it arises;
- labour should be represented on the directorates through the Unions;
- every citizen should have two days rest in seven, and an annual holiday with pay.

It is a great credit to Temple's realism and judgement that many of these recommendations were implemented by the post-Second World War governments. What is of particular importance to us today is Temple's methodology: that he did not simply draw up the list on his own but responded to the advice of those who were more informed on the relevant issues.

At one point he did not want to include his programme in the book, thinking that it was too partisan a view. He sent it to Keynes to be peer reviewed and Keynes persuaded him to include it, writing persuasively that

I can see no reason at why you should not print this Appendix. On the contrary I much hope that you will include it. Unquestionably it is interesting and will add reality to the book. Indeed, I am rather at a loss to know why you should not print it. You will not expect me to agree with all the details, but I am in general sympathy with your approach. It represents a middle position which, in my judgment, much needs emphasizing and bringing before the public. I am sure it will be unserviceable to suppress it ... your later suggestions are interesting and, put in an Appendix with your modest preamble, are not likely to be thought unduly dogmatic or trespassing on professional ground.[57]

Keynes is therefore showing that Temple's programme, arising out of consultation and mediation, acquired a representative significance within the political debate of the time. He may also have supported it because it showed how economics needs moral grounding. As he pointed out elsewhere, most early economists were churchmen and 'along the line of origin at least, economics – more properly called political economy – is a side of ethics'.[58]

The appropriateness of including the programme was confirmed by Tawney who, after the publication of *Christianity and Social Order*, wrote to Temple in the following encouraging way:

> *Christianity and Social Order* has just arrived. Thank you so much for it. I think it is good and will do good. You have a wonderful gift of packing essentials into a small compass, without giving the impression of excessive compression. Nearly everything I should desire is here, though, of course, much of it would bear expanding, and will be expanded by others. I am glad, too, that you put the 'Programme' into an Appendix ... It adds a note of realism, without in any way preventing the reader who may not accept particular suggestions from accepting the general course of your argument.[59]

Temple's consultative methodology, guided by fundamental theological and social principles and drawing on the insights and recommendations of those better informed about the practicalities of forming policy recommendations on a range of social issues, produced a programme recognized as having not only general goals but the teeth of specific and highly relevant practical proposals, the 'realism' described by Tawney.

This chapter has revealed a responsiveness in Temple's social vision that needs recognition. While he began with fixed ideas about the dominance of the state over the life of society and the individual we have seen how he revised and sometimes with humility abandoned these in response to the dramatic and tragic times in which he lived. He appreciated more and more the need for the state to serve every citizen rather than the citizen to serve the state. This led him to formulate the concept of the welfare state, one that would become hugely influential in the years after his death. He also increasingly recognized the persistence and intractability of human sin, requiring a realistic vision of how things could be different, rather than the presentation of any kind of utopian vision. All of this led him to formulate a social vision based on some general and wide-ranging social principles and with some practical policy recommendations that had teeth, an approach which would catch the imagination of many during the war years, as seen in the Royal Albert Hall in the Introduction above. We also saw how he sought and received the guidance of those better informed about economic and social issues, thus giving his vision a basis in the work of others, a collaborative and authoritative vision.

Overall in this long and central chapter of this book, we have seen Temple move from a prescriptive to a responsive vision, one forged in response to the events and needs of his time, leading him to step back from some of his early views and to draw on the expert advice of others, to give that vision direct relevance and purchase. Recalling the Introduction to this book and its description of Robert K. Greenleaf and Ken Blanchard's model of servant leadership, all this therefore shows Temple offering a rich and impressive example of Blanchard's servant leadership, namely insight into the way things are with a compelling vision of the way they could be, with the principles, values and specific goals that are needed to get there, and the hands-on leadership of listening to others, revising proposals and encouraging others to turn that vision into reality.

Notes

1 G. W. F. Hegel, *Philosophy of Right* (trans. T. M. Knox), Oxford: Oxford University Press, 1952, paragraph 260.

2 Bernard Bosanquet, *The Philosophical Theory of the State*, London: Macmillan & Co., 1923, p. 172.

3 F. H. Bradley, 'My Station and Its Duties' in *Ethical Studies*, Oxford: Oxford University Press, 1927, p. 174.

4 William Temple, *Mens Creatrix. An Essay*, London: Macmillan, 1917, p. 218. See also pp. 186, 224, 252, for the italicized formula.

5 Temple, *Mens Creatrix*, p. 224.

6 Temple, *Mens Creatrix*, p. 225.

7 William Temple, *The Education of Citizens* (Address), London, 1905, p. 4.

8 Hegel, *Philosophy of Right*, para. 155 and 'Addition'.

9 William Temple, *The Nature of Personality*, London: Macmillan, 1911, p. 60.

10 Temple, *Mens Creatrix*, p. 224.

11 John Neville Figgis, *Churches in the Modern State*, London: Longmans Green and Co., 1913, p. 79.

12 Figgis, *Churches in the Modern State*, p. 171. This makes him seem today to be a very contemporary political theorist and has led some commentators to describe him as a 'pluralist' in distinction from the British Idealist political philosophy that influenced Temple and others, e.g., Matthew Grimley, *Citizenship, Community and the Church of England: Liberal Anglican Theories of the State between the Wars*, chapter 2 especially pp. 70–2.

13 William Temple, *Christianity and the State*, London: Macmillan, 1928,

p. ix. For further discussion of Temple's relationship with Figgis see my chapter 'John Neville Figgis and William Temple: A Common Tradition of Anglican Social Thought?' in Paul Avis (ed.), *Churches in a Pluralist World: The Thought and Legacy of John Neville Figgis, CR*, Leiden: Brill, 2022.

14 Temple, *Christianity and the State*, p. 106.

15 Temple, *Christianity and the State*, pp. 109–10.

16 Temple, *Christianity and the State*, pp. 169–70. See Grimley, *Citizenship, Community and the Church of England*, p. 1.

17 William Temple, *Citizen and Churchman*, London: Eyre and Spottiswoode, 1941, pp. 26, 35.

18 Temple, *Christianity and the State*, p. 170. See further pp. 160–77.

19 Temple, *Christianity and the State*, p. 173.

20 Temple, *Christianity and the State*, pp. 174–5.

21 William Temple Papers Vol. 67, p. 125, printed in Spencer, *Christ in All Things*, pp. 198–203, especially p. 199.

22 Letter (1942) in the William Temple Papers at Lambeth Palace Library, Vol. 47, p. 93.

23 William Temple, *Nature, Man and God*, Gifford Lectures, London: Macmillan, 1934, p. 451.

24 F. A. Iremonger, *William Temple, Archbishop of Canterbury: His Life and Letters*, London: Oxford University Press, 1948, p. 537.

25 William Temple, *Christus Veritas: An Essay*. London: Macmillan, 1924, p. 88.

26 William Temple, *Christianity and Social Order* (new edition), London: Shepheard-Walwyn and SPCK, 1976, with Foreword by the Rt Hon. Edward Heath and Introduction by Professor R. H. Preston, p. 60.

27 Temple, *Christianity and Social Order*, p. 60.

28 Temple, *Christianity and Social Order*, p. 65.

29 Temple, *Christus Veritas*, p. 88.

30 Temple edited this periodical between 1920 and 1927. Many of the articles that he wrote for it were reprinted in *Essays in Christian Politics*, including 'Christian Social Principles', pp. 9–18.

31 Temple, *Christianity and Social Order*, pp. 62–3.

32 Temple, *Christianity and Social Order*, pp. 63–6.

33 Temple, *Christianity and Social Order*, p. 62.

34 Temple, *Christianity and Social Order*, p. 58.

35 Temple, *Christianity and Social Order*, p. 67.

36 Rowan Williams, 'From Welfare State to Welfare Society: the contribution of faith to happiness and well-being in a plural civil society', *Crucible: The Journal of Christian Social Ethics*, January-March 2009, p. 52.

37 Williams, 'From Welfare State to Welfare Society', p. 52.

38 Temple, *Christianity and Social Order*, p. 69.

39 Chris Baker, book review, williamtemplefoundation.org.uk/book-review-christ-in-all-things-spencer-williamtemple, 2005.

40 Temple, *Christianity and Social Order*, p. 70.

41 Temple, *Christianity and Social Order*, pp. 70–1.

42 Temple, *Christianity and Social Order*, p. 73.

43 Temple, *Christianity and Social Order*, p. 75.

44 R. H. Tawney, 'William Temple – An Appreciation', *The Highway*, January 1945, p. 45.

45 William Temple, *Christ in His Church*, diocesan charge, London: Macmillan, 1925, p. 80.

46 Temple, *Christ in His Church*, p. 82.

47 Temple, *Christianity and Social Order*, p. 37.

48 For a discussion of Tawney's connections with Temple see Spencer, 'R. H. Tawney and Anglican Social Theology', *Crucible*, January 2018. Temple made the following comment on Tawney's book *Equality*: 'I agree about Tawney. To be quite truthful I was bitterly disappointed with *Equality*. The whole of the main contention could have been put on to ten pages. And the sustained, rather contemptuous, irony infects the whole style. It is one of the worst written books that I ever saw from the pen of a capable writer.' William Temple Papers, Vol. 30, p. 230.

49 Temple, *Christianity and Social Order*, p. 96.

50 William Temple, *The Kingdom of God*, Lectures. London: Macmillan, 1912, p. 74.

51 Temple, *Christianity and Social Order*, pp. 96–7.

52 On Cripps and Temple see Matthew Grimley, 'Anglicans, reconstruction and democracy: the Cripps circle, 1939–52', in Tom Rodger et al., *The Church of England and British Politics since 1900*, Woodbridge: The Boydell Press, 2020.

53 Jose Harris, *William Beveridge: A Life*, Oxford: Clarendon Press, 1997, pp. 110–13.

54 In a letter of 1943, Temple expressed his support for Beveridge's proposals: 'I believe myself that the Beveridge plan at any rate can be so administered as to increase actual liberty, for it seems to me that the primary necessity for effective liberty is security as regards the basic consumer goods.' *Some Lambeth Letters*, p. 91. On the connections between Beveridge and Temple see Spencer, 'William Temple and the Beveridge Report', *Crucible: The Journal of Christian Social Ethics*, July 2022, Norwich: Hymns Ancient and Modern.

55 Malcolm Brown, 'Politics as the Church's Business: William Temple's *Christianity and Social Order* Revisited', p. 167.

56 See Ronald Preston's Introduction in Temple, *Christianity and Social Order*, p. 7.

57 J. M. Keynes letter to Temple, William Temple Papers, Vol. 46, pp. 378–82.

58 In Robert Skidelsky, *John Maynard Keynes 1883–1946: Economist, Philosopher, Statesman*, New York: Penguin, 2003, p. 708.

59 R. H. Tawney letter to Temple, William Temple Papers, Vol. 46, p. 383.

8

A path to political leadership

William Temple was not only a thinker who forged a social vision but a political activist who sought to provide leadership to church and society to turn that vision into reality. This chapter looks at his life in the political arena, beginning with his early political commitments and tracing the growth of his leadership through the ups and downs of the 1920s and 30s to the mature leadership that he provided during the war years, the leadership so vividly seen at the Royal Albert Hall in September 1942.

Early commitments

First of all, where should he be placed within the spectrum of political positions, from Fascism on the extreme right to Communism on the extreme left? As always in this book we are interested in seeing the change and development in his views, so we begin by asking this question of his early life, in the Edwardian era before the watershed of the First World War.

Given what we have already seen of his social vision it seems likely that he was a Christian Socialist, but earlier commentators do not agree on this. Joseph Fletcher[1] and Peter d'A. Jones[2] assume that Temple was a Christian Socialist. John Oliver, on the other hand, uses the title only for the movement of 1848–54 associated with F. D. Maurice and his associates;[3] Edward Norman denies that he was a socialist.[4]

What does Temple himself say? An early piece on the relationship of the Church and the Labour Party, written for the *Economic Review*, appears to be unambiguous:

Socialism ... is the economic realization of the Christian Gospel. There is no middle path between the acceptance of Socialism and the declaration that the Gospel cannot be applied to economics, and this is Manicheism. The alternative stands before us – Socialism or Heresy; we are involved in one or the other.[5]

This is an extraordinary statement in so many ways, another indication of Temple's assertiveness as a young man,[6] but the association of socialism with Christian doctrine recalls Maurice and suggests a connection with him. This is strengthened by an earlier statement in the article: 'we must substitute a co-operative basis for the existing competitive basis of society'. What he means is expanded in a pamphlet he wrote for the Australian Student Christian Union on *Principles of Social Progress*:

> You will notice that individualism as a principle would tend to lay all the stress upon the element of competition, and Socialism as a principle would tend to lay all the stress upon the element of co-operation ... in this, as in all other aspects, Socialism is the higher ethical doctrine.[7]

Temple's socialism, then, is very far from the Marxist socialism associated with economic redistribution. For Temple it is all about applying the principle of cooperation to the life of society. Comparison of his words with Maurice's own definition of Christian Socialism in the first *Tract on Christian Socialism* of 1850 shows his closeness to Maurice: 'I seriously believe that Christianity is the only foundation of Socialism and that a true Socialism is the necessary result of a sound Christianity.' A key definition of socialism then follows: 'The watchword of the Socialist is CO-OPERATION; the watchword of the anti-Socialist is COMPETITION. Anyone who recognizes the principle of co-operation as a stronger and true principle than that of competition, has a right to the honour or the disgrace of being called a Socialist.'[8]

Temple broadly followed in the footsteps of Maurice, shown by his connection with those who built on Maurice's Christian Socialism, in particular Henry Scott Holland and Charles Gore, the two founders of the campaigning Christian Social Union in 1889 who, as we saw in Chapter 1, also had a profound influence on his faith. Temple joined the CSU when a student and helped to organize one of their exhibitions highlighting the exploitation in sweatshops in Britain.[9] His debt to Scott Holland, as to Gore, is clearly acknowledged,[10] and Temple's biographer mentions that between 1907 and 1917 Gore had 'a growing influence ... on his social thinking'.[11] This was the period in which Gore published a radical and influential report on property with its critique of the notion of private property.[12]

This influence bore fruit between 1909 and 1917 when Temple helped to lead a group of scholars and members of the Student Christian Movement who studied and wrote about competition in society, publishing a set of essays in 1917 called *Competition: A Study in Human Motive*. This has been described as an outstanding contribution to Christian social thought[13] showing how the group as a whole and Temple in particular were engaging in a critique of the competitive economic system in ways that Maurice would have supported.

Then at the end of the First World War, Temple started to support the Labour movement openly as troops demobilized and unions started to organize workers for membership of the party. Writing in the *Daily News* he commented:

> The Church has not been without prophets; much of what is now becoming accepted doctrine finds its origin in F. D. Maurice. Bishop Westcott was a prophet, as we become more sure with every year that separates us from his death. Lately we lost in Henry Scott Holland a man of the authentic fire and vision of the true prophet.[14]

B. F. Westcott was a biblical scholar and Bishop of Durham, and Scott Holland had been dean of St Paul's Cathedral. Temple states that 'these saw in what we now call the Labour Movement the working of the Holy Spirit who is given to the Church'. This warm endorsement is then developed with a description of the Labour Party that reveals Temple's own political outlook:

> Now the Labour Movement is essentially an effort to organise society on the basis of freedom and fellowship. As such it has a right to claim the sympathy of the Church. The Labour Party is a different thing: that is a political organisation, and the Church as a whole must not be attached to any political party – not even to the Tory Party. But Churchmen ought to consider very carefully the formulated programme of the Labour Party, and whether individually they should subscribe to it. Here is a party who has at least put forward an outline scheme of reconstruction in national and international life. It is a scheme based on moral ideals.

For Temple there is an imperative in all this:

> We must not support it merely because we sympathise with the motives behind it: but if we believe that those motives are, on the whole, applied with wisdom we have no right to stand aside, we must go in and help.[15]

Temple *did* believe they were applied with wisdom and so he joined the party. He also announced this to the Church of England's Convocation.

He remained in the party for seven years, continuing his membership as he moved to Manchester to be bishop there. He resigned in 1925 over inconsistency in the party's policy in the Far East and as a result of dis-appointment over its parliamentary achievements,[16] but he continued to feel more sympathy with the Labour Party's general programme than with that of any other political group, though he was not always ready to give Labour leaders the active help they sought from him.[17]

In the 1920s he would still use term 'Christian Socialism' occasion-ally, such as in an introduction to a volume on the nineteenth-century Christian social reformers. In this he identified his own growing concern with 'principles of social application', which we examined above, with a broadly defined Christian Socialism:

> What then are the Christian principles in question? The asking of those questions is the beginning of Christian Socialism (which, of course, does not historically represent any prejudging of the question, What should be the relation of Christianity to the proposals of economic socialism in any of its forms?).[18]

Temple therefore drew a distinction between economic socialism and an ethically defined Christian Socialism and identified himself with the latter.

But in this same period as he began to formulate his social principles he began to move away from the language of cooperation and competition. In its place, as we have already seen, beginning with articles he wrote in the 1920s for the journal *The Pilgrim*, he gave priority to 'liberty' rather than 'cooperation', then 'brotherhood or fellowship', then 'the duty of service' and finally 'sacrifice' (later dropped from the list). They are placed in this order because Temple had come to appreciate that any kind of meaningful relationship, whether of cooperation or fellowship, presupposes freedom.[19] In a decade which saw the rise of Soviet totali-tarianism in Russia and Fascist authoritarianism in Italy, his thinking was evolving. Nevertheless, a continuing connection with Maurice is still seen in the way he mentions 'brotherhood' in the second principle. For Maurice this was a key characteristic of society, reflecting the Fatherhood of God over all.[20]

Temple later repudiated any idea of preaching socialism: this is 'a thing I have never done and never would do!'[21] presumably referring to eco-nomic socialism rather than cooperative socialism. But he was still in contact with Labour members of the national government, among others, as he drew up his programme in *Christianity and Social Order* for post-war reconstruction, as we saw in the chapter above.

Political interventions

COPEC

How did these commitments translate into action? When Temple became Bishop of Manchester he gained a platform from which to launch political campaigning. This happened through the massive Conference on Christian Politics, Economics and Citizenship (COPEC) which met in Birmingham in April 1924. The idea behind it had been hatched in 1919 when Temple was at Westminster, and Gore had strongly encouraged it. The proposal was to 'seek the will and purpose of God for men and women in every relationship of their lives', political, social, industrial and the rest. Whereas previous conferences and reports had looked at individual issues and problems, none had attempted an overview. The problems of industry were to be seen alongside the problems of education, housing and international relations, so that the whole field might be grasped. Four years were allowed for study and campaigning in all the denominations (including the Roman Catholic Church, although it withdrew just before the conference). Twelve commissions were set up, 200,000 questionnaires were processed at 75 centres, and the whole of 1923 was spent in studying the replies and producing the commissions' reports. Twelve book-length reports were produced which, according to John Kent, 'summed up one side of the social thinking which had gone on in the English churches since the beginning of the nineteenth century, and nothing quite like them has been produced since'.[22] They proposed various resolutions, which the conference slightly amended and passed. Temple became chairman of the movement and chaired the conference itself, which had 1,400 delegates, 80 of which came from outside the British Isles. When he opened the conference, he described two motivating forces behind the whole event: 'We represent here to-day the consequence of a spiritual movement in the Church prompted by loyalty and hope, and a spiritual movement in the world prompted by disillusion and despair ... Our aim is to hear God speak.'[23]

The conference was run smoothly, with Temple using his excellent chairing skills to keep the proceedings focused and purposeful. It ended with a general call

> on all Christian people to do all in their power to find and apply the remedy for recurrent unemployment, to press vigorously for the launching of efficient housing schemes, whether centrally or locally, and to secure an immediate extension of educational facilities, especially for the unemployed adolescents, whose case is perhaps the most deplorable

of all the deplorable features of our social life today ... we urge the immediate raising of the school leaving age to sixteen, and the diminution as rapidly as possible of the maximum size of classes.[24]

But the conference did not lead to a movement for change. This may have been because the final resolutions were too general and did not, for example, propose an actual scheme for tackling unemployment. Nor did the politicians of the day respond: the Labour government of Ramsey MacDonald was about to collapse and be replaced by the Tory government of Stanley Baldwin. Nor was Temple able to secure the support of Archbishop Davidson and thereby give the conference an official standing in church life. COPEC should not, though, be dismissed out of hand. Adrian Hastings wrote that its

> immediate consequences were small. Its importance lay within a longer process of adult education whereby the leadership, clerical and lay, of the Church was being weaned from high Tory attitudes to an acceptance of the Christian case for massive social reform and the development of a welfare state. In this it and its like were almost over-successful.[25]

This long-term success will become apparent as we proceed.

The Miners' Strike

The lack of immediate political influence of Temple and those in the churches he represented is shown by what happened around the Miners' Strike of 1926. The background to the strike was the disorganization of the coal companies and the fact that they were struggling to survive: the owners became determined both to reduce pay and lengthen the working day (even beyond the legal limit). The miners decided to strike because conditions of work were harsh and pay was already barely lifting them out of poverty. Their slogan became 'Not a penny off the pay, not a minute on the day.' The government could have resolved the dispute, but all it had proposed before the strike, in the Samuel Report, was a curb on lengthening the working day. No new money would be given, no national reorganization or nationalization of the industry would take place, no rise in miners' wages would be allowed. Neither the owners nor the unions were willing to accept this and hence the strike took place.

When the miners stopped work, their action prompted a General Strike, a stopping of work by all the unionized workers in the country. The General Strike collapsed after ten days, however, and the miners had to continue with their strike on their own. It continued for six more months although, in the end, they were driven back to work by starvation.

As the strike wore on, Temple joined a group formed by the Industrial Christian Fellowship (ICF), the successor to the Christian Social Union, that included Gore, other bishops and Nonconformist leaders, who decided to act as mediators between the miners and mine owners. They approached both parties. The miners were now willing to reconsider the Samuel Report but the mine owners were not. The group then went to see the Prime Minister, Stanley Baldwin, to put the case for the government pushing through an adapted version of the Samuel proposals (substituting a bank loan for state subsidies to the mining industry). Temple reports that 'Baldwin was very nice personally, but was not disposed to budge.' Temple saw that the government wished the churches would keep out of the whole business, for it believed that the churches were implicitly encouraging the miners to continue the strike.

What should the group convened by the churches do then? P. T. R. Kirk, the convenor of the ICF, wanted the group to side with the miners in their push for the Samuel proposals. Temple and the others did not agree. He later explained that while

> the Church, acting for goodwill, may pass on technical proposals tend-
> ing to promote [a settlement], it is quite another thing for the Church
> to take the field saying that some technical proposal (e.g. a loan) is
> certainly the righteous line of action. Cook [the miners' leader], of
> course, will call us rats if we do not fight; and perhaps will be right to
> do so: but we *must* stick to our own job.[26]

Temple, then, was prepared to bring to light and expose a social injustice, in this case the plight of the miners, even to the extent of taking it to the highest levels of government and suggesting a certain course of action to overcome it. But at this stage of his career, he did not see his role as one of organizing a strong enough campaign to push through its proposals. He backed down from a messy fight.

The intervention by the church group has been heavily criticized. At the time there were many in the churches (including, it seems, Davidson),[27] as well as many outside, who agreed with the government and thought the intervention needlessly prolonged the strike by raising the hopes of the miners that they had support from the churches. In other words, the economic realities facing the mining industry should have been allowed to take their course sooner rather than later: the miners should have been forced to accept a reduction in pay and a lengthening of the working day (to an impossible degree) because there was no alternative!

From the other side, the failure to side with the miners has been heavily criticized by more recent commentators, notably Adrian Hastings. In his *History of English Christianity*, he wrote that 'It would seem that this was the real moment of Church failure and that Temple, more than anyone, was responsible for it.' What should happen, Hastings asks rhetorically, when reconciliation is impossible because one party (the owners) are sitting on the backs of the other (the miners).

> In some sense liberation [for the miners] has to come first, but to help with that can mean an at least temporary commitment to one side and to particular policies, not just general principles. If the churchmen were not willing to go so far because it was not their 'own job', then they could have better stayed out of the whole thing.[28]

Temple and the other bishops therefore pleased no one with their intervention. Later he admitted that the group had not intervened in a very skilful way with the detail of the proposals and that they had not known all the relevant information at the time they intervened.[29] He also later ruefully reported that when Stanley Baldwin the Prime Minister asked how the bishops would like it if he asked the Iron and Steel Federation to revise the Athanasian Creed, 'this was acclaimed as a legitimate score'.[30]

However, within a longer-term perspective, a more positive assessment emerges. While at the time the group's intervention failed in its objectives, it did pioneer, in a real and public way, the kind of mediating role the churches came increasingly to play in twentieth-century British political life, more successfully during the war years and more recently with the 1985 report *Faith in the City*. Temple's group became involved in the coal strike and failed in that involvement, paying a price, but they were seen, at least, to be trying to move things forward. Through their intervention it can be argued that the leadership of churches were growing into a role that initially had been pioneered by Cardinal Manning in the London dockers' strike of 1889, one of no longer simply supporting the political and economic establishment of the day but becoming a positive critic of that establishment, committed to improving the lives of ordinary people. This was a role that would grow with increasing effectiveness. Temple and the others in the 1926 group were, to their credit, in some ways leading the churches towards a new kind of presence in British society.

But after the coal strike, Temple largely withdrew from deliberate political intervention on social issues. It may have been because he had had his fingers burnt or it may have been because he became increasingly involved in the ecumenical movement. Furthermore, he was also drawn into the muddle over parliament's rejection of a revised version of the

Book of Common Prayer in 1928 and 1929. This took up a considerable amount of his time.

Reporting on unemployment

It was not until 1933 that he again became involved more overtly in the political process. This time it was unemployment that caught his attention. He was distressed and angry at the level and severity of unemployment in Britain, and above all upset that it prevented those affected from contributing to the life of their communities. He saw the need to work collaboratively with a team and called together a group of academics and church people to investigate the issue thoroughly and scientifically. They secured the financial backing of the Pilgrim Trust and began the research. At about the same time Temple published a letter in *The Times* calling on fellow Christians to write to their MP, asking that the reversal of recent cuts in benefit to the unemployed should take precedence over tax cuts for the better off in the forthcoming budget. Neville Chamberlain, the Chancellor, told Temple to stop interfering. Temple wrote back unapologetically saying that he had every right to invite people to forgo a benefit to themselves in favour of helping the less fortunate. It was an ineffective plea as far as the government was concerned but, again, Temple was allowing a critical yet constructive Christian voice to be heard at Westminster.

Much more effective was the report itself, published in 1938, 450 pages in length, with the title *Men Without Work*. It drew on studies on unemployment in Blackburn, Deptford, Durham, Leicester and Liverpool in England and the Rhondda in South Wales. The inquiry looked at those who had been unemployed for over a year and looked at the causes and symptoms of the problem. There were sample investigations of personal cases and examination of the relief work already being provided for the unemployed. When the report was published it was welcomed as a significant piece of scientific and human research.[31] It reminded a wide body of people of the plight of the unemployed and spurred both government and voluntary bodies to provide support for the setting up of 1,500 occupational centres in areas of high unemployment, not least in South Wales. With the publication of the report and through his enabling leadership, Temple's own standing as an informed and effective advocate of social justice rose considerably in government circles. It was, perhaps, a sign of a more effective kind of political leadership that he was now offering.

Men without Work, while leading to the better treatment of many who were already unemployed, could not and did not confront the underlying economic and social reasons that had produced widespread unemployment. It did not yet move society as a whole towards a more equitable social order. Temple's involvement in social reform, in other words, had not yet completed the circle, a circle which began with analysing society and understanding the need for reform but which needed to come round to pushing through that reform. He had patiently and impressively built up a vision of society as it could become, based on his theological convictions, one which resulted in him formulating the social principles. He had begun to work out the practical implications of those principles, seeing the need for radical reform of the social and educational structures of society. But in the 1930s he had not yet developed the practical policy recommendations found in his programme at the end of *Christianity and Social Order* and, crucially, he and his allies had not yet organized a campaign to press for their implementation. The upheaval of the Second World War would create the conditions in which this would become possible and in which Temple's responsive leadership would find its most effective expression.

Mobilizing a campaign

As the reality and disruption of war took hold in Britain, the director of the Industrial Christian Fellowship, Prebendary Kirk, approached Temple and together they decided there was no time to lose in beginning to think about what kind of society should be built after the war. How were the resources of the nation going to be distributed? What about health care and education? What about the living conditions in which people would grow up and live? It was well known that the opportunity for social reconstruction, presented at the end of the First World War, had been squandered. What was going to happen this time?

Temple knew that leadership must be provided and he believed the church should speak out on behalf of the poor as well as the rich in society. How, though, was he going to rise to this challenge? This time he decided not to launch his own personal initiative promoting his own ideas but to begin with consultation. Even as the war was commencing, long before moving from York to Canterbury, he and Kirk started to plan the Malvern Conference.[32] The aim of the conference would be to consider, from an Anglican standpoint, the fundamental ordering of the new society that would emerge from the war effort and to consider 'how Christian thought could be shaped to play a leading part in the reconstruction after the war is over'. An impressive group of speakers was brought to Malvern for three days in January 1941, including John

Middleton Murry, T. S. Eliot, Dorothy Sayers, Sir Richard Acland MP, the philosopher Donald Mackinnon and the social theologian V. A. Demant. There was an array of bishops present and, according to John Kent's researches, about 200 clergy and laity.[33]

The programme of the conference was overloaded and there was little opportunity for discussion. Acland created division among those present with his view that common ownership of the nation's principal industrial resources was a matter of fundamental Christian principle. The issues raised by Demant, Mackinnon and Murry were not addressed, and by the third day of the conference the participants were dazed and exhausted. But on the last night of the conference, Temple was able to write a series of conclusions, which he then presented to a surprised conference the following morning, suggesting that they expressed the common mind of the assembly. Temple's ability to sum up disorderly discussions in an orderly way has already been noted and at Malvern this ability had one of its finest hours. His conclusions were widely welcomed, except that the resolution on common ownership, the most contentious issue at the conference, had to be revised. It had reflected Acland's argument about the need for common ownership and stated that the vesting of the principal industrial resources of the country 'in the hands of private owners is a stumbling block ... contrary to divine justice, making it harder for men to live Christian lives'. The conference members, in an amendment proposed by Bishop Bell, substituted the much vaguer words 'may be' for 'is'.[34] But the final resolution still upheld the important principle that there should be social limits on the freedom of private capitalism, an idea Temple gives voice to in the Pathé film clip mentioned in the Introduction.

Despite the poor management of the conference and the vagueness of the final resolution, the conference had a significant impact: 'As far as the Church of England was concerned,' writes John Kent, 'Malvern undoubtedly expressed a resurgence of the more radical Anglican attitudes to unemployment and poverty which had dropped into the background after 1926.'[35] And, as Kent shows, for Temple it was the start of a movement for social reform. This is seen in a letter to Kirk in the month after the conference where he speaks of 'the movement' and the need to keep a broad range of support behind it, including from Anglo-Catholics and Evangelicals and those in the centre as well as on the left of politics.[36]

The increasing strength of the movement is seen the following summer when Kirk informed Temple that the Industrial Christian Fellowship had printed and distributed 200,000 copies of a brief summary of the conclusions of the conference. Temple went on to write a 16-page summary of the conference, which sold 30,000 copies, and in that same summer planned further meetings in London with a small hand-picked group to discuss practical objectives for reform, the objectives that became 'A Suggested Programme' in *Christianity and Social Order*. That book was itself written in the summer and autumn of 1941 and explicitly drew on the work of the Lambeth Conferences of 1897, 1908 and 1920, and the work of ecumenical conferences commissions. Temple states at the beginning of the book that 'reference to these will shew that the principles which I lay down are not an expression of a purely personal point of view but represent the main trend of Christian social teaching'.[37] In this he drew on a number of theological traditions giving prominence, for example, to the idea of natural law alongside his own Christian social principles, and also of current academic and governmental expertise, as we have already seen, through consultations with economists such as Keynes and Alice Lascelles and other academics such as Tawney, and Professors Mouat Jones and Henry Clay.[38] Temple's proposals were peer reviewed in this way, as we have seen. He was clearly determined to draw up a practicable programme, with specific proposals for eradicating poverty and unemployment, but one which would be supported by a broad range of opinion. He was clearly determined that the opportunity of the moment should not be lost (as it had after the Miners' Strike of 1926). He was going to make a deliberate attempt, through consulting, discussing, editing, writing, corresponding and speaking up and down the country, to influence national political life, and all of this on top of his existing duties as an archbishop.

And, as reported in the Introduction, it began to work. Not only was the Malvern material being bought and read but *Christianity and Social Order* went on to sell 139,000 copies. His social thought was clearly being absorbed by a wider public than the restricted church circles that had previously read his books. And when, in the same year that it was published, Temple planned some mass meetings to raise the profile of his agenda, he had no trouble in attracting Cripps and Acland, as well as other church leaders, to share his platform. As already described in the Introduction of this book the meetings were organized under the banner heading of 'The Church Looks Forward' and were organized by Kirk and the ICF, beginning with the Royal Albert Hall meeting in September 1942, then Birmingham (November 1942), Leicester (February 1943), Edinburgh (June 1943), and ending with a youth rally back in London (October 1943). The halls were filled with people eager to hear his message, as the Pathé film clip vividly shows.

The first Royal Albert Hall meeting was also to have some dramatic repercussions in the press. Temple not only made his comments about the right and the duty of the church to lay down principles for the ordering of society, and to criticize the capitalist system for attempting to privatize everything it possibly could, but he also mentioned that there had been a great amalgamation of banks in the last 50 years with the issuing of credit becoming monopolized within a few private hands. He continued with a very bold suggestion:

> Now it is surely a primary political principle that, when, something which is universally necessary becomes a monopoly, that monopoly should be taken under public control. In my judgment at least – I don't claim that it is worth much, but I want to offer it you – in my judgment at least it should now be regarded as improper for any person or corporation to issue new credit; as it was in the Middle Ages for any private person or corporation to mint actual money, for the two are equivalent. And so I should like, I confess, to see the banks limited in their lending power to sums equivalent to that which depositors have entrusted to them, and all new credit to be issued by some public authority.[39]

The hesitant way in which these remarks were made belies the radical nature of their proposals. Temple was advocating a major intervention by the state in the banking system and proposing that in significant ways it take command of the financial sector.

There was consternation from various quarters of the City of London. It seemed to some that the archbishop did not know what he was talking about. He was either naïve or an agent for Marxism. What did he think he was proposing? The letter pages of the press were filled, first with protest and then with defence of Temple's words. *The Times* published a selection of letters on several consecutive days and hardly a newspaper or magazine did not comment. The story was sent around the English-speaking world and publicized as far away as Nebraska and New South Wales. Temple's own mail bag was filled and so were those of the other speakers that night.

Iremonger comments on the correspondence that in Temple's technical arguments and in his use of technical terms 'there can be little doubt that he went astray. (This becomes even clearer from the many subsequent letters that passed between him and his friends and correspondents among the bankers.)'[40] However the points he was making had been included in *Christianity and Social Order* and had been peer reviewed by the economist John Maynard Keynes among others, so there is some doubt about Iremonger's 'little doubt'. It does seem clear that Temple was making a bold and even visionary statement, one intended to show the whole way the Christian conscience was confronting the entrenched forces of capitalism with the demand for a more just and equitable world.

Those who supported Temple saw it in this way. Robert Lynd wrote that Temple had 'taken the only step possible to a modern Christian leader in demanding that politics and economics should be christianized'.[41] A cartoon in London's *Evening Standard* showed that Low the cartoonist believed Temple's speech was more than just one proposal for the reform of credit laws. It was instead 'the Christian aim' for post-war reconstruction, in the hands of the Primate of All England, facing down the bulldogs of high finance. An editorial in the *Spectator* wrote that the 'effect of the controversy, indeed, is to impress on many people who had overlooked it that the new Primate is a man of great knowledge and brilliant intellect, as well as of abundant moral courage'. It also thought that support for Temple's speech far outweighed the criticism it evoked.[42]

Temple himself saw his banking proposals, disingenuously, as nothing more than his own personal views given to illustrate the principles on which a Christian social order could be founded. But, as many pointed out, it was impossible for the Archbishop of Canterbury just to give his own personal views. The person and the office were as one. Nevertheless, through the controversy he stood his ground and said that he had issued his challenge to stir consciences and provoke attention.[43]

Did the Royal Albert Hall speech enhance the campaign that had begun at Malvern and continued with other speeches up and down the country? Did Temple provide visionary leadership for the nation, or was he engaging with subjects he had no right to speak about? Some commentators side with Temple's critics at this point. Norman, for example, calls Temple's views on banking 'absurd'.[44] Hastings calls them 'a bee in his bonnet'.[45] But his supporters at the time, as we have seen, thought he was doing what was right. And there is evidence that other younger observers were also inspired by his words, from both the left wing and the centre ground of politics.

From the left came David Jenkins, who later became the Bishop of Durham and himself no stranger to controversy. At the centenary of Temple's birth in 1981 he wrote the following autobiographical words:

As a teenager I attended the Albert Hall meeting which Temple addressed, along with others including Sir Stafford Cripps, and what I drew from this, as well as what I read of his utterances and writings, was a clear understanding that we should be deeply Christian and deeply concerned with current affairs. Christianity was neither a purely private religion nor a merely spiritual religion. This was so because of the nature and purposes of the God to whom Christianity was a response. Temple was, surely, a powerfully devout man, and the demands which he put before one were clearly religious, devotional, and godly. But godliness required concern for the affairs of society because men and women were so socially shaped, and often socially distorted, and because the transcendent God was committed to worldly particularities for the furthering of his purposes and the sharing of his love.[46]

There is not much here about Temple's views on banking but, instead, the subject of the reminiscences is the whole orientation of the Christian towards the world he or she lives within. Temple's words on the banking system did not make Jenkins question Temple's credibility. His speech as a whole inspired Jenkins to enter into the struggles of making society conform more closely to the love of God, providing tangible leadership in the middle of wartime.

From the centre ground of politics the Conservative politician and future prime minister Edward Heath expressed similar sentiments:

> The impact of William Temple on my generation was immense ... The reason was not far to seek. William Temple was foremost among the leaders of the nation, temporal or spiritual, in posing challenging, radical questions about the nature of our society. Most important of all, he propounded with lucidity and vigour his understanding of the Christian ethic in its application to the contemporary problems which engrossed us all.[47]

The movement which had begun at Malvern, then, leading through *Christianity and Social Order* to 'The Church Looks Forward' campaign, clearly touched and inspired a great many people, from a variety of standpoints, to pick up the torch offered by Temple. If further proof of the impact of his leadership was needed, the constructive work of the wartime and post-war governments in Britain can be cited. Within the space of five years many of the social and economic objectives advocated by Temple had been achieved. These included the passing of a comprehensive education act by the national government in 1944 and various reforms by the Labour government between 1945 and 1951 including nationalization of principal industrial resources such as the coal industry and transport, major improvements to social security, widespread house building and most impressively of all the creation of a national health service. Taken as a whole these measures amounted to the creation of the welfare state. There were, of course, other powerful forces behind these developments but William Temple and those who worked with him provided a collaborative and responsive leadership within British public opinion which helped to make them come about.

Notes

1 Joseph Fletcher, *William Temple: Twentieth-Century Christian*, New York: Seabury, 1963.

2 Peter d'A. Jones, *The Christian Socialist Revival 1877–1914*, Princeton: Princeton University Press, 1968.

3 John Oliver, *The Church and Social Order: Social Thought in the Church of England 1918–1939*, London: A. R. Mowbray, 1968, pp. 2–24.

4 E. R. Norman, *Church and Society in England, 1770–1970: A Historical Study*, Oxford: Clarendon, 1976, p. 281.

5 William Temple, 'The Church and the Labour Party', *The Economic Review*, Vol. XVIII, 15 April 1908, p. 199.

6 Rowan Williams has provided the following wry comment on this assertion: 'Now over the years, I have become reasonably expert in the sort of things you probably ought not to say if you want to be Archbishop of Canterbury, so you might be surprised to hear that these words were spoken by William Temple in 1908, the future Archbishop of Canterbury, arguably the greatest archbishop of the 20th century ...' ('The challenge of affluence', 2019).

7 William Temple, *Principles of Social Progress*, Melbourne: Australian Student Christian Union, 1910, p. 12.

8 F. D. Maurice, *Tracts on Christian Socialism*, London: Bell, 1850, p. 4.

9 F. A. Iremonger, *William Temple, Archbishop of Canterbury: His Life and Letters*, London: Oxford University Press, 1948, p. 329.

10 'Introduction' in H. Martin (ed.), *Christian Social Reformers of the Nineteenth Century*, London: SCM Press, 1927, p. vii.

11 Iremonger, *William Temple*, p. 332.

12 Charles Gore (ed.), *Property: Its Rights and Duties*, London: Macmillan and Co., 1913.

13 Oliver, *The Church and Social Order*, p. 11; see pp. 10–14.

14 Temple, 'The Church and Labour', *Daily News*, 14 May 1918.

15 Temple, 'The Church and Labour'.

16 Iremonger, *William Temple*, pp. 333, 509.

17 Iremonger, *William Temple*, pp. 509–10.

18 Martin (ed.), *Christian Social Reformers*, p. 7.

19 Martin (ed.), *Christian Social Reformers*, pp. 1, 12.

20 T. Christensen, *Origins and History of Christian Socialism 1848–53*, Aarhus: Universitetsforlaget, 1962, p. 137.

21 Temple, letter to Mr Skuse, William Temple Papers, Vol. 47, p. 223.

22 John Kent, *William Temple, Church, State and Society in Britain 1880-1950*, Cambridge: Cambridge University Press, 1992, p. 116.

23 Iremonger, *William Temple*, p. 335.

24 Kent, *William Temple*, p. 125.

25 Adrian Hastings, *A History of English Christianity 1920–2000*, London: SCM Press, 2001, p. 179.

26 Iremonger, *William Temple*, p. 340.

27 Kent, *William Temple*, pp. 138, 139, 142.

28 Hastings, *A History of English Christianity*, p. 191.

29 Iremonger, *William Temple*, pp. 342–3.

30 William Temple, *Christianity and Social Order*, Shepheard-Walwyn and SPCK, 1976, p. 29.

31 William Temple, *Men without Work*, Cambridge University Press, 1938.

32 Cosmo Lang, the then Archbishop of Canterbury, also turned his mind to the future just three months after the start of the war, but without drawing on the views of others through organizing a conference or consultation. See Robert Beaken, *Cosmo Lang, Archbishop in War and Crisis*, London: I. B. Tauris, 2012, p. 196.

33 Kent, *William Temple*, pp. 150, 157.

34 Iremonger, *William Temple*, p. 431. See further Temple, *Malvern 1941*, 1941.

35 Kent, *William Temple*, p. 161.

36 Kent, *William Temple*, p. 163.

37 *Christianity and Social Order*, p. 27.

38 *Christianity and Social Order*, p. 27.

39 William Temple, *The Church Looks Forward*, London: Macmillan, 1944, p. 112

40 Iremonger, *William Temple*, p. 579.

41 Iremonger, *William Temple*, p. 581.

42 Iremonger, *William Temple*, p. 581.

43 Iremonger, *William Temple*, p. 582.

44 Norman, *Church and Society in England 1770–1970*, p. 323.

45 Hastings, *A History of English Christianity*, p. 398.

46 David Jenkins, editorial, *Theology*, September 1981, pp. 321–2.

47 'Foreword', Temple, *Christianity and Social Order*.

9

Called into ecumenical leadership

William Temple's leadership in the British political arena, important as it was, was only one of several ways he made a material contribution to church and society at the mid-point of the twentieth century. Another was to the ecumenical movement. Indeed some historians, such as Frances Knight, regard this part of his legacy as the most important of all.[1] She introduces his contribution in its early twentieth-century context: 'He was in the right place at the right time.' This began with his involvement as an usher in the first big ecumenical activity of the new century, the Edinburgh Missionary Conference of 1910, which

> gets together missionaries from all over the world who [then] after the First World War realise they are not going to convert the whole world to Christianity but what they can do is get along better with each other. He moves into being a leading figure in the various ecumenical movement's congresses and conferences which happen in the twenties and thirties which then culminate in the [founding of the] World Council of Churches in the 1940s.

Knight then describes the transformative outlook that Temple brought to all this:

> He is an incredibly Anglican establishment figure … and yet he says in his enthronement sermon in 1942 that the really exciting thing that is happening in Christianity is that sense of it becoming a worldwide brotherhood of people who recognise each other and acknowledge each other, and that Christianity is seen as being much bigger than just the denomination that you belong to, which was the feeling widespread up to that point. So he opens it out from the church equals the Church of England or the Roman Catholic Church or the Methodist Church to the church is actually a worldwide Christian society.[2]

This portrait raises a key question for any analysis of William Temple's ecumenical leadership. What led such a quintessentially Anglican figure, who had been brought up at the heart of the English establishment, to become such an influential servant of cross-denominational ecumenism? It is this question which this chapter addresses.

We begin by investigating Temple's early life. Even though he was brought up in bishops' palaces and had an ever-confident disposition, there was significant unease and questioning of Christianity in his formative years, as we have already seen in the letters he wrote when an undergraduate. These were letters he wrote to his friend John Stocks in 1901 and 1902 attempting to persuade him to seek ordination. They reveal Temple's own criticism of the Church that his father was currently leading. They give real insight into his outlook at this formative moment of his life: 'I mean that the Church – and consequently the nation – is in a very critical state: I mean that it is doing very nearly as much harm as good – and perhaps more. And this because of its narrow spirit.' Temple cites an emotional form of preaching as part of the problem, and baldly states that 'anything more hostile to the New Testament than our modern English religion is hard to conceive'. Such narrowness needs a strong response: 'Well, I believe that the only thing that can save us is a vigorous attack from within the Church on the existing conceptions of religion.'[3]

In another letter, one that is worth quoting again, Temple revealed the theological outlook that lies behind this strong criticism:

> The Christ men believe in and worship is to a great extent a myth and an idol – very different from Him who lived and died 'to bear witness to the truth', and Whose Spirit lived and spoke in Socrates and Buddha and Mahomet [sic.] as it did also in Hosea and Luther and Browning. Men do not realize that Christ requires a good life and not church-going, and knowledge of God more than communicating.[4]

It was not only the current practice of the Church of England that Temple was questioning, then, but the basic understanding of Christ found in most churches. He was wanting to transcend the idea that Christ can be found only in institutional Christianity and was advocating an inclusivist understanding of Christ's presence in the world: the Lord does not belong just within narrow ecclesiastical circles but to all humanity, including those of other faiths.

The question then became: how was Temple going to promote this passionate inclusivism? And the answer was not at first very encouraging. We have already seen how the early years of his career saw him veer towards a conventional ecclesiastical path, from don to headmaster to rector of a smart London parish, rather than follow his calling to a more radical and prophetic kind of ministry. But then from 1917 he began to strike out on his own, first by resigning his incumbency to lead the Life and Liberty movement and then, when Bishop of Manchester, to spearhead a number of radical initiatives such as the COPEC movement and the subject of this chapter, the building of bridges with other churches.

Promoting an ecumenical Anglicanism

A precondition of genuine ecumenism is that those who engage in it are prepared to recognize the authenticity of other traditions and denominations. How did Temple, so much the product of the Church of England's version of Anglicanism, come to promote an ecumenically-minded Anglicanism? It is clear he did not follow his mentor Charles Gore, who was emphatic in his upholding of the Catholic nature of Anglicanism in distinction from the churches of the Reformation. When Bishop of Manchester, Temple engaged with leaders of other denominations, both Protestant and Roman Catholic, and it is in this period that we see him come to articulate an inclusive version of Anglicanism. This is found in his address to the annual diocesan conference of the Manchester clergy in 1925 on the vocation and destiny of the Church of England. The diocesan conferences were one of the principle ways he sought to connect with and influence the clergy of his diocese. In this address he described what he understood to be the vocation and destiny of the church to which they all belonged. Its vocation, he believed, was derived from its history. This history was of a church that was heir to the continuous history of Christendom and, also, heir to that 'new birth' which is called the Reformation:

> Both of these must be borne in mind, for both of them are equally essential to the constitution, doctrine, and work of the Church of England as it has constantly represented itself from the time of the Reformation onwards.[5]

In the 1925 address as a whole, however, he emphasized the importance of the Reformation over what came before it. While an earlier reforming movement of the eleventh century is commended for its right intentions in recovering the spiritual character of the church and its fidelity to the New Testament, it nevertheless 'did not go deep enough ... it did not reach the roots'. Consequently, it was followed by a sharp decline which led to a 'decay which made the Reformation inevitable'. For Temple, the sixteenth-century Reformation marked the recovery of two fundamental principles of Christian life: the supreme authority of scripture, and the duty of private judgement (or what Temple prefers to call the freedom of the individual religious life). Describing the first, Temple made a distinction between the authority of scripture and its interpretation: the interpretation of scripture may vary both from person to person, and from one age to another, and scripture does not make any claim to describe the whole truth concerning God and his dealing with the world. But its supremacy remains none the less, for it is there, and there only, that we find God's teaching coming into its 'fullness' with the light blazing out in all its glory, in the Person of Jesus Christ.[6]

The other principle Temple described as the duty of everyone 'sincerely to make up his mind what it is that God says to him through the Scriptures'. But Temple did not see this as taking place by means of the individual alone. The believer will do it 'in the fellowship of his fellow-seekers in the Church; he will allow to the witness of the Church's authority, if he is wise, a weight which will override any mere whims of his own mind'. But then 'he will recognise the duty of making up his own mind and of appropriating for himself, as far as the Holy Spirit enables him, the truth that is given to the world through the Scripture'.[7]

And so Temple's emphasis on the Reformation did not lead him to an individualistic view of how scripture should be interpreted. The scriptures are paramount and have their own authority, an authority worthy of respect, but are handed on by the corporate life of the church guided by the Holy Spirit. Ultimately the individual conscience could set aside the tradition of the church, but only when there was good reason and when others in the fellowship supported that. Scripture and conscience were the ultimate sources of authority but tradition had an important role to play as well.

For Temple these principles were embodied in the Church of England. Its vocation and destiny was to live by them and in them, 'to offer the fullness of God's help to every soul but never to dictate to any soul precisely how that soul may best receive the benefit'.[8] The Church was to embody a freedom in its life that would be different from a strict and military discipline based on the fulfilling of clear-cut duties. It would be a freedom that would allow 'a fullness of individual apprehension and appropriation', by which he meant that it would really allow those within it to adopt and own the Christian faith for themselves.

And this vocation meant that the Church of England was in a good position to respect and appreciate other Christian outlooks, not least the traditional Catholic churches of East and West and the Protestant churches of the Reformation. It was this that allowed it to reach out to both traditions. Towards the end of his address he described how as a church we hold out, as it is commonly said, a hand upon both sides to the other great Christian bodies. We can hold out a hand both to the ancient Churches of the East and to Rome on the one side, and to all those who with us are heirs of the Reformation on the other; and in that we have a position unique in Christendom, the full value of which can only be realised for the universal Church so far as we are true to both sides of our own tradition.[9]

Ecumenism, then, could have a natural and central place in the life of Anglicanism because this tradition was based itself on the coming together of different traditions. Anglican church leaders could reach out, engage in dialogue and draw more closely together with the leaders of other churches because that was the inherent nature of Anglicanism. In this address therefore we see how ecumenical commitment, for Temple, would become part and parcel of being an Anglican Christian. It was to be at the heart of church life.

Temple, however, went on to qualify his ecumenical commitment in a significant and subtle way, one which some of his Protestant friends did not agree with. It concerned Anglicanism's inherited sacraments and especially its episcopal ministry. In the Lambeth Conference of 1888, these two elements had been declared to be two of four essential ingredients or 'articles' of unity across churches.[10] But many Protestant churches do not have bishops and have different understandings of the nature of the sacraments. Should Anglicans insist that they take on these articles for the sake of unity, which they are unlikely to do, or should Anglicans downgrade and even dispense with them for the sake of forging unity?

Temple's own answer to this recurrent and challenging question was given in its most extended form in one of his 'charges' to the clergy of York Diocese when he was Archbishop of York. In a carefully constructed and extended address,[11] which needs to be quoted at some length, he began by resoundingly condemning church disunity for the way it prevented common witness, common fellowship at the Lord's Supper and common mission work:

the world cannot see even such unity as exists among Christians so long as they are unable to join together at the Table of the Lord. Where there are many Churches in the same place, they obscure instead of manifesting the one Christ ... A vast amount of the material resources available for the Work of the Christian Community is frittered away through the overlapping of organisation, the needless multiplication of places of worship with consequent waste of man-power, and the loss of efficiency through the need to weigh irrelevant considerations.[12]

The need for effective evangelism and ecclesial efficiency demanded that churches come together. But Temple then states, surprisingly, that 'there are prices too high to pay [for Christian unity]. The severed parts of the Universal Church are trustees for the treasures of their own spiritual tradition, and must bring these with them to the reunited fellowship of the future.'[13] So he is not advocating *uniformity* across the churches but a *unity of differences*, a much more difficult proposition, which brings him to the question of the episcopate.

Later in the charge, in order to prepare his ground, Temple looks to the book of Acts and the subsequent story of Christendom which shows that there 'was a fellowship of believers with the Apostolate [the body of the apostles] as its focus of leadership and authority'. He sees an interdependence between the apostles and the wider group of believers:

> Neither did the Apostles gather the Church about them in obedience to an authority which they independently possessed, nor did the society of believers confer upon the Apostles an authority originally inherent in the body as a whole. But the Church was born with the Apostolate as an integral part of it, providing leadership and exercising authority with a general consent that was grounded in a universal sense of what was fit. This was the inevitable and unquestionably (as I think) intended result of our Lord's own action in forming the Apostolate; thus the differentiation of Clergy and Laity within His Church is of His own making.[14]

Temple then argues that the episcopate carried forward this interdependent structure down the centuries, quoting an ecumenical text to support this point: episcopacy does this '"in its continuity of succession and consecration," (*Report on the Ministry* of the Lausanne Conference on Faith and Order, p. 115) as its central principle of Order. The Anglican Communion still uses the Historic Episcopate in that way.'[15]

This means episcopacy needs to be part of a reunited church and when 'we are asked why we should insist upon its acceptance by others before we can establish full intercommunion with them' the answer is that episcopacy conveys the authority of the universal church as handed down since the time of the apostles, an authority 'which, therefore, can only be rightly administered by those who hold the Church's commission to do so'. So, later in the address, Temple states that:

> The Church is the repository and trustee of God's self-revelation. Its ministers do not represent a local group; they are the appointed agents of the Universal Church for the proclamation of the revelation and dispensing of the means of grace which are entrusted to that Universal Church.[16]

This means that churches in which 'the full system of the historic Church has been maintained, their very office bears this testimony'. Therefore the priest 'who preaches and celebrates does so as the organ of the Universal Church; the office of the Bishop who ordained him is, in part of its very essence, constituted by, the commission to commission others on behalf of the Universal Church.'[17]

On the other hand, churches that do not have the historic episcopacy have a 'defect of authorisation' which 'leads to a lowered sense of the spiritual importance of authorisation'.[18] He is not arguing that they cannot receive the grace of God through their ministry and sacraments but that, to be faithful to what has been handed down, they should receive episcopacy back into their life. He later adds, however, that

> I make no claim to perfection for the Anglican Communion. I know that we are the poorer for lack of gifts which our Free Church friends possess in greater abundance. I do not claim that our ministry is fully representative; the refusal of recognition by Rome, even though we believe it to be mistaken, would alone prevent that. For the only fully representative Ministry would be one 'acknowledged by every part of the Church as possessing not only the inward call of the Spirit, but also the commission of Christ and the authority of the whole body.' (Lambeth Conference 1920, Resolution 9.6)[19]

Temple then summarizes this difficult but important argument:

> [It] is of the essence of episcopacy that the bishop acts for the whole Church, not for any section of it. Where any great part of the Church refuses to recognise a bishop or the commission bestowed through him, the commission is to that extent defective, not in authority (which comes from Christ alone) but in effectiveness. If some part of the Church has failed to maintain the episcopate in its continuity of office and conse-cration, it has lost the agency through which the claim to issue the com-mission of the whole Church is made. God may (and we know He does) bless the ministries serving those parts of the Church ... But this does not constitute the commission given to and on behalf of the Universal Church, and to treat the two as identical is the way, not to secure union, but to new disunion whenever some strong conviction is formed by any group of Christians.[20]

Here, then, was an aspect of Anglicanism that Temple was not prepared to surrender in ecumenical reunion. He came to welcome the exchange of pulpits between ministers of the different churches but he could not accept the interchangeability of eucharistic ministry. On his belief that, ultimately, the eucharistic ministry of the non-Catholic churches was not effectively authorized, and that episcopacy was necessary to the preservation of the true order of the Church, he was vigorously challenged by the American theologian Reinhold Niebuhr,[21] but he held his ground and showed that his ecumenical leadership was based on a firm but carefully qualified commitment to church unity. This also shows that he did not simply believe in the complementarity of different denominational traditions but had a more nuanced view of how those traditions should come together, with some important adjustments required by some of them.[22]

Overall, then, we see that Temple's ecumenical Anglicanism was not one of dissolving difference into uniformity but of endeavouring to be faithful to what had been handed down while actively seeking unity with other churches. This was not an easy calling at all, and he could not and did not please everyone, which makes his historic and widely welcomed contributions to ecumenism, the subject of the next section, all the more remarkable.

Bringing churches together

What was Temple's practical contribution to ecumenism? His first involvement was as a steward at the Edinburgh Missionary Conference in 1910, already mentioned above. This made him aware of an emerging movement among missionaries for the churches to work more closely together for the evangelization of the world. As a young man he also supported the ecumenical Student Christian Movement, having become a member when at Oxford and then becoming one of its most regular speakers at its annual conferences in Swanwick in Derbyshire. Many of the student leaders of the SCM in the 1920s and 1930s were inspired by Temple to work for unity among the churches in their subsequent careers, among them Lesslie Newbigin, Ambrose Reeves, Oliver Tomkins and Ronald Preston. And as Bishop of Manchester he supported discussions exploring the possibility of reunion of churches within the British Isles.

Temple's international leadership really began to take shape in the late 1920s. This is seen in his participation in the Jerusalem missionary conference of 1928, which was a follow up to the Edinburgh conference and which brought together official denominational representatives rather than just missionary societies. The conference took place during the British protectorate of Palestine and delegates were accommodated in military huts on the northern slopes of the Mount of Olives. Conditions were basic: there were no baths and no electricity. Candles were used for lighting and on one occasion the draught in Temple's hut was so strong that the candle he used for lighting would not burn properly on the table and he reported to his wife that he had put it on the floor, himself lying on his tummy on the floorboards, to write his letters.[23] During the conference he visited Tabgha and Capernaum and described Lake Galilee as 'most beautiful, and full of a delicious peace. When the sunset light fell on the Eastern hills the steep sides were much greener than I had seen before, though the rock comes through a great deal. The red in the Northern parts became glorious.'[24] Of Jerusalem itself he wrote, 'I shall not forget the 20 minutes or so that I spent all alone in Gethsemane, looking across at the dome in the Temple area. It is the one thing that has given me "feelings" in Jerusalem.'[25] However, what was most important about the conference was the recognition of Temple's ability to formulate concluding statements in which every point of view was woven into a coherent whole. This was noticed and appreciated, resulting in his being called to draft the concluding 'Message' of the conference, a statement which apparently satisfied both the progressives and the conservatives. Temple's ability to serve ecumenism in this attentive yet proactive way was beginning to reveal itself. As a whole the Jerusalem conference showed that, from now on, there was a willingness in both the older and younger churches to attempt to work together in missionary work around the world.

This calling would find more significant expression in the Faith and Order Movement, a coming together of Protestant churches to share and resolve the theological and ministerial differences between them. The first significant Faith and Order conference was at Lausanne in 1927 and the second in Edinburgh in 1937. Temple was present at both. At the first he was again responsible for drafting the message of the conference, which was widely applauded. The conference agreed that the Apostles' Creed and the Nicene Creed expressed the faith of all the churches represented, and that a future unity must rest on the basis of the historic episcopate. Temple considered these achievements to have been very significant. His gifts of attentive listening and proactive assimilation led in 1929 to his being elected the chairman of the Faith and Order continuation committee. Thereafter he always attended its annual meetings, mostly on the continent of Europe, and chaired the executive committee, at which most of the important preparatory work was done. At one of these meetings Temple described to his wife how, at a lunch in a hotel in Denmark,

[E]ach person's plate was replenished from some other as soon as his last mouthful of the last was off it. I got off lightly with bits of smoked salmon, lobster, chicken and assorted vegetables – mercifully small portions of each. Then came a great dish with several kinds of cheese and several sorts of salad. There is a lovely instrument like a fish-slice with a bent down flange in it which cuts shavings of cheese with delightful ease.

We got over knotty points in the Agenda until tea-time.[26]

Temple's considerable skill in guiding discussion and producing comprehensive statements at the end resulted in his being elected the chairman at the world Faith and Order conference in Edinburgh in 1937. This conference passed a final 'affirmation' that bears Temple's theological stamp:

> We are divided in the outward forms of our life in Christ, because we understand differently His will for His Church. We believe, however, that a deeper understanding will lead us towards a united apprehension of the truth as it is in Jesus. We humbly acknowledge that our divisions are contrary to the will of Christ and we pray God in His mercy to shorten the days of our separation and to guide us by His Spirit into fullness of unity.[27]

This statement does not pretend that differences do not exist between the churches and does not try to ignore them. But it places great store in the power of dialogue and agreement between the churches, so that such differences could be overcome in time and that a full unity could come about. This placing of hope in the power of reasonableness and in what the future could bring is very characteristic of Temple, and it became characteristic of the whole Faith and Order movement in the mid-twentieth century. It shows how his leadership was so well matched to the ecumenical needs of the time.

His most significant contribution, however, was to help form the idea of a world council of churches, the most enduring ecclesiastical development of the 1930s. Once again this was not through political campaigning or high-profile public speaking but through the collaboration of backroom committee work. He worked closely with two influential figures in the international ecumenical movement: J. H. Oldham, a slightly deaf Free Church of Scotland secretary of the International Missionary Council, who later became chairman of research in the Life and Work arm of the ecumenical movement, and William Paton, an English Presbyterian who had been a missionary in India and was Oldham's forceful successor at the International Missionary Council. Oldham, Paton and Temple have been described by Hastings as 'the ecclesiastical statesmen of Protestant Europe, dexterously creating the structures for the Church of the future'.[28] Of the three it was Temple who became the public representative. But the turning point in all this was not a grand public meeting but a gathering at his home at Bishopthorpe outside York.

The background to this was the widespread perception that the Faith and Order movement had overlapping concerns with the Life and Work movement, another attempt to bring Protestant churches together. In the 1920s Archbishop Nathan Söderblom of Sweden had begun to push for a League of Churches to bring all the leaders together, and then in 1929 a co-ordination commission was set up between Faith and Order and Life and Work, to work together in certain areas. Other ecumenical bodies were doing similar things. Edward Loane has provided the following revealing account of what happened next, based on correspondence in the archives of the WCC:

> These shared synergies and pressures led Temple to host a crucial meeting in May 1933 at his home of Bishopthorpe. The meeting was small and unofficial but was attended by ten key leaders of the ecumenical organisations ... Temple later described the meeting as 'a group of friends concerned in international work who met at my invitation to see whether we could make our arrangements more economical or more effective by any sort of co-operation'.[29]

Temple's primary helper in arranging the meeting was Henri Henriod, who described the occasion as 'a godsend in the present troubled and chaotic conditions, when the future of most of our oecumenical movements may be at stake'.[30] It is important to remember that the Nazis were seizing power in Germany at this time and the future of Europe was looking very bleak. Various papers were prepared for the meeting, including one by William Adams Brown who proposed the forming of 'a World Council of Christian Churches' to facilitate the organic union of the whole church. The meeting produced a number of resolutions. Loane comments that, 'While the meeting at Bishopthorpe did not produce immediate practical results, Visser 't Hooft is correct in identifying it as a turning point for the movement. From the conference, a dedicated and representative group, albeit unofficial, was focused on reorganising the ecumenical movement.'[31]

This was followed three months later by another meeting in Paris at which a proposal was made to merge Faith and Order with Life and Work in due course, and then Temple instigated a successful drive to raise funds for financing the next stage of Faith and Order's work. At another informal meeting at Princeton in 1935 Temple then took the lead in proposing an 'interdenominational, international council representing all the churches'. In July 1937, he chaired the so-called 'Committee of Thirty-Five meeting', at Westfield College, London, which formulated the precise proposal for a 'World Council of Churches'. This was subsequently accepted by the international ecumenical Life and Work conference at Oxford (chaired by Bishop Bell of Chichester) and by the world Faith and Order conference in Edinburgh in 1937; Temple preached the sermon at its opening service in St Giles Cathedral, Edinburgh, in 1937.[32] The sermon was a rousing call for renewed commitment to Christian unity in the increasingly bleak environment of Nazi-dominated Europe. The next year at Utrecht, Temple was elected chairman of the provisional World Council's central committee, with Wim Visser 't Hooft, Oldham's assistant, as one of two general secretaries, and Paton as the other.

As an archbishop, he was the most senior church leader to be involved in these discussions and this partly explains his rise to leadership of the movement. But his rise was also due to his considerable skills as an advocate of ecumenism and, underlying his involvement, to his own theology of the church which, as we have seen, was one that accepted other churches as fellow pilgrims along the way. Hastings writes that, 'It is unlikely that the World Council would have been proposed, agreed to, and brought into existence without his combination of authority and persuasiveness.'[33] If Temple had lived he would almost certainly have become the first president of the World Council of Churches when it was formally constituted in 1948. Loane comments that its establishment 'should be considered one of Temple's greatest achievements'.[34]

It can be added that all the contact between European churches that this process entailed in the war years brought about a very different set of relationships than during the First World War. 'The nationalistic orientation of the churches during the First World War was not repeated in the Second. The response was primarily due to the ecumenical bonds that had been built in the inter-war period.'[35] Temple's warm sentiments to Christians in Germany in a Christmas broadcast in 1941 show this very well:

I am most happy that it falls to me as Chairman of the Provisional Committee of the World Council of Churches in process of formation to add these closing words of greeting to our fellow Christians in Germany. The project of the World Council is a result and expression of that growth in fellowship which, all over the world, has been uniting Christians to one another in ever-deepening unity. Thirty years ago it could not have been conceived as possible: now it is an achievement on the point of being consummated ... I think of many very dear German friends, whom I yearn to meet again, knowing that when we meet it will be to find our fellowship in allegiance to Christ unbroken and undiminished.[36]

In the British Isles

Temple also reached out to the Roman Catholic Church which was not part of these discussions. In February 1939, he wrote to the Cardinal Secretary of State at the Vatican informing him of the plans to establish the WCC and expressed the hope that it might be possible to exchange information on matters of common interest and that the WCC 'should have the help from time to time of unofficial consultation with Roman Catholic theologians and scholars.' Several months passed before an answer was received but the answer was that the cardinal saw no obstacles in the way of carrying out Temple's proposals.[37] His hand of friendship had not been rebuffed and in an era in which there was an immense divide between their respective communions this was of some significance.

He also began to work with the Roman Catholic leader in England and Wales, Cardinal Hinsley. They shared a platform at the Royal Albert Hall with the Chief Rabbi and Herbert Morrison the Labour politician at the end of 1938, calling for a national response to the persecution of the Jews. Then, after the outbreak of war, Temple and Hinsley, who now shared a friendship with each other, signed a joint letter to *The Times* with other religious leaders, supporting the Pope's five peace points as 'the only sure foundation for a European peace'. This showed how the ecumenical fraternity was now being widened to include the Roman Catholic Church in England. Finally, Temple, who in his thirties had claimed to be the only English clergyman who had read Thomas Aquinas' *Summa Theologiae* from end to end, addressed an audience of English Dominicans at the London Aquinas Society in October 1943 on 'Thomism and Modern Needs'. It was a sympathetic appreciation of all that the father of contemporary Thomist theology could give to the production of a new 'map of the world'. A former president of the society wrote that Temple's words reflected 'the prevailing spirit of collaboration among Christians and of co-operation in all charity'. When Temple died, Hinsley's successor, Archbishop Griffin, described how with the talk Temple was 'breaking new ground with his eager and adventurous mind and that warm charity which drew new friends to him all through his life'.[38]

At the same time as the plans were being laid for the WCC, the churches in the British Isles were also reaching agreement, after protracted discussions, on the establishment of a British Council of Churches (but without the Roman Catholics). Temple was part of these discussions and supported the plans. In 1940 he had proposed a resolution at the Church Assembly of the Church of England welcoming the establishment of the World Council and paving the way for its counterpart in the British Isles, and this had been passed. Then at the climax of this process, in September 1942, he preached at the service of the inauguration of the British Council in St Paul's Cathedral. His sermon explained why it was so important that the different churches, which had distinctive principles and commitments, should nevertheless come together in a body like this:

> [I]n days like these, when the basic principles of Christianity are widely challenged and in many quarters expressly repudiated, the primary need is for clear and united testimony to Christianity itself. The difference between Catholic and Protestant is very small as compared with the difference between Christian and non-Christian, between those who do and those who do not believe that in Jesus Christ God 'hath visited and redeemed his people'.
>
> Our differences remain: we shall not pretend that they are already resolved into unity or harmony. But we take our stand on the common faith of Christendom, faith in God, Creator, Redeemer, and Sanctifier; and so standing together we invite [all] to share that faith and call on all to conform their lives to the principles derived from it.[39]

The sermon was the culmination of all his efforts, national and international over the previous 15 years, to call the churches together. The work showed that in this respect he was not just someone who talked about a future Christian unity in a theoretical way but gave equal attention to the practical business of convening, chairing and implementing the means of bringing it about.

In general it is clear Temple was not responsible for initiating the ecumenical movement: the delegates at the Edinburgh conference in 1910 were responsible for that. He was not, then, a herald or prophet of the ecumenical ideal. But he was responsible, along with Oldham and Paton, for decisively moving the Protestant churches towards an enduring structural expression of it, and he and they became its instruments. Of the three, furthermore, he was the only one to truly straddle the Faith and Order movement (from the Lausanne conference onwards), the international missionary movement (from the Jerusalem conference onwards) and the Life and Work movement (through his drafting of the final 'Message' of the Oxford Conference of 1937). Looking back on the development of the movement Visser 't Hooft commented that 'William Temple had a unique place in the ecumenical movement. He belonged to all parts of it.'[40]

While his achievements did not stop the churches being divided from one another (in some ways the divisions became more intractable during the war years, as John Kent shows),[41] they did facilitate the churches beginning to work together in a structured and committed way and this, in the light of previous bitter divisions between them, was a historic contribution to Western Christianity.

Temple's pioneering ecumenical leadership was rooted in an early passionate inclusivism, but really developed after he had become a church leader and was called to engage with the leadership of other denominations. He could have just managed these contacts in a business-like way, like his predecessors at York and Canterbury, letting others take the initiative and ensuring that the privileged status of the established church was not undermined. But this is not the figure who has emerged in this chapter. On the one hand Temple developed an ecumenically-orientated understanding of Anglicanism which did not avoid the difficult challenge of remaining faithful to its apostolic inheritance while, on the other hand, he worked collaboratively and constructively to integrate and carry forward the aspirations of the ecumenical movement itself. His outstanding contribution was in backroom committee work, such as at the Bishopthorpe gathering, of being able with patience and forbearance to hear and distil the essence of what others were bringing to the table and then forging statements or resolutions that carried forward this ecumenism towards the establishing of the World Council of Churches and the British Council of Churches, as well as forging better relationships with the Roman Catholic Church. William Temple's kind of leadership is therefore being revealed as having a multifaceted character: of being able to be expressed on public platforms in front of massed audiences (as we saw in earlier chapters), influencing the political life of the nation *and* of finding expression in the painstaking engagement of committee discussion and negotiation, waiting with humility for the right moment to draw together the thinking of others and make proposals that would bring divided churches together with purpose and resolve.

There are two other major arenas that Temple played a part in, the teaching forums of the church and the social and political life of the nation in wartime, especially through the media of radio and print. What kind of leadership did he exercise within these?

Notes

1 Temple, according to Knight (as quoted in the introduction above), is 'the most significant person in the history of twentieth-century Anglicanism in the first half of that century'. Knight goes on to say that 'his legacy is first of all ecumenism and, secondly, a belief that Christianity has to be about social justice.' Frances Knight, 'Why study William Temple?'

2 Knight, 'Why study William Temple?' The sermon is printed in Temple, *The Church Looks Forward*, pp. 1–7, in which he describes the ecumenical movement as the 'one great ground of hope for the coming days – this world-wide Christian fellowship, this ecumenical movement, as it is often called', p. 3.

3 F. A. Iremonger, *William Temple, Archbishop of Canterbury: His Life and Letters*, London: Oxford University Press, p. 98.

4 Iremonger, *William Temple*, pp. 102–3.

5 'The Vocation and Destiny of the Church of England', reprinted in *Essays in Christian Politics*, London: Longmans Green and Co., 1927, p. 192.

6 'Vocation and Destiny', p. 197.

7 'Vocation and Destiny', p. 198.

8 'Vocation and Destiny', p. 202.

9 'Vocation and Destiny', pp. 205–6.

10 The Chicago–Lambeth Quadrilateral is Resolution 11 of the 1888 Lambeth Conference, in which the bishops resolved that 'in the opinion of this Conference, the following Articles supply a basis on which approach may be by God's blessing made towards Home Reunion:

(a) The Holy Scriptures of the Old and New Testaments, as 'containing all things necessary to salvation' [Article VI], and as being the rule and ultimate standard of faith.

(b) The Apostles' Creed, as the Baptismal Symbol; and the Nicene Creed, as the sufficient statement of the Christian faith.

(c) The two Sacraments ordained by Christ Himself – Baptism and the Supper of the Lord – ministered with unfailing use of Christ's words of Institution, and of the elements ordained by Him.

(d) The Historic Episcopate, locally adapted in the methods of its administration to the varying needs of the nations and peoples called of God into the Unity of His Church (Anglican Communion 1888).

11 'Reunion and Validity', reprinted in *Thoughts on Some Problems of the Day*, Diocesan charge. London: Macmillan, 1931, pp. 88–132.

12 Diocesan charge, p. 89.

13 Diocesan charge, p. 91.

14 Diocesan charge, pp. 104–5.

15 Diocesan charge, p. 105.

16 Diocesan charge, p. 115.

17 Diocesan charge, pp. 115–16.

18 Diocesan charge, p. 121.

19 Diocesan charge, p. 130.

20 Diocesan charge, pp. 131–2.

21 See Reinhold Niebuhr's fascinating account of their discussions in Iremonger, *William Temple*, pp. 493–4.

22 Edward Loane has recently provided a richly informative and critical account of Temple's ecumenical thought and work, which the following paragraphs will draw upon. However, at several points in the book he characterizes Temple's ecumenical ecclesiology as 'complementarian', which does not really give proper recognition to the argument we have just seen Temple making. See *William Temple and Church Unity*, Palgrave Macmillan, 2016, pp. 85, 95, etc. See also Paul Avis, 'William Temple: Pioneer and Pillar of Christian Unity', *Ecclesiology*, 12 October 2020.

23 Iremonger, *William Temple*, p. 396.

24 Iremonger, *William Temple*, p. 394.

25 Iremonger, *William Temple*, p. 397.

26 Iremonger, *William Temple*, pp. 403–4.

27 Iremonger, *William Temple*, pp. 426–7.

28 Adrian Hastings, *A History of English Christianity 1920–2000*, London: SCM Press, p. 302.

29 Loane, *William Temple and Church Unity*, pp. 159–60.

30 Loane, *William Temple and Church Unity*, p. 160.

31 Loane, *William Temple and Church Unity*, p. 160.

32 William Temple Papers, Vol. 68, pp. 207–26, reprinted in Spencer, *Christ in All Things*, pp. 154–60.

33 From 'William Temple', *Dictionary of National Biography*, Oxford.

34 Loane, *William Temple and Church Unity*, p. 165.

35 Loane, *William Temple and Church Unity*, p. 176.

36 Broadcast 25 December 1941, printed in *Is Christ Divided?*, pp. 112–13, reprinted in Stephen Spencer, *Christ in All Things*, Norwich: Canterbury Press, 2015, pp. 160–1.

37 Iremonger, *William Temple*, p. 412.

38 Iremonger, *William Temple*, p. 421.

39 Sermon at the inauguration of the British Council of Churches, 23 September 1942, St Paul's Cathedral, in the William Temple Papers, Vol. 69, pp. 59–62, reprinted in Spencer, *Christ in All Things*, pp. 162–3.

40 'The Genesis of the World Council of Churches', p. 713.

41 John Kent, *William Temple*, Cambridge: Cambridge University Press, 1992, pp. 99–109. Kent emphasizes the failure of the provisional committee of the WCC to get agreement from the European churches about war aims and peace aims in the conflict. But the very existence of such a committee within the broader context of long-standing and bitter church division before these years is perhaps the more impressive fact.

From logic to imagination

By the time Temple moved to York as its new archbishop he had been out of academic life for almost 20 years. But he remained committed to fulfilling one of the elements of his calling when an undergraduate: the theological task of rethinking and teaching the Christian faith in the terms of modern thought. We see this in the 1930s in a number of very significant ways, each for a different kind of audience. The first was his mission addresses to student audiences, most notably in the 1931 Oxford Mission, published as *Christian Faith and Life* (1931). The second was a return to fundamental questions of philosophy and natural theology in the Gifford Lectures in Glasgow, which were published as *Nature, Man and God* (1934). And the third was an exposition of John's Gospel, to groups of clergy and laity at different times and in different places, an exposition that was put into print in his best-selling *Readings in St John's Gospel* (1939 and 1940). These three works represent the pinnacle of Temple's teaching ministry, but what kind of teacher did he become in this last full decade of his life?

Mission addresses

Temple took every opportunity to travel up and down the country to speak about the Christian faith to young people. He would speak every summer at the Student Christian Movement camp at Swanwick in Derbyshire. He would visit different universities to address their Christian societies. He also travelled to the United States on three different occasions, speaking to students as well as to teachers.

The most famous of these encounters was the Oxford Mission of 1931. F. R. Barry, who was the vicar of the University Church, described the background to the mission as being 'the disillusioned aftermath of the first war'. At Oxford,

[R]eligious and moral life was at a low ebb. College chapels were virtually empty. Christianity was almost a dirty word. Christian belief was commonly regarded as the refuge of the mentally second-rate – few, anyhow, were prepared to take it seriously. The job of the University Church, in that context, was to get Christianity back upon the map – to exhibit its relevance to the life of Oxford and as something intellectually respectable.[1]

Temple spoke at the first mission to the university since the war. He spoke on eight consecutive nights in the church. He spoke without movements or mannerisms, with hands resting lightly on the lectern in front of him, standing motionless except for an occasional tilt of the head or the raising of a hand to adjust his glasses. He spoke of God's purpose for the world and how God had a purpose 'for us as part of His purpose for the world'.[2] As was often the case, he presented a sense of the sweep of history, past, present and future, to inspire and motivate his audience to make a committed response. He spoke of the place of Christ within this history, and of Christian morality, sin, repentance, the cross, the Holy Spirit, prayer, the sacraments and the Church. Through all of this he was able to present the Christian faith as a rational and coherent philosophy of life. And, apparently, he startled his hearers by his obvious and profound belief in aspects of Christianity which many of them had dismissed. John Adam, one of the undergraduates who attended the mission, wrote the following description:

> The church was packed with hundreds of undergraduates, thronging to hear him. He was large of stature and the picture of this great figure, high above us in the pulpit, is one I shall never forget. Unlike many missioners, Temple was not an emotional preacher. His powerful appeal was primarily to the head. It aimed to challenge, deepen and straighten our Christian thinking, belief and standards of life, and only then to stir our emotions. In all his eight addresses there was this element of challenge and every night, following the address, there was time for quiet reflection – silence, punctuated by quotations from Scripture, which helped to shape our prayers and our resolve. The silence ended with a prayer and a blessing and we all went out into the Oxford night stimulated, challenged and deepened, many of us with a new approach to faith and life.[3]

This vivid description shows how a key part of Temple's advocacy was an appeal to the powers of reason in his listeners, creating the space and opportunity for their informed response, rather than seeking to build emotional pressure to bring about commitment. It was an approach that respected the autonomy and integrity of those he was addressing, offering them a gift rather than making a demand, an apt reasonableness. But there was something more as well, an element not present in Temple's earlier lectures and addresses, the time of silence and reading of verses from scripture at the end of each address, described by Adam. This was very significant and showed a recognition that advocacy of the Christian faith depended not only on logic but on allowing the imagination to play a part, that faculty of going beyond what is apparent to grasp intuitively a bigger picture, in this case to grasp the cosmic significance of Christ and his invitation. It is possible to see Temple's love of poetry, especially of the Romantic poets mentioned in the first chapter, influencing his teaching ministry in this kind of way. Coleridge had been a leading advocate of the place of the imagination in Christian theology and here we see Temple in a small but significant way providing an opportunity for this to take place.

The creation of space for a freely chosen response to his talks was especially seen on the last night of the mission when Temple spoke of the need for his hearers not to practise their faith in isolation but to bring themselves into the Christian society, the church, which many had dismissed. He described how the church existed not for its own sake but to serve a greater purpose, the coming of the kingdom of God.[4] This was similar to one of the most famous statements he ever made, one that is nowhere in print but was made at a number SCM meetings, that 'the Church is the only institution that exists primarily for the benefit of those who are not its members'.[5] Temple then asked his student audience to remember that

> the supreme wonder of the history of the Christian Church is that always in the moments when it has seemed most dead, out of its own body there has sprung up new life; so that in age after age it has renewed itself, and age after age by its renewal has carried the world forward into new stages of progress, as it will do for us in our day, if only we give ourselves in devotion to its Lord and take our place in its service.[6]

This was followed by what became a famous moment towards the end of the evening. When the hymn 'When I survey the wondrous cross' was being 'roared out', Temple stopped the organ and the singing and asked the students to read the words of the last verse to themselves. Then, if they meant them with all their heart to sing them loudly, if they did not mean them at all not to sing them, and if they meant them even a little and wanted to mean them more, to sing them very softly. There was silence while everyone read the words and then a spontaneous and hushed whispering of 'Love so amazing, so divine, demands my soul, my life, my all.'[7]

Barry described how the mission touched and changed the lives of a large number of undergraduates, to the extent that many of them offered themselves for ordained ministry after leaving university. Adam was one of those. The mission 'was, indeed, a decisive moment in the history of that generation ... It was when the tide began to come in.'[8] This is confirmed by Hastings who describes the mission as the first sign of a revival in Anglican Christian life after the scepticism of the 1920s.[9] It was, as well, a moment when we see Temple's own gifts as a teacher develop in an important way, with his utilizing of the faculty of imagination alongside the logic of reason. In these addresses he not only made a case for the Christian faith but gave his audience the space and opportunity to imagine its scope and significance, so paving the way for a response of faith.

The text of his addresses also became very popular. It was reprinted 16 times between 1931 and 1957 and reissued again in 1963 and 1994, the last time in an edition edited by the author Susan Howatch. This is because *Christian Faith and Life* gives one of the clearest and most concise summaries of Temple's reasoned faith. It shows that despite the problems with aspects of his philosophical writings mentioned above his thought could still be powerfully persuasive through its combination of reason and suggestion. Another good example of this is in Temple's teaching about the nature of true prayer with its emphasis on seeing Christ with the inner eye:

Praying is speaking to God; so the first necessity is that you should be directing your mind towards God. That is the best part and most important part of prayer anyhow, and without it all the rest is useless. The great aim is union with God, and the first need is that you should be, so far as you are capable, with open face gazing upon Him. And then, when you have remembered what you know about God (which is not difficult, because He has given us the portrait of Himself in Jesus Christ, and though you cannot see God you can always remember Jesus Christ; so you should never begin to pray until you have the figure of Christ before your mind, and should pray to God as you see Him there); then you turn to the things you will pray for, and this is to be after the manner of the Lord's Prayer.[10]

A philosophical theology

Temple was invited to return to the borderlands of philosophy and theology in the Gifford Lectures delivered at Glasgow University at intervals between 1932 and 1934. The moment was a good one for him to deliver this prestigious series of lectures. He was now well established in his new role as Archbishop of York and he and his wife were settled in their new home at Bishopthorpe. He was freed from the time-consuming work of managing a large urban diocese. He had a certain amount of time for reading and writing, though apparently he was in the habit of writing out his next lecture on the train from York to Glasgow. He was aware that his previous essay on the philosophical foundations of theology, *Mens Creatrix*, had been written in disconnected moments of a busy life in London and had suffered as a result. He would have been keen to have another go at the pre-eminent intellectual concern of his life.

In the preface to the printed version of his lectures, *Nature, Man and God* of 1934, Temple explains that his method is not to construct, stage by stage, a philosophical fabric where each conclusion becomes the basis of the next advance. Something more complex is being attempted: 'My own endeavour is rather to provide a coherent articulation of an experience which has found some measure of co-ordination through adherence to certain principles.' This immediately shows how he was not attempting to work deductively as in a mathematical equation but asking his readers to use the different chapters and principles to imagine the whole outlook he was advocating. The argument would stand or fall as a whole insofar as his readers would be willing to make this leap in their minds and hearts and see how all the parts of the argument fitted together.

But logic still plays a central place in the book, where he draws a comparison between his approach and the dialectical materialism of Marx, Engels and Lenin who, he recognizes, make a strong appeal to the minds of his contemporaries. He wishes to present a dialectic that has a greater range of apprehension and is more thorough in its appreciation of the interplay of factors in the real world than that of Marxism.[11] In other words the spiritual as well as the material dimension of life is to be included.

The method he was proposing can be explained by returning to the common root behind both Marxism and Temple's own Idealist philosophical background, namely Hegel's philosophy and especially his belief in historical development being fundamental to the constitution of reality (sometimes called historicism). Hegel offered a way of interpreting and unifying human experience and the reality behind it. He did this through positing the concept of '*geist*', the German word for spirit, seen as a kind of controlling presence within human culture, at work through human affairs and historical development. He saw the conflicts, struggles and resolutions of human history as the working out of an overarching dialectical process, involving the three responsive steps of thesis, antithesis and synthesis at every turn.

Marx and his disciples retained the grammar of Hegel's philosophy while replacing the vocabulary, as it were. They continued to see an unfolding dialectical process at work in history but saw the controlling dynamic behind this as the economic struggle of the working classes for a class-free society. History was still seen as purposeful and progressive but in a materialist rather than a geist-led way.

Temple also thought easily and naturally within the historicist grammar of Hegelian philosophy. His project was the attempt to update its Idealist vocabulary, as it were, with ideas and ways of thinking drawn from Christian belief and to do so in a way which accounted for a greater range of human experience than Marxism. He was also seeking to build on the outlook of A. N. Whitehead's *Process and Reality*, which he respected greatly. Temple agreed with many aspects of Whitehead's process thought but felt that at crucial points in the argument Whitehead did not sufficiently recognize the separation of the Divine Mind from the world.

The areas he included in his study of dialectical realism, as he now called it, were similar to those he discussed in *Mens Creatrix*. In the first half of the book he began with the fact of evolution as revealed by science.[12] He sought to trace the scope and limits of human knowledge within this evolutionary process, and the likelihood of a unifying Mind lying behind the unfolding reality of the terrestrial world. He discussed the place of truth and beauty within this scheme and the key significance of value as a concept which can explain why things are the way they are. He traced the place of freedom and determinism for individuals within the evolutionary process. Towards the end of that section, he concluded that reality gives grounds for believing in a transcendent Mind or, as he now says, a personal Spirit, over and above the process of development. All of this was a well-worn path for Temple but here expounded at greater length and in a more measured way than in *Mens Creatrix*.

Then, in the second half of the book, he worked in the other direction. He asked his readers to begin by imagining a transcendent Mind at work through the whole cosmic process, and then see how this makes sense of the world around us. He sought to trace the ways such a mind is immanent within that process and can be known by finite minds. He discussed the nature of a particular revelation, which he famously defined as not being a set of propositions held as truths but as the *coincidence* of divinely guided events with minds divinely illuminated to interpret those events.[13] This again opened the way for human imagination to play a part in grasping the truth of divine revelation, for Temple was implying that it was through the believer being inspired to imagine a connection between historical events and the cosmic divine meaning behind them that he or she experienced divine revelation. Temple also discussed human finitude, the relationship of divine grace and human freedom[14] and eternal life. He characteristically argued that all values ultimately exhibit a *commonwealth* of value and that this shows the presence of a transcendent Mind at work in the universe. He argued that human history also ultimately exhibits a dependence on eternity, though recalling his early historicism, he also said that history is necessary and essential to the eternal and that in an important sense it 'makes' eternity.[15]

Then, in a famous and brilliant aside, which was meant as a deliberate rebuff to Marxism, he presented Christianity as the religion that best expresses both a materialist and spiritual understanding of reality:

> It may safely be said that one ground for the hope of Christianity that it may make good its claim to be the true faith lies in the fact that it is the most avowedly materialist of all the great religions. It affords an expectation that it may be able to control the material, precisely because it does not ignore it or deny it, but roundly asserts alike the reality of matter and its subordination. Its own most central saying is: 'The Word was made flesh,' where the last term was, no doubt, chosen because of its specially materialistic associations. By the very nature of its central doctrine Christianity is committed to a belief in the ultimate significance of the historical process, and in the reality of matter and its place in the divine scheme.[16]

Marxists would argue that Christianity underplays the fundamental economic processes that govern the life of nations and people. But Temple was arguing that the ministry of Christ, the Word made flesh, addresses and redeems the material lives of people in ways that Marxism barely touches. He was not, though, presenting a deductive argument to prove that he was right and the Marxists wrong, but instead seeking to describe and offer a whole conception of material and spiritual reality that was broader and richer than the one they were offering, one to be inhabited as a whole.

At the end of the book he summed up his view of reality with a new and evocative concept, one that has been quoted by many subsequent commentators, that of the universe being sacramental.[17] He defined a sacrament as 'the spiritual utilisation of a material object whereby a spiritual result is effected'.[18] In other words, it is an instance where matter becomes an 'effectual expression' or 'symbolic instrument' of spirit: the spirit is first and last, but matter is its vehicle. He then applied this idea to the whole of the created universe: 'the view of the universe which I have called sacramental asserts the supremacy and absolute freedom of God; the reality of the physical world and its process as His creation; the vital significance of the material and temporal world to the eternal Spirit.'[19] But how is the world a sacrament of the Spirit?

> God, who is spirit, is His eternal self in and through the historical pro-
> cess of creating a world and winning it to union with Himself. His
> creation is sacramental of Himself to his creatures; but in effectively
> fulfilling that function it becomes sacramental of Him to Himself – the
> means whereby He is eternally that which eternally He is.[20]

This concept allows Temple to avoid falling into the traps of pantheism, of merging the universe with God, and of dualism, of separating the two. As in a sacrament, where there is a material component, such as water or bread and wine, and a spiritual reality, the presence and grace of God, with the material component being an effective vehicle of the spiritual reality, so for Temple the material reality of the universe, in all its awesome scale and beauty, effectively conveys the presence and grace of God. But sacraments require the believer to make an imaginative leap of seeing God in the bread and wine and in the water of baptism, so the same must be the case for those who accept Temple's concept of the sacramental universe. We therefore see how the culmination of the argument in *Nature, Man and God* moves from the logic of reason to an appeal to the imagination.

In this discussion, it is clear that the Idealist philosophy in which Temple was trained is no longer controlling the outcome. He is showing how the mysteries and depths of sacramental religion are playing a key role in his argument, one which depends on the reader to willingly make the connections between them and what he is proposing.

This illustrates an important comment on *Nature, Man and God* made by the distinguished German theologian Emil Brunner in a personal letter to Temple. Brunner argued that Temple had failed properly to distinguish true natural theology, which relies simply on logical argument and generally accepted facts, from Christian theology and dogmatics, which are regulated by Christian beliefs:

> So, for instance, your conception of religion is determined *a priori* by
> Christian faith, and is deduced from it; the same applies to your con-

cepts of sin, love, personality, etc. This means, however, that in these passages your natural theology is natural only in appearance, whilst it is in truth Christian. In the third and final part of your book, your expositions are substantially, even predominantly, nothing more nor less than Christian dogmatics, even though the difference in method is repeatedly stressed.[21]

While, then, *Nature, Man and God* could not convince the unbeliever of the truth of Christianity, it did construct a philosophical path into the insights of the Christian faith for those who would willingly take that path with some leaps of imagination and faith.

Dorothy Emmet, a philosopher of the generation that followed Temple's, captured this very well when she wrote that Temple's philosophical writings stand as an impressive exposition of a reasonable faith.[22] In other words, Temple may not convince the sceptic but he certainly impresses the sceptic and makes him or her seriously engage with the issues of religion. Furthermore, Emmet suggested, some aspects of Temple's scheme could be carried forward even if his metaphysics ultimately could not. She quoted a letter that Temple wrote to her in 1942 which shows Temple now thinking that the Gifford Lectures did not describe reality as it is but reality as it will become in God's own time. The letter comes from the same period when Temple was rethinking his whole approach to theology, quoted in Chapter 6 above, and it employs one of his favourite analogies also quoted in that chapter, a play performed in a theatre:

The particular modification (in my thinking) to which I am feeling driven is not substantial, though I think it is very important. It is a much clearer perception of what is worked out in the Gifford Lectures about process and value. What we must completely get away from is the notion that the world as it now exists is a rational whole; we must think of its unity not by the analogy of a picture, of which all the parts exist at once, but by the analogy of a drama where, if it is good enough, the full meaning of the first scene only becomes apparent with the final curtain; and we are in the middle of this. Consequently the world as we see it is strictly unintelligible. We can only have faith that it will become intelligible when the divine purpose, which is the explanation of it, is accomplished ...

All this is really there in the Gifford Lectures, but I don't think the total presentation in that book or in *Christus Veritas* sufficiently gives this impression of a dynamic process and leaves too much that of a static system.[23]

Temple therefore still believed in a profound and unifying meaning within the universe but now he saw that this would only become clear in the future (a position not unlike that of Teilhard de Chardin). *Nature, Man and God* could still contribute to this future-orientated view of the world but only after some revision. Its argument would now have to be read as an extended description of the contours of such a hoped-for world, a world which would eventually produce a society of spirits united in a commonwealth of value.

Temple's ongoing commitment to philosophy, then, a commitment which had sought to describe the world both as it was and as it was becoming, would now have to be directed mainly to the latter. But this, at least, would give it a more visionary character: he would now be describing a new world, one that was growing out of the present world but was not always visible within it. His philosophy would now be explicitly based on an imaginative faith and so would be better described as philosophical theology. It had, of course, always been based in some degree on his own faith but now he was clearly recognizing and embracing that self-consciousness.

Meditating on the Fourth Gospel

The development of Temple's teaching ministry from one based on philosophical logic to one based on the use of the imagination is most clearly seen in its third instantiation in the 1930s, his exposition of John's Gospel. Introducing the book that lays this out, he wrote that 'for as long as I can remember I have had more love for St. John's gospel than for any other book', and that 'with St. John I am at home'. His exposition, which had begun to be formulated at St James's, Piccadilly, was especially developed when he addressed clergy on retreat or laity at conferences and in services. He came to write the exposition down in the late thirties 'in odd half hours', as he admitted, and it was published in two parts, the first in 1939 and the second in 1940, as *Readings in St John's Gospel*. It is not a presentation that drew on the New Testament scholarship of his time and so did not attempt to resolve any of the critical and exegetical questions surrounding the Gospel. It was deliberately a reading of the text as it stands and drew, for its inspiration, as much on Temple's own living experience of Christ as on the text itself. In his comments on one passage in the Gospel he gave a description of what the whole book was doing. Writing on John 1.14 he comments,

... as we read the story, though it all happened long ago, we apprehend present fact. It is not only the record of a historical episode that we read; it is the self-expression of that God 'in whom we live and move and have our being'; so that whatever finds expression there is true now, and the living Jesus who is 'the same yesterday and today and for ever' still deals with our souls as He dealt with those who had fellowship with Him when He *tabernacled among us.* Our reading of the Gospel story can be and should be an act of personal communion with the living Lord.[24]

The reader, then, must make an imaginative connection between what is in the text and what is happening in their own life in the present. If that connection is made then the exposition comes to life. Through its following of the unfolding story of Christ's ministry, death and resurrection, and the dialogues that intersperse it, it uncovers and describes not only the ways Christ related to his disciples but also the ways he relates to believers today. Using the text of the Gospel as a peg Temple draws on his own and others' experience of Christ to present the living truth of the Christian gospel, which is Christ himself. In the introduction he describes his method of reading and writing in the following terms: 'I am chiefly concerned with what arises in my mind and spirit as I read; and I hope this is not totally different from saying that I am concerned with what the Holy Spirit says to me through the Gospel.'[25]

While this kind of reading does not remove the need for the logic of philosophy, because on its own it does not make a case for belief, it does lead the willing reader far beyond the results of that kind of logic. Temple describes how this type of reading leads to a direct encounter with the truth itself, because that truth is a living person. Writing on John 14.6 and the words 'I am ... the truth' he states:

Truth is the perfect correlation of mind and reality; and this is actualised in the Lord's Person. If the Gospel is true and God is, as the Bible declares, a Living God, the ultimate truth is not a system of propositions grasped by a perfect intelligence, but is a Personal Being apprehended in the only way in which persons are ever fully apprehended, that is, by love.[26]

The use of logic was not the way, ultimately, to know God. The knowledge of God would come through a loving relationship, of seeing and knowing the one who lies behind all the outward changes and chances of life – of imaginatively knowing God as one adorable being, as in a committed relationship with another person. God would be known through a holistic response of body, mind and spirit, with Christ opening the door to that:

'He that hath seen me hath seen the Father.' Those are the words that we long to hear. We cannot fully grasp that supreme truth, as we should if our discipleship were perfect. We need to hear them over and over again, to let the sound of them constantly play upon our ears, the meaning of them perpetually occupy our minds, the call in them unceasingly move our wills ... In adoration, in supplication, in dedication, let us take care always to address ourselves to God as He is seen in Jesus Christ. Never ask in prayer for any blessing till you are sure your mind is turned to Jesus Christ; then speak to God as you see Him there.[27]

The truth of the incarnation, then, was to be grasped in the same way that the disciples came to know Christ, though stepping out in faith and accompanying him through his life, death and resurrection, but now through imagining it rather than literally on the roads and lanes of Palestine. The incarnation was to be known in its depths through the practice of faith rather than just in the description of faith. The story within John's Gospel, as it unfolds in Temple's hands, provides a model of such practice.

It is also important to acknowledge how Temple recognizes the darkness and unintelligibility of the world in this exposition, in line with his letter to Dorothy Emmet quoted above. In one of the most evocative passages in the book he quotes John 1.5, 'the light shineth in the darkness, and the darkness did not absorb it' and asks the reader to

Imagine yourself standing alone on some headland in a dark night. At the foot of the headland is a lighthouse or beacon, not casting rays on every side, but throwing one bar of light through the darkness. It is some such image that St. John had before his mind. The divine light shines through the darkness of the world, cleaving it, but neither dispelling it nor quenched by it.[28]

Temple explains that

This darkness in which the light shines unabsorbed is cosmic. St John is most modern here. The evil which for him presents the problem is not only in men's hearts; it is in the whole ordered system of nature. That ordered system is infected; it 'lieth in the evil one' (1 John 5.19). St John might have had all the modern problem of the callousness and cruelty of nature [as seen in earthquakes, droughts and pandemics as well as in human cruelty and evil] before his mind.[29]

His image of the beacon, though, shows how Christ the light of the world can still shine through this profound darkness:

> Take any moment of history and you find light piercing unillumined darkness – now with reference to one phase of the purpose of God, now another. The company of those who stand in the beam of the light by which the path of true progress for that time is discerned is always small. Remember Wilberforce and the early Abolitionists; remember the twelve Apostles and the company gathered about them. What is seen conspicuously in those two examples is always true.[30]

But the end of the 1930s in Europe were especially dark times. Temple responds reflectively:

> As we look forwards, we peer into darkness, and none can say with certainty what course the true progress of the future should follow. But as we look back, the truth is marked by beacon-lights, which are the lives of saints and pioneers; and these in their turn are not originators of light, but rather reflectors which give light to us because themselves they are turned towards the source of light.[31]

And so 'the one great question for everyone is whether he will "walk in darkness" or "walk in light" (1 John 1.7; 2.10,11).'[32]

The book offers many practical suggestions about how to start 'walking in the light'. One memorable example comes from someone he knew who moved into a poor district of the East End of London in order to serve its people. This person found he could do nothing so long as he came to 'offer service'. But everything changed when he moved into a flat and needed to borrow a hammer: 'he went to borrow one from the people in the flat below. At once the relationship was different. There was something that they could do for him.' Temple then makes a connection with how God relates to us:

> So the Almighty God seeks to win us to fellowship with Himself by putting some part of His purpose into our hands. 'The kingdom of heaven is as when a man, going into another country, called his own servants, and delivered unto them his goods' (St Matthew 25.14). That is the way in which God is King; and He takes that way because it is the way of fellowship. He who might be all-sufficient to Himself, entrusts His purpose to us. He makes Himself dependent upon us, as the Lord was dependent on the woman [at the well in John 4] for the quenching of His thirst. He asks for our service.[33]

But Temple does not leave it there. He turns back to the believer recalling how a sense of unworthiness often grows in their own heart:

> But how can that be? *How is it that thou askest of me?* Thou canst do all things. I have nothing. I am not fit to offer the meanest service. Surely God will first require, and help me to form, a character worthy to serve Him, and then appoint me my task.[34]

But there is a firm reply to this: 'No; in point of fact it is only through service that such a character could be formed.' Temple recalls the insight that, 'Christ did not first make His disciples saints and then give them work to do; He gave them work to do, and as they did it other people (though not themselves) perceived that they were becoming saints.' So, for the believer today,

> The service that He asks of me is a real service, not fictitious; yet it is for my sake, and out of love for me, that He so orders His world as to need my service. That is how it is that *He* asketh of *me*. Also because He loves us, He rejoices that we should be 'fellow-workers' with Him (1 Corinthians 3.9). If He were not Love He would have no need of us; it is His love that needs us. And behind His request is the love that prompts it – the love which He is ready to give me, the gift of God.[35]

In this exposition, then, we have the privilege of seeing into the heart of Temple's own personal faith where fellowship, service and love are intimately related, in fact they are facets of one compelling divine and human reality. Here are the roots of the servant leadership we are exploring throughout this book.

Readings in St John's Gospel has proved to be one of Temple's most enduring books. It was not his most popular book when it was published (that was to be *Christianity and Social Order*) but it stayed in print longer than any other (for 60 years after being published). It was a presentation of the Christian faith that did not seek to prove a case and make the sceptical come to faith but, in line with other examples of Temple's teaching in the 1930s, invited the reader to open their inner eyes, the eyes of their imagination, to the person of Christ and to his way and then to follow that way in their hearts and minds. In this, it provided another example of Temple's mature approach to leadership, of serving through open invitation and encouragement rather than through deliberately challenging his listeners and readers to change their outlook. It has continued to do this ever since, despite some aspects of its style and presentation becoming dated. Rupert Hoare, a biblical scholar and great-nephew of Temple, has written, 'Dated they may be, in relation to critical biblical scholarship, where many of Temple's judgements now seem naïvely conservative. But the book remains a source for meditation from which many people continue to derive inspiration: his exposition opens the scriptures for us now, as it did at the time.'[36]

And so, surprisingly, it was this volume, rather than the more rigorous and weighty *Christus Veritas* or *Nature, Man and God*, that went furthest to fulfilling his early ambition of restating Christian belief in a powerful and inspiring way for his contemporaries. In other words, he most strongly restated the Christian faith not through the strength of his philosophical arguments but, with the help of St John, through a reasoned and evocative description of his own living relationship with Christ.

Notes

1 William Temple, *Christian Faith and Life*, London: SCM Press, 1963, p. 11.

2 Temple, *Christian Faith and Life*, p. 126.

3 From notes given to the author.

4 Temple, *Christian Faith and Life*, p. 132.

5 Jack Keiser, who worked with Temple as a student in SCM and was associated with the William Temple Foundation after Temple's death, reported to Ronald Preston and Malcolm Brown that Temple used the expression, virtually or precisely in the oft-quoted words, three or four times in his recollection, in informal question-times (as reported by Malcolm Brown to the author in an email 25 July 2018).

6 Temple, *Christian Faith and Life*, p. 133–4.

7 F. A. Iremonger, *William Temple, Archbishop of Canterbury: His Life and Letters*, London: Oxford University Press, 1948, p. 378.

8 Iremonger, *William Temple*, p. 377.

9 Adrian Hastings, *A History of English Christianity 1920–2000*, London: SCM Press, 2001, p. 257.

10 Temple, *Christian Faith and Life*, pp. 113–14.

11 William Temple, *Nature, Man and God*, Gifford Lectures, London: Macmillan, 1934, pp. ix–x.

12 A. R. Peacocke described William Temple's percipience in detecting those broad features in the new knowledge of his day – mostly from the sciences – that theology needed properly to respond to. See 'The New Biology and *Nature, Man and God*', p. 29.

13 Temple, *Nature, Man and God*, p. 312. See further Temple's essay in *Revelation*, ed. Baillie and Martin, 1937.

14 Presented and discussed by Ellen T. Charry, 'The Beauty of Holiness: Practical Divinity', pp. 219–20, 239–42.

15 Temple, *Nature, Man and God*, pp. 448, 451.

16 Temple, *Nature, Man and God*, p. 478.

17 See, for example, the engaging analysis of Deborah Guess in 'The Eco-theological Significance of William Temple's "Sacramental Universe"', *Journal of Anglican Studies*, May 2020.

18 Temple, *Nature, Man and God*, p. 491.

19 Temple, *Nature, Man and God*, p. 493.

20 Temple, *Nature, Man and God*, p. 495.

21 Iremonger, *William Temple*, pp. 531–2.

22 Iremonger, *William Temple*, p. 535.

23 Iremonger, *William Temple*, pp. 537–8.

24 William Temple, *Readings in St John's Gospel*, London: Macmillan, 1945, p. 14.

25 Temple, *Readings in St John's Gospel*, p. xiii.

26 Temple, *Readings in St John's Gospel*, p. 223.

27 Temple, *Readings in St John's Gospel*, p. 225.

28 Temple, *Readings in St John's Gospel*, p. 7.

29 Temple, *Readings in St John's Gospel*, pp. 8–9.

30 Temple, *Readings in St John's Gospel*, p. 8.

31 Temple, *Readings in St John's Gospel*, p. 8.

32 Temple, *Readings in St John's Gospel*, p. 9.

33 Temple, *Readings in St John's Gospel*, pp. 66–7.

34 Temple, *Readings in St John's Gospel*, p. 67.

35 Temple, *Readings in St John's Gospel*. For an illuminating exposition of the connections between this book and Temple's social thought, especially his social principles of freedom, fellowship and service, see Rupert Hoare, 'William Temple's *Readings in St John's Gospel* and Social Ethics', *Crucible: The Journal of Christian Social Ethics*, Jan.–Mar. 2003, Norwich: Hymns Ancient and Modern, pp. 299–306.

36 Hoare, 'William Temple's *Readings in St John's Gospel* and Social Ethics', p. 299.

11

Leadership in wartime

At the outbreak of war

The 1930s was a decade of increasing tension in British politics. The rise
of the Nazis in Germany following the taking of power by the Fascists
in Italy came to change the whole political landscape. After the economic turmoil of the great crash in 1929 and the need for strong national
leadership, especially in the face of Soviet communism in Russia, the rise
of Hitler and his regime had seemed to some on the right in Britain a welcome development. Some church leaders, not least Bishop A. C. Headlam
of Gloucester, had also welcomed it. But when in the second half of the
decade the true nature of Hitler's aims became clear, opinion in political
circles divided sharply and this was reflected in the churches.

One response to the prospect of war was the rise of the Peace Pledge
Union, a campaign launched at the Royal Albert Hall in 1935 to oppose
rearmament and any thought of fighting. It was led by Dick Shepperd, a
charismatic priest who had worked with Temple in the Life and Liberty
movement. Shepperd had since become Dean of Canterbury. The PPU
gained the support of a wide range of opinion, including the biblical
scholar C. H. Dodd, the theologian Donald Mackinnon, church leaders
such as George Macleod and Donald Soper, George Lansbury of the
Labour Party among politicians, Vera Brittain, and non-Christian academics such as the philosopher Bertrand Russell. Its leaders recalled the
horrors of the First World War and the movement was determined they
should not be repeated. It also believed that a gentleman's agreement
could be reached with Hitler and Mussolini, an agreement that would
make war unnecessary.

The other response was the rejection of pacifism and support for rearmament in the hope that this would deter Hitler. Karl Barth, who
had worked in Germany in the thirties and had to flee to Switzerland,
and Reinhold Niebuhr in the United States, both rejected pacifism. In
Britain this became the majority view and that of many church leaders.
What of William Temple? He had argued for the rights of conscientious

objectors during the First World War and had often spoken in support of the League of Nations and its attempts to bring countries to negotiation rather than conflict. But he did not embrace pacifism. In a York diocesan leaflet of November 1935, he once described pacifism as being heretical in tendency. He did not repeat this charge but during the war he did argue, more persuasively, against a pacifism which saw the killing of German soldiers as breaking the law of love. He argued that the question was not simply how Britain could show love to Germans: Britain also needed to show love to Frenchmen, Poles, Czechs and Germans, all at the same time. If it could be said that Britain was fighting to overthrow Nazi tyranny and secure for all Europeans a greater measure of freedom, then resistance to Germany by force was a way of loving Germans themselves as well as others: 'In the world which exists, it is not possible to take it as self-evident that the law of love forbids fighting. Some of us even hold that precisely that law commands fighting.'[1]

In the mid-1930s, however, no one wanted war. Neville Chamberlain's policy of appeasement towards Hitler received widespread support. When, after the Munich agreement of September 1938, he returned to Britain with the famous words that he had brought back 'peace with honour ... peace in our time', the nation generally and enthusiastically welcomed it. Most church leaders also welcomed it: Chamberlain was applauded by Cosmo Lang, the Archbishop of Canterbury, who declared that 'This is the hand of God.' George Bell, the Bishop of Chichester, who was in close contact with the German Confessing Christians (who opposed Hitler) and who had protested against the Nazi's arrest of Pastor Niemöller, also agreed with Lang, as did Cardinal Hinsley the Roman Catholic leader. Even Herbert Hensley Henson, the contrary Bishop of Durham, who was under no delusions about the true nature of Nazism and its anti-Semitism, was uncomfortably silent.

On 9 November 1938 there was a dramatic change with *Kristallnacht*, the burning of 119 synagogues and the arrest of 20,000 Jews in Germany. The true character of Nazi intentions towards the Jews could no longer be ignored. Even so, German church leaders, including the leaders of the Confessing Church, issued no condemnation; nor did Bishop Bell, who took his lead from them. He remained an appeaser even after the declaration of war with Germany. Among the wider public and within the churches, however, the whole atmosphere began to change steadily and determinedly against appeasement. When the Germans invaded the rump of Czechoslovakia, in March 1939, the coming of a European war was finally recognized as being only a matter of time.

The invasion of Poland, of course, finally provoked the outbreak of war. Chamberlain's policy of appeasement was in tatters. The country was now ashamed of the Munich agreement; Lang was dismayed and silent throughout 1939. The turmoil in Europe had compromised all church leaders in one way or another, the pacifists of the PPU as well as the non-pacifists who had turned to appeasement. Even the non-appeasers like Henson who had not risen to the challenge of the hour in 1938 were implicated. Adrian Hastings asks, 'What indeed is the peace-seeker to do when faced with "the phenomenon of Hitler"? That question, unanswered then – or answered diversely by equally Christian and conscientious men – remains unanswered still.'[2]

Temple was part of all of this: he had accepted appeasement in 1938 (though without the enthusiasm of Lang) and, like other church leaders, had not really responded to the increasing persecution of the Jews in the 1930s. In these respects he was a creature of his time. But, with the outbreak of war between Britain and Germany on 3 September 1939, it is clear that Temple suddenly and impressively offered a fresh kind of leadership. One month after the declaration of war, while still Arch-bishop of York, he was invited to broadcast an address to the nation on the BBC. He spoke about the spirit and aims of Britain in the war. He avoided the kind of jingoism that many churchmen had preached at the beginning of the First World War. With his natural and steady delivery, he spoke with reason and feeling, beginning by pointing out the con-trast between the atmosphere now and what it had been in August and September 1914, at the outbreak of the First World War, when there had been some high spirits and exhilaration. This time there was less excite-ment but more resolution. He described how 'for months the public mind has been habituated to the thought that war might become an evident duty'. Now, he said, this public mind

> ... is completely void of excitement. There is a deep determination, accompanied by no sort of exhilaration, but by a profound sadness. Men are taking up a hateful duty; the very fact that they hate it throws into greater relief their conviction that it is a duty. It is a duty first to Poland; but that is rather the focus than the real essence of our obliga-tion ... for our purpose is to check aggression, and to bring to an end the perpetual insecurity and menace which hang over Europe, spoiling the life of millions, as a result of the Nazi tyranny in Germany.[3]

Temple then highlighted the impressive way that young people were now willingly enlisting in the armed forces to fight the Nazis:

> We enter the war as a dedicated nation; and it is this fact which has called forth the response of the younger generation in so marvellous a

manner. It is one of the most remarkable features of this crisis that it has found our young folk more ready to serve their country in arms in its service of a cause than ever they were, or could have been roused to be, for any imperial interest. No doubt there is in the background the reflection that, if the Nazi tyrants are again successful in aggression, our turn is not far off. But this is very much in the background. The prevailing conviction is that Nazi tyranny and aggression are destroying the traditional excellences of European civilization and must be eliminated for the good of mankind. Over against the deified nation of the Nazis our people have taken their stand as a dedicated nation.[4]

The last sentence recalls his distinction between the power state and the welfare state, a connection he explicitly made in another address on the same subject in 1941.[5] He then laid out 'seven shameful events' over the last eight years that showed the criminality of the Nazi regime, the last of which was the pogrom against the Jews on *Kristallnacht*. Temple argued (as Churchill was later to do) that the government should make no terms with Hitler or his government, because they were simply not trustworthy. He also argued that whatever terms were made with a future German government these should include 'no kind of advantage for ourselves and no humiliation for the German people'.[6] He finished by calling for a congress of nations not to repeat the mistakes of the treaty of Versailles in which Germany was punished for its role in the war but for all nations *including Germany* to negotiate a peace agreement:

> When the fighting stops, the terms of peace shall be drawn up in a true Congress of Nations, in which Germany – freed from the Nazi tyrants – shall take her place among the rest, but in which also the rights of Czechs and Poles shall have a first claim to consideration.[7]

Finally, Temple outlined a bold and long-term vision for Europe:

> Many of us hope that the Congress will pave the way for that Federal Union of Europe in which we see the only hope of a permanent settlement. But that is a large question, and certainly Europe cannot be federated until it is pacified.[8]

This broadcast therefore caught the meaning of the moment, being the mood of many British people in their sadness and in their determination to fight, and it presented a clear outline of the causes of the war along with a reasoned and principled description of its aims. In a distressing and potentially chaotic moment Temple was able to draw out a sense of moral purpose that brought clarity and resolve. Iremonger indicates that Temple's words crystallized what many were feeling and thinking at that time and the broadcast turned him into a national leader overnight.[9] Also it was heard throughout the British dominions, including Canada and Australia, giving him an international standing. He seemed to become the voice of the Christian conscience at a turning point in British history. This was seen in a small way the following day when he took the chair at a National Society of Education conference, when Lord Sankey, a senior judge and Labour politician, said, 'Before even the Minutes are read, I want in the name of all here – and I believe of all Englishmen – to thank our chairman for his broadcast last night.'[10]

In other words, Temple's words, rooted within the stark constraints of the outbreak of war, were able to find within those constraints a moral and even a spiritual dimension that would otherwise have remained hidden. They showed that there was a conditional Christian authority behind the declaration of war and that there was a clear and positive aim for the conflict. The broadcast, then, was able to draw out some purpose in a dire situation and so prepare people for the hard times that lay ahead. It therefore shows Temple embodying a kind of leadership that is anchored within a body, in this case British society, finding a positive and constructive current within that body so that this would set the tone and guide its actions. It is clear that Temple's awareness of the thoughts and feelings of those around him allowed him to do this, showing how he was in touch with their sentiments and at their service. The address, then, is a telling example of a servant leadership that responds to the needs of the moment, of providing support more than resistance and of encouragement more than judgement.

In the middle of war

But as the war progressed, was Temple able to sustain and strengthen this kind of responsive and collaborative leadership, or did the constraints of his position hamper and restrict what he was able to offer and even compromise it?

Early signs were promising. In 1940 we see him collaborating with other English church leaders to publish a letter supporting Pope Pius XII's five-point peace plan for ending the war and creating a just peace. This was instigated by Edith Ellis, a remarkable and formidable Quaker who approached Cosmo Lang, the Archbishop of Canterbury, and would not give up until Lang agreed to coordinate the letter. The Pope's plan had been published at the end of 1939 and there was now an opportunity for Roman Catholic and Free Church leaders to come together with the archbishops to support it. The letter was finally published in *The Times* in December 1940. Robert Beaken, in his account of Lang's role in all this, reports that at one of the lowest moments of the war the letter had a powerful effect on public opinion: 'It was the first time that the arch-bishops of Canterbury and York, a cardinal archbishop of Westminster [Hinsley], and the moderator of the Free Churches Council had signed such a joint letter about agreed religious matters, and it was hailed by members of all denominations.'[11] A group of MPs and even Winston Churchill, the recently installed Prime Minister, expressed appreciation. Ellis and Lang were central to the letter's publication but Temple's involvement needs to be recognized as well.

Temple's vision of the post-war world was developing all the time, and this is seen in a set of talks on BBC radio that he gave in September and October 1940 on 'The hope of a new world'. In these talks he ranged widely over the state of culture, politics, the nature of freedom, wor-ship and prayer, the requirements of international justice, social justice in ownership and industry, education and the foundations of a Christian civilization, all this with reference not just to the war but with a longer-term perspective stretching back to the nineteenth century.[12] The talks had an explicit grounding in Christian faith and practice, suggesting they were primarily for a Christian and church-based audience even though broadcast on the BBC. The talk on 'Prayer and its answer' includes one of the most evocative definitions of worship to be found anywhere:

> For to worship is to quicken the conscience by the holiness of God, to feed the mind with the truth of God, to purge the imagination by the beauty of God, to open the heart to the love of God, to devote the will to the purpose of God. All this is gathered up in that emotion which most cleanses us from selfishness because it is the most selfless of all emotions – adoration.[13]

The talk also reflects helpfully on how God answers prayer. It describes the way that in answer to prayer much of God's actions in the world 'appears to us as coincidence'.[14] This recalls one of Temple's most famous sayings of all, one which does not appear in his books: 'When I pray, coincidences happen. When I stop praying, the coincidences stop happening.'

In some ways the talks feel like a first run at what would become Temple's Penguin Special of 1942, *Christianity and Social Order*. How-ever, that later volume is much more clearly addressed to a general readership without strong Christian belief, and it spends much more time justifying the right of the church to speak out on political and economic issues. This was astute given that much of the population did not go to church and it is probably one of the reasons for the book's much greater popularity. Another reason is that it was more clearly a collaborative effort: as we have seen it came out of the Malvern Conference, and Temple drew on various expert advisers for the content of the argument. Also, as we also saw, he worked with the Industrial Christian Fellowship on 'The Church Looks Forward' campaign to promote its aims from 1942–3.

By 1942 there was little doubt that after the retirement of Lang as Archbishop of Canterbury, Temple would replace him. This duly happened in April 1942, though Temple himself had not been sure it would happen.[15] Churchill did not admire Temple's views on social reform, nor his lack of bellicosity, and he had no interest in Temple's theology nor in his leadership of the ecumenical movement. Nevertheless, he had to agree to the translation of Temple from York to Canterbury as no other bishop in the Church of England had Temple's stature and authority.

Temple and his wife moved from the tranquillity of Bishopthorpe outside York to Lambeth Palace in London. Iremonger provides the following description of the sad state of their new home which had recently been bombed by the Luftwaffe:

> Part of the roof of Wren's library had been burnt away, 2,000 books were now ashes, and 3,000 more were jumbled together in a sodden heap on the floor. Piles of smashed furniture and pictures torn by the blast lay in a litter of broken glass and rubble, the great drawing-room was a mere gaping hole, and the chapel was open to the sky.[16]

Temple and his wife set up their living quarters on the ground floor and with a chaplain, a secretary, two domestic staff and a gardener got on with their duties. Some time later he reported that some flying bombs had landed nearby:

> [L]ast Friday morning there was one just across Lambeth road ... which blew in all the windows facing that way as well as a good many others, and shook down several ceilings; it blasted the back door clean off its hinges on to the ground and it jammed the front door and the big gates in Morton's Tower so that they would not open ... Nobody to do with us was hurt, though one man was killed in the garage across the road where the bomb actually fell. Of course it all causes much inconvenience, but for us nothing worse than that, so far, and this hideous house stands like the Rock of Gibraltar![17]

Iremonger adds that when the last of these bombs fell he had just finished shaving and was getting ready for his bath. 'He scrambled out into the passage, and a second later a good part of the ceiling collapsed.'[18]

Weekends at Canterbury were a welcome relief from all this, though the city was also bombed soon after they arrived. The enthronement ceremony took place in the cathedral on 23 April 1942 and was restrained and in keeping with the conditions of wartime.[19] The end of the war was still a distant prospect but Temple characteristically spoke of the future with hope. As we saw above, he used his sermon to point to the ecumenical movement and describe it as 'one great ground of hope for the coming days – this world-wide Christian fellowship, this ecumenical movement, as it is often called'.[20]

He spent more time at Canterbury than his predecessors but also travelled continually. He would move around the country on crowded buses and trains in the blackout. It was clear that as Archbishop of Canterbury he became wholly identified with the war effort of the British people.

Interventions

The campaign for post-war social reconstruction was the most significant of Temple's initiatives as Archbishop of Canterbury, but not the only one. He had a wide range of other interests and causes, some of which he had taken on when still at York. He wrote many letters to the press on different subjects, and to government ministers, ambassadors and civil servants. He probably over-extended his advocacy and made it less effective than it could have been, but some of the support he gave was politically and morally significant.

He would be informed, for example, of the plight of an individual or group in mainland Europe. At one point it was the threat of famine to the people of Belgium. On another occasion it was the fate of an individual German pastor. In response to the first he gave his support to the efforts of Bishop George Bell of Chichester to secure famine relief, trying to get around the block which the Foreign Office put in their path when it said that any relief must not 'help the enemy'. With regard to a German pastor who had been arrested by the Nazis he began correspondence in November 1939 and was still writing letters about this in 1942.

His response to two issues is especially revealing of his leadership. The first was his response to the increasingly horrific plight of the Jews. When, towards the end of 1942, it was confirmed that there was a deliberate Nazi plan to exterminate the Jews of Europe, Temple returned to the Royal Albert Hall a month after his 'Church Looks Forward' speech and spoke with passion:

> We are witnessing such an eruption of evil as the world has not seen for centuries. What is happening in Europe is so horrible that the imagination refuses to picture it. Our people as a whole remain very largely unaware of it. And even when we are aware, it is difficult to feel the horror which is appropriate to the facts.[21]

Temple pointed to the plight of many peoples across Europe, 'of Poles and Czechs, of Greeks and Yugo-Slavs, of Norwegians, Dutch and Belgians' but then stated that

> there is one people which has no national home, which lives among other peoples as in some sense their guests, ready to be most loyal citizens to whatever extent the opportunity is opened to them, but true with a constancy that claims our admiration to their own great culture and tradition. Upon this people – the Jews – the fury of the Nazi evil has concentrated its destructive energy. It is hard to resist the conclusion that there is a settled purpose to exterminate the Jewish people if it can be done.[22]

He cited the example of French Jews being deported: first the men, then the women and then even children, sent to the east where thousands had already perished. He was speaking

> ... to express our horror at what has been and is being done, our deep sympathy with the sufferers, our claim that our own Government should do whatever is possible for their relief, and our steadfast resolution to do all and bear all that may be necessary to end this affliction.[23]

A few weeks later it became clear that most of Poland's three million Jews had already been wiped out. On 5 December he wrote to *The Times* expressing 'burning indignation at this atrocity, to which the records of barbarous ages scarcely supply a parallel'.[24]

What could be done? The Allied forces were in a position to rescue those Jews who were yet to be sent to the camps. Those in Bulgaria, Hungary and Romania would have been the easiest to save. Churchill wanted something to be done but his wishes were disregarded by the Allied command. Under American leadership it was not prepared to deviate from its war effort and attempt such a rescue.[25]

Temple had at first tried to put pressure on the government with private correspondence, to ministers and to Churchill. He asked what the government was going to do about this outrage. In reply, they tried to divert Temple with their own questions: 'Had the Archbishop considered the possibility of an anti-Semitic outbreak in England which might follow on from some special favour being shown to Jews?' Or, 'Was there not the danger of giving Hitler an excuse for further barbarities if he could point to British acts of charity and tell his people that the Jews were now seen to be the friends of Britain and therefore the enemies of the Fatherland?'[26]

Finally on 23 March 1943, Temple publicly called for action. In a long and detailed speech in the House of Lords, one of his most important in that chamber, he moved a motion calling for 'immediate measures, on the largest and most generous scale compatible with the requirements of military operation and security, for providing help and temporary asylum to persons in danger of massacre who are able to leave enemy and enemy-occupied countries'. He quoted the estimated number of Jews who had been massacred 'before which the imagination recoils', and made several suggestions for government action, including the appointment of a senior official to oversee the measures. He concluded,

> We know that what we can do is small compared with the magnitude of the problem, but we cannot rest so long as there is any sense among us that we are not doing all that might be done ... We at this moment have upon us a tremendous responsibility. We stand at the bar of history, of humanity, and of God.[27]

The government's reply, as was often the case, was that the best way of helping the Jews was to win the war and all the attention of the government would be on this rather than special relief efforts for those Jews imprisoned by Hitler. Temple's response to this hopeless line of reasoning was not to slacken his efforts but to continue with writing letters and pressing for action. Whether or not his vociferous intervention would be effective at any given moment 'it ought to be said for the sake of the principles of justice itself, and I shall continue the advocacy which I have endeavoured to offer hitherto'.[28]

The political importance of Temple's stand, in the middle of what has since come to be known as the Holocaust, should not be overemphasized. He was not able to get the British government to do anything very effective about the concentration camps nor even to bomb the railway lines into the camps. The limits of his political leverage were clear. He probably knew that being even more outspoken in public would have been even less effective in the conditions of wartime, as Bishop Bell found when he publicly condemned the Allied obliteration bombing of Dresden (see below). What can be said is that Temple was not silenced by the constraints of his position but spoke out with anger against an unspeakable crime against humanity. This in turn shows that his leadership was not quiescent but vigorous and outspoken when it needed to be. Furthermore, it was recognized as such by the World Jewish Congress on Temple's death. An official statement from that body said that he would be

> [P]articularly mourned by the Jewish people whose champion he was ... Profoundly conscious of the physical suffering of the Jews, and acutely sensitive to its spiritual significance, he was at all times ready to make every contribution to the alleviation of the great tragedy that had befallen a great people.[29]

The second of Temple's responses that should be mentioned was his response to the Allied strategy of obliteration bombing. This strategy became known to the British public in the middle of 1943 and it became clear that many thousands of German civilians would be killed as Allied bombs flattened the centres of different cities. Bishop Bell asked Temple for support in his campaign to stop it. Bell's argument was that 'to bomb cities as cities, deliberately to attack civilians, quite irrespective of whether or not they are actively contributing to the war effort, is a wrong deed, whether done by the Nazis or by ourselves'.[30] This stance was deeply unpopular at the time and Bell became a *persona non grata* in the corridors of power for the rest of the war. Some believe that it may have cost him being made Archbishop of Canterbury after Temple's death. But, subsequently, as the terror and ineffectiveness of the obliteration bombing has become better known, Bell's costly stand has become correspondingly more respected.

Temple, though, refused to support Bell on this issue: 'I am not at all disposed to be the mouthpiece of the concern which I know exists, because I do not share it.'[31] To another correspondent he explained that

> I wrote ... to the Secretary of State for Air to ask if he could assure me that the principles governing [the Allied] choice of objectives remained unaltered, and he replied that they were unaltered. All that has changed is the scale; and that seems to me irrelevant, except as a factor to balance against the probable gain. If it appeared that this method of warfare – always directed to the checking of the enemy's war effort – led to a break up of the enemy's war machine without the years of slaughter probably involved in an invasion of Germany on land, it would seem to me certainly justified – supposing we are justified in fighting at all.[32]

Temple, then, saw no moral differentiation between the bombing of German cities and the kind of bombing of military sites that had preceded it. He believed the government when it said that military objectives were still determining the strategy. The only judgement to be made was a military one, as to whether this type of bombing would actually bring the war to a swifter conclusion. On this type of judgement, he did not have or claim any expertise and so was unwilling to oppose the strategy. Subsequent findings have questioned the military effectiveness of the strategy, but Temple could not have known these and so at one level his reasoning cannot be questioned.

In another letter on 30 August he admitted that talking about this issue in these ways 'always seems horribly cold-blooded in view of the horrible facts with which one is dealing'. But he maintained his position, arguing that the strategy was justified because it was directed to military objectives even though there were inevitable tragic consequences in the deaths of civilians. On the other hand, a strategy of dropping bombs 'merely with the object of killing the general population would not be legitimate'.[33]

Temple's logic is clear and in its own terms cannot be faulted. He was not aware of any good reason to question the government's word when it said the bombing was not intended primarily to kill the civilian population. But, compared to Bell, Temple can be criticized for a lack of imagination about what was happening on the ground. Bell had been wrong about Hitler's true intentions[34] and wrong about the effectiveness of appeasement, but on this issue he has subsequently been vindicated: he grasped what obliteration bombing was doing to the people of Dresden and the other German cities targeted in this way, as opposed to what it meant in the heads of Allied military strategists. He saw that it amounted to killing the general civilian population for its own sake and, with undeniable courage and at cost to himself, he said as much. The government failed to take heed and, on this occasion, so did Temple. Temple's approach to national leadership in wartime on this occasion constrained him more than it should have done. It was not his most impressive hour.

Reforming education

As the war progressed and an Allied victory looked increasingly likely the government began to prepare for post-war reconstruction. A renewal of school education was long overdue and Temple offered important leadership on this issue, one that had been close to his heart since WEA days.[35] R. A. Butler, the government minister who was president of the Board of

Education, set about drawing up proposals for a new national framework for schools, to come into effect at the end of the war. Up to this point, schooling had been divided between church schools, whether Church of England or Nonconformist or Roman Catholic, and schools funded by the state. In the inter-war years, the funding of state schools had significantly overtaken that of church schools and many of the latter had fallen into a poor state of repair, both in the quality of the teaching and of the buildings. The Church of England alone had 400 school buildings on the Board's 'blacklist'. Up to now, however, the churches had kept a distance from the state in order to preserve the religious character of the education they were providing, and they had kept their distance from each other in order to preserve their denominational identities. In 1918 they had blocked an earlier attempt at reform. But it was now obvious that they lacked the resources to bring their own schools up to national standards. What was to be done?

Butler published his proposals on educational reconstruction in July 1943; he published a bill to go to parliament the following December. He proposed, significantly, raising the school-leaving age to 16 and maintaining the dual system of church schools on one side and state schools on the other, but with the state and the churches coordinating the services they provided. This meant that both the churches and the state would provide education for whoever lived near their schools, and the church schools would be brought into a national framework. The churches would also have to make sure their schools achieved certain minimum standards. This would be expensive, but Butler also proposed that the churches could either hand their schools over to the state or the state would fund 50 per cent of the cost of modernizing and maintaining the church schools. Furthermore, he proposed that it now be compulsory for state schools to provide for an act of worship in the school each day and that religious instruction be included within the state curriculum (though parents could withdraw their children from this if they wanted). The bill therefore represented a certain amount of give and take for both the churches and the state. It would require some new funding from the churches for their schools but it would also bring significant extra funding from the state.

When the bill was published there was concern from the Nonconformists that in some areas their children would have to attend a Church of England school. Also from some non-church teachers in the state system there was consternation that they would have to lead prayers. An earlier bill proposing education reform, the Birrell bill of 1906, had been wrecked by quarrelling between the churches. What would happen this time?

Two views quickly developed. Many in the educational world, including a number of Temple's colleagues in the WEA, hated the idea of a dual system of education, with the continued existence of church schools: there should be one modern system for all children. On the other hand, many in the churches were unhappy with the idea of relinquishing control of their schools to the state and wanted the dual system to continue. Which side would Temple take? How would his kind of immersed and accommodating leadership express itself within this polarized debate when finding common ground that was not an option. As Archbishop of Canterbury, he was president of the National Society, which had oversight of Church of England schools, and so at its annual conference in June 1942 he spoke about the challenge of responding to the government's initiative:

> Well … if we are to meet that challenge we must do it much more thoroughly than merely by saying 'We believe in the dual system', or 'We believe in Church Schools'. We must say what it is about the dual system that we believe in and why the thing we believe in can be secured by the dual system and in no other way. We must say what it is about Church Schools that we believe in, and to what extent it is true that that can be secured by Church Schools and in no other way.

Temple, then, was not simply weighing in on one side or the other but challenging his own church people to be clearer about which aspects of current provision should be retained and which handed over. He then described his own position, which on one hand was to support the dual system:

> I would very daringly suggest that one value of the dual system is its duality. I wish to suggest that there is a very great advantage in the educational field in maintaining real variety of type, with a considerable measure of individual liberty and autonomy. Many of the non-provided schools represent that element in our system at the present time, and we want to find a way of retaining, quite apart from all religious interest in the matter – of retaining, and, if it may be, of extending this element of freedom and autonomy in the individual schools.[36]

But on the other hand, he accepted the need for an overall state system that would ensure consistently high standards across the country. He saw that churches were not able to maintain their schools on their own but needed to work with the state as partners and, if unable to meet the challenge, hand their schools over to the state. This is what he advocated as Butler finalized his educational bill which would maintain the dual system within one framework. Speaking at a WEA conference in February 1944, Temple again argued that there should be schools of a variety of types with a considerable measure of individual autonomy. He believed that Butler was offering a positive and generous way forward for church schools and, equally importantly, he believed that the general raising of the school-leaving age to 16 would be a significant step forward for English society as a whole. When he spoke to his diocesan conference in Canterbury in October, supporting Butler's proposals, this was the point he emphasized above all others: 'it is the most essential element of the Bill'.[37]

Temple spoke for the bill in the Church Assembly, which accepted it. He chaired meetings with Nonconformist educationalists so that agreement on some of the details of the bill could be reached. He also spoke to church and non-church audiences up and down the country advocating its proposals. Tawney movingly describes one such address:

> The last public gathering at which I heard Temple speak was a conference of representatives of Labour and educational organisations, with Sir Walter Citrine [a trade union leader] in the chair, to demand the passage of the Bill at any early date. He was greatly overburdened at the time and, as usual, arrived late. He spoke simply, avoiding technical details, and making no attempt to give the impression of special knowledge. The effect of his speech on the audience was due to his transparent sincerity and to the fervour of moral conviction with which he spoke: it was, I think, profound.[38]

Temple's final advocacy for the bill was in the House of Lords. One of those there reported that his speeches for the bill 'were notably successful and he spoke with great authority'.[39] When the bill returned to the House of Commons, in a two-day debate, 20 out of the 31 speeches were concerned with the religious issue, which showed how important it was. But there was none of the bitterness between denominational traditions that had wrecked the Birrell bill. In the end, the main parts of the bill were all passed, including the requirement to have a daily act of corporate worship in state schools (though the school-leaving age was not actually raised to 16 until 1972).

Historians have recently given a very positive assessment of this intervention. Simon Green comments that the Act was 'something of an Anglican triumph' for it cemented in legislation 'peculiar privileges' for the Church in terms of religious education for the rest of the century and beyond.[40] Stephen G. Parker and Rob Freathy comment that 'with a very fair wind, Temple was able to negotiate the salvation of the "dual system" by the creation of the new categories of voluntary school, "Aided" and "Controlled", with the latter category preserving Church schools but reducing costs by bringing them under LEA [local education authority] control.' Furthermore, the Act not only imposed a daily act of corporate worship across all schools but made religious instruction in the classroom a requirement across all schools, replacing informal and uneven provision. He helped to put in place ways in which Christianity could 'be caught (through collective worship and across the educational experience) as much as taught [in the classroom], especially with the expansions to the school system and a further raising of the school leaving age'.[41] The Education Act of 1944 brought two Anglicans, Temple and Butler, together in common purpose towards 'the provision of a traditional Christian education through the novel instruments of a secular welfare state'.[42] Parker and Freathy comment that the Act 'established in law what many Anglicans had fought for since the beginning of state-funded education [in 1870]: guarantees for their own schools and a good deal of influence over religious education in the rest'.[43]

Temple's final act of political intervention, then, was sophisticated, committed and ultimately successful. It shows how his approach to leadership was not simply to accommodate the interests of his own constituency, as it were, but to forge an alliance with the state so that there could be benefits all round, for the general population above and beyond the church. His intervention showed that his kind of leadership could sometimes be about looking beyond the immediate to wider and longer-term interests. His immersive leadership was not simply one of reacting to pressures but of taking the initiative in a strategic way in partnership with others. It was very different from his first foray into politics during the miners' strike in 1926 which, with other bishops, had been reactive and unaware of the power dynamics in that polarized crisis. It was fitting, perhaps, that Temple's career should conclude successfully in this way and on the issue with which it had begun, education.

Temple did not himself see his career finishing at this point. The next step, he believed, was proper provision of adult education, and he became involved with setting up a central organization to help local authorities find the resources and skills they needed to provide the kind of rich and diverse educational opportunities the 1944 Act was requiring. Sadly, his death in October 1944 prevented him from taking this work forward.

Notes

1 William Temple, 'A Conditional Justification of War', *Religious Experience*, London: James Clark, 1958, pp. 172–3.

2 Adrian Hastings, *A History of English Christianity 1920–2000*, London: SCM Press, 2001, p. 343.

3 Temple, 'The Spirit and Aims of Britain in the War', reprinted in Stephen Spencer, *Christ in All Things*, Norwich: Canterbury Press, 2015, pp. 193–4.

4 Spencer, *Christ in All Things*, p. 194.

5 'The Real Meaning of the War', 1941 printed in Spencer, *Christ in All Things*, pp. 199. See above, pp. 100–1.

6 Temple, 'The Spirit and Aims of Britain in the War', reprinted in Spencer, *Christ in All Things*, p. 196.

7 Spencer, *Christ in All Things*, p. 197.

8 Spencer, *Christ in All Things*, p. 198.

9 F. A. Iremonger, *William Temple, Archbishop of Canterbury: His Life and Letters*, London: Oxford University Press, 1948, pp. 540–1.

10 Iremonger, *William Temple*, p. 541.

11 Robert Beaken, *Cosmo Lang*, London: I. B. Tauris, 2012, p. 199.

12 Printed in William Temple, *The Hope of a New World*, London: SCM Press, 1940.

13 Temple, *The Hope of a New World*, p. 30.

14 Temple, *The Hope of a New World*, p. 34.

15 He wrote to his brother on 27 January 1942 that, 'I shall be surprised if just at this moment the "powers" select me for Canterbury. Some of my recent utterances have not been liked in political circles, and it would be thought by some that to choose me now is to endorse them. I don't deny I should like to be asked! But if I were, I should have to go; and I do not think I should like the job there as much as the job here. Anyhow – it's as it will be.' Temple, *Some Lambeth Letters*, p. 1.

16 Iremonger, *William Temple*, p. 596.

17 Iremonger, *William Temple*, pp. 619–20.

18 Iremonger, *William Temple*, p. 620.

19 See Pathé news clip, www.youtube.com/watch?v=SOsSjVvGvRY.

20 William Temple, *The Church Looks Forward*, London: Macmillan, 1944, p. 3.

21 Speech of 29 October 1942, printed in Spencer, *Christ in All Things*, pp. 203–4.

22 Spencer, *Christ in All Things*, p. 204.

23 Spencer, *Christ in All Things*, p. 204.

24 Hastings, *History of English Christianity 1920–2000*, p. 376.

25 Hastings, *History of English Christianity*, pp. 376–7.

26 Iremonger, *William Temple*, p. 565.

27 Iremonger, *William Temple*, pp. 566–7.

28 Iremonger, *William Temple*, p. 567.

29 Iremonger, *William Temple*, p. 567.

30 Hastings, *History of English Christianity 1920–2000*, p. 378.

31 In R. C. D. Jasper, *George Bell*, Oxford: Oxford University Press, p. 276.

32 William Temple, *Some Lambeth Letters*, Oxford: Oxford University Press, p. 103.

33 Temple, *Some Lambeth Letters*, pp. 106–7.

34 Karl Barth wrote to Bell in the following way: 'Dear Bishop, I think you are too much a British gentleman and thus unable to understand the phenomenon of Hitler.' Hastings, *History of English Christianity 1920–2000*, p. 343.

35 On Temple's educational work as a whole, see John Sadler, 'William Temple's Educational Work and Thought', Taylor and Francis Online.

36 From 'Our Trust and Our Task', the presidential address delivered at the annual meeting of the National Society, 3 June 1942, in *The Church Looks Forward*, pp. 46–53.

37 Iremonger, *William Temple*, pp. 573, 575.

38 Iremonger, *William Temple*, p. 575.

39 Iremonger, *William Temple*, p. 577.

40 S. J. D. Green, *The Passing of Protestant England* (Cambridge, 2011), p. 215, quoted in Stephen G. Parker and Rob Freathy, 'The Church of England and religious education', p. 206.

41 Stephen G. Parker and Rob Freathy, 'The Church of England and religious education', p. 208. Parker and Freathy go on to describe the increasing difficulties of implementing this as the 1950s gave way to the 1960s, long after Temple's death in 1944.

42 S. J. D. Green in Parker and Freathy, 'The Church of England and religious education', p. 209.

43 Parker and Freathy, 'The Church of England and religious education', pp. 209–10.

12

In the end

Last days

During the years of war, Temple steadily increased his level of public engagements. At York he had had time to prepare the Gifford Lectures and the *Readings in St John's Gospel*. When he moved to Canterbury there was no time for writing or academic lecturing. The only volume to be published was a collection of sermons and addresses, a book which took its title from 'The Church Looks Forward' campaign. He felt that with so many men and women in the armed services giving their lives to the service of their country he could hardly do less himself. And so he would speak as often and in as many places as the hours of the day would allow him. Between speaking he would write his letters, in his own hand, to everyone who wrote to him and to many others as well.

On one occasion in Coventry, between 4pm and 10pm, Temple spoke at three meetings and attended a reception. There was an interval of 50 minutes in the six hours and this, his host reports, he filled by writing letters, 14 in all. Randall Davidson had had the measure of Temple many years earlier when he said, 'The trouble with dear William is, he is so kind that he cannot say No.'[1] This became even more true during the years at Canterbury.

He loved the work, of course. One colleague wrote how Temple was due to attend a meeting in central London on the day a terrifying daylight air raid took place. The meeting had to take place in a basement shelter that was not particularly safe:

> After a quarter of an hour, during which the elements of a snack lunch were provided, Temple appeared, his arrival heralded down the basement stairs by characteristic gusts of laughter. I don't think that we got much further that day in the definition of war aims, but I do know that Temple's presence acted as a vivifying tonic on every human being present in that by no means agreeable situation, from the youngest typist up to the research director.[2]

All this work inevitably took its toll. It had begun to do so before he moved to Canterbury. To his brother, in 1941, he confided that, 'We have kept our Silver Wedding here to-day in great restfulness; we are both tired, so having kept the day clear we slept nearly all the afternoon in the garden.'[3] In the last couple of years his gout began to return more regularly and each time more painfully. This was not helped by the disturbed nights at Lambeth with flying bombs frequently falling nearby. Temple had to sleep on a sofa in the ground floor passage of the palace, where there was a domed roof which had so far stood up to the shock of bomb explosions near by. The previous chapter gave an account of the damage that the bombs did (pp. 170-1). Temple wrote to his brother that there was a flying bomb 'which broke all our windows on that side of the house, and some others; then there was one in the bombed part of St Thomas' Hospital which did a little damage, but nothing very serious; there was one in Lambeth Walk, just behind the railway embankment, which broke a few more on the other side of the house ...'.[4] All this added to the pressure Temple was under.

But he did take holidays, and he and his wife frequently visited the Isle of Wight, the Lake District, the valley of the Kennet and the Quantocks. In the Lakes he would always wear an old Norfolk jacket whose original colour might have been anything from grey to green. Sandwiches would stick out of one pocket, maps from another and on his head an old hat with holes in it. He would forge slowly up the fell tracks but liked to leap down them on the way back (at least when he was younger). After the walks his companions remembered his appetite for tremendous farmhouse teas of bread and butter, cream, bilberry jam and apple pastry. One of his fellow walkers wrote what has become a famous story of a walk at Buttermere:

William knew the Lakes intimately and was a stalwart and steady walker. Having more to carry he progressed more slowly than the rest of us. One hot morning Tawney, Bell [not the bishop], and I, having reached the summit of Great Gable, watched William climbing steadily upwards and 'larding the lean earth' as he came. When he reached the rock on which we were sitting, he sat heavily down, wiped his brow and exclaimed: 'Thank God, I do *not* believe in the resurrection of the *flesh*!'[5]

That was before the move to Canterbury. In these years he and his wife would get away on their own, especially to a holiday cottage at Weacombe in Somerset, for rest and the opportunity to be with each other. They talked of his retirement and he of his plans to write a book on the Holy Spirit. But the gout returned when he was back at work: it always seemed to do so when he was under pressure.

At the beginning of September 1944 it returned again, this time more severely than ever before. He was unable to use his legs and had to be carried into Canterbury Cathedral when the clergy of the diocese assembled for a synod. This meeting had been planned for months and he was determined to give his address. In this, his last public engagement, he spoke of the need for the clergy to find inward strengthening through regular prayer, meditation, penitence and retreats, for 'Apart from Me, ye can do nothing.' He then urged the parochial clergy to undertake evangelism; such evangelism should be directed especially towards those men and women who would be returning from war service and whose habits of a lifetime had been broken by the war. He asked deaneries to establish evangelism committees and parishes to call groups of men and women to visit and encourage the returnees to respond. He told the clergy that if ever they thought that he could help them in any difficulties of their own they were to let him know, and 'if you would at all like to come and talk them over, ask for an appointment without any hesitation. It may have to be fixed for some weeks ahead, for my engagement book gets very full; but it can always be arranged. After all, it is what I am here for!'[6]

He also issued a pastoral letter to be read at the main service in all the parishes, calling on all parishioners to share in this great evangelistic calling. In the letter, in characteristic vein, he wrote how God

> was putting before us a great opportunity. Let us all dedicate ourselves anew and pray for the guidance and strength of His Holy Spirit that we may use this time, when a new fashion of life must needs be formed, in the way that will most set forward His glory and the true welfare of all His people.[7]

After the end of the war members of a specially appointed commission responded to Temple's call by publishing the report *Towards the Conversion of England* and promoted it across the dioceses.[8]

Three days later he wrote to his brother that the attack of gout had returned 'in prodigious violence, and I have now got acute gout in both knees, which, as you can imagine, is quite immobilising ... at present I am able to make no plans'.[9] Nevertheless, over the next two days he saw some ordination candidates while sitting up in bed, and then called them all to sit round him while he delivered his address to them. This was his last ministerial act.

Two young girls, Zoë and Nancy Brennan, knowing that Temple was ill, took some grapes to his house. He was emphatic that the grapes should not be put on a plate but left in the children's basket, just as they had brought them, and he sent them this reply:

Dear Zoë and Nancy
I am sorry to be so late in writing to thank you for so kindly sending me those grapes. It has not been easy to write till now, and even to-day I cannot do much. But the horrid thing does seem to be going away and though I still have a lot of discomfort, the really bad pain seems to be over.
   Thank you so much.
   Yours sincerely,
   William Cantuar[10]

He was then taken for rest and treatment to Westgate, where he remained. His 63rd birthday fell on 15 October. A few days later he wrote to Lang (the retired archbishop) that the gout was being kept alive by a sub-acute streptococcal infection and that this must be tackled first. However, there was to be no chance to do that. On the 26th, in the morning, he was struck by a pulmonary embolism caused by a blood clot. He said that he felt very faint and his wife hurried to get help. A doctor was at hand and did what he could. '"Are you in great pain?" he asked, to which Temple replied: "No, but I can't breathe." A few minutes later he was dead.'[11]

News of his death was met with shock and disbelief in Britain and around the world. To many it seemed that he had been taken just as his greatest work was beginning. His funeral took place in Canterbury Cathedral a few days later and then, as he had wished, he was cremated. His ashes were laid beside the grave of his father in the cloister garth at Canterbury.

But Temple would not have wanted news of his death, shocking as it was, to lead to any kind of despair. A few months earlier, in a letter to a mother grieving the loss of her son, he had written in a clear yet profound way:

I cannot say how deeply I sympathise with you in your sorrow and the shock that it has brought to your faith. I trust that as time heals the surface of the wound, which of course it does, though never perhaps its depth, you will see things in a rather different proportion and be able once more to trust in God.
   If we are Christians, we cannot possibly suppose that we have a right to expect God to save either us or those we love from death. If He, as St. Paul puts it, 'spared not His own Son', it is quite clear that the way of suffering may be the way by which we are to fulfil His purpose. When

Our Lord says that God cares even for the sparrows, He does not for a moment conceal or ignore the fact that they do fall to the ground and die; what He says is that when this happens, it is within the loving care of the Father of all creatures. And Christ, by His Resurrection, has made clear to us that death after all is not the end, nor of necessity any great evil; it is the one thing in life that some time or other we all have to face; it is therefore part of God's ordering of the world for us, and we must trust to Him not so much to save us from it but to uphold us through it and beyond it.

I hope that as you think of these things you may begin once again to feel that your only son is still in God's keeping as truly as when he was here, and that you too are in His keeping and can look forward to the happiness of renewed fellowship in God's closer presence in the world beyond.[12]

Prelate or servant?

How is such a figure to be summed up within church and national life? Should it be as an ecclesiastical statesman like his predecessor Randall Davidson who moved easily and frequently in the corridors of power, or as an influential social theologian like the powerfully outspoken American preacher and writer Reinhold Niebuhr, or as a great reformer like William Wilberforce battling against the slave trade, or Lord Shaftsbury fighting for factory reform? He is an important but difficult figure to sum up. As mentioned in the Preface, Adrian Hastings compared Temple with Charles Gore and Michael Ramsey, two other twentieth-century Anglican figures who combined theological influence with practical leadership: 'Temple remains the man "in the middle", his time cut off in war, still the most enigmatic of the three, the most difficult to make up one's mind about.'[13]

Much of the story told by this book might seem to confirm this statement. He achieved so much, yet what was his pre-eminent contribution? His philosophical theology was impressive in its scope and accomplished in its expression and yet, as we have seen, did not quite succeed in achieving the goal it set itself. His leadership and reform of the church, in the Life and Liberty movement, then as a diocesan bishop, then archbishop, was important in updating some of the structures (the dividing of the Diocese of Manchester being the clearest example) but it did not institute and carry through a general reform of the Church of England. His successor, Archbishop Geoffrey Fisher, would do more of this than he. Temple's work for social reform, whether through COPEC or the

Malvern Conference or even 'The Church Looks Forward' campaign did not bring immediate results in parliament in the way that Wilberforce had done, though it did have a significant general influence on what happened after the war. His interventions in the politics of his time were few and far between (compared with Davidson's) and for most of his career (up to the outbreak of the Second World War) relatively meagre in their results. His role in the emergent ecumenical movement was crucial, along with that of J. H. Oldham and William Paton, but his contribution was essentially one of bringing people together and building bridges between churches rather than of creating the ecumenical ideal in the first place. He did not plant the ecumenical movement although he certainly watered it. And his work as a Christian social theologian, while important as an example of practical theology in making connections between philosophy and theology on the one hand and social and economic policies on the other, did not itself create an influential school of thought in the way that Niebuhr or Jacques Maritain had done. Temple was great in so many ways, possibly more ways than any other contemporary church leader in Britain or around the world, but pre-eminent in none of them.

Nevertheless, this kind of statement does not capture the full significance of the man. There was something about the way he combined all these things which suggests that there was more to him than the sum of these different parts. Hastings put it this way: 'There have been more convincing philosophical theologians, more effective social reformers, greater preachers, more-single-minded ecumenists, but no one who combined all these skills to so high a degree and who so steadily matched his leadership with the hour.'[14] Frances Knight also focuses on the significance of his leadership: 'He was academically active but it was his work making things happen, being involved in organisations and in being an incredibly energetic figure that is really at the heart of his legacy.'[15]

These assessments helpfully draw our attention back to the person as a whole and to the kind of leadership that he provided, but they also raise the question of *how* he matched his leadership with the hour and *how* he made things happen. It is this question that this book has sought to address.

The chapters above have provided a set of windows on to his leadership but, looking back at them as a whole, they do not offer a single answer to this question. There is variety and complexity in what they reveal. For example there is the figure we encountered at the start of this book, on the platform of the Royal Albert Hall in September 1942, a larger-than-life figure demonstrating a commanding kind of leadership, holding the banking world to account and demanding change, apparently a powerful prelate of the church laying down moral law on the basis of the church's own authority. Such outspokenness was also seen in his response to the Holocaust, from the same platform and then from within the House of Lords, not silenced by the constraints of his position but speaking out with anger against an unspeakable crime against humanity. This showed that his leadership was not quiescent but vigorous and dynamic when it needed to be.

But other chapters of this book have revealed a different side to Temple, one based on a natural humility seen early in life when he was open to and glad of the formative influence of Albert Mansbridge and the Workers Education Association. It was seen when he experienced the disappointment of being turned down for ordination, accepting the decision of his diocesan bishop and turning to other avenues. It was seen in the way his rise to senior leadership during his thirties was far from straightforward, even for someone with so many gifts, his lack of success as a headmaster showing that he had much to learn, not just to follow in the footsteps of his great father. Temple must search for his own way forward and at certain moments break with the expectations of his upbringing, which he finally did when he took on the leadership of a campaign to reform the church, a role that began to fulfil his early sense of calling.

Temple's addresses and writings have also appeared to be doing different things. On the one hand the major works of philosophical theology appear to compel their readers to accept a complete map of reality, a Christocentric metaphysics, argued on the basis of logical reasoning. The scope and range of their arguments are broad and seemingly unanswerable. Yet, on the other hand, when the content of the arguments are analysed something else is being attempted, the establishing of some common ground with his listeners and readers so that a conversation can take place and an offer made of a worldview, broad in its scope, to those who are interested in exploring it.

Furthermore, while the case that he makes for a Christocentric metaphysics was not convincing for some, as commentators have subsequently pointed out, his philosophical works show a committed and sustained collaboration with the outlook of his listeners and readers. In his letter to Ronald Knox he had stated, after all, that 'I am Jones', a contemporary person of learning seeking the truth, and this conditioned his whole approach. His intellectual leadership, then, was not one of compelling his audience to change their minds but one of *offering* a different and rich way of understanding the world around them and of the place of the Christian faith within that.

As we turned to his work as Bishop of Manchester a collaborative approach to leadership also began to emerge, especially when compared with his predecessor. It was seen in the way he served the life of the diocese through entrusting others with the work of the boards, committing himself to mission and teaching such as at the Blackpool missions and through demonstrating the virtues of pragmatism and patience when the diocese needed to be divided. He also had a winning humility, described in Lancashire as being 'without side', though in some respects he was not as personally collaborative as he could have been. While his ministry did not always touch the hearts of people it did touch the minds of many and especially of his clergy and it was notable how he proactively empowered the female lay workers and deaconesses in ways which were ahead of their time and widely appreciated.

This book, then, has uncovered two William Temples, the prelate and the servant. And some of the chapters have begun to explain why this is so, because they have shown how he gradually become more and more of the latter. This was seen in some of his shorter and more popular books in the 1920s which showed him combining big metaphysical themes with more intimate pastoral teaching, such as on the connection between prayer and love, showing an increasing warmth and encouragement in his writing, a feature that would become characteristic of much of his later speaking and writing, showing a gradual shift from academic lecturer to pastorally-minded teacher.

Theologically, we found a figure who was prepared to keep searching and reflecting, one who did not rest on the laurels of his major publications but who kept digging for the truth. His humility was seen in the way he was prepared to critique and in some respects put to one side his earlier work in philosophical theology. The disposition of a student was seen in the way, when archbishop, he was eager to learn from younger theologians in order to respond to the challenges of that time. All of this showed his preparedness and commitment to put himself at the service of others for the forging of a truthful vision.

With his views on society, we saw Temple move from his early historicist and collectivist outlook, prescriptive and in places colonialist, to a responsive vision, especially in the early 1940s in response to the events and needs of his time, drawing on the expert advice of others, to give that vision direct relevance and purchase. He was clearly determined to draw up a practical programme, with specific proposals for eradicating poverty and unemployment, but one which would reflect a broad range of opinion. After some missteps earlier in his career over the Miners' Strike, we saw a much more joined-up approach, with the collaborative movement that began at Malvern and continued through 'The Church Looks Forward' campaign, a well-judged and ultimately very influential initiative.

Temple's involvement in ecumenism clearly influenced him in this direction as well, for here was a movement which depended on listening, mutual learning and sensitivity to the views of others. We saw him carefully reconsider Anglicanism in ways that attempted to be faithful to what had been handed down while actively seeking unity with other churches. This was not an easy calling at all, and he could not and did not please everyone, but he was not going to dissolve difference into uniformity. In meetings with other churches he worked collaboratively and constructively to integrate and carry forward the aspirations of the ecumenical movement itself. We saw how his outstanding contribution was in backroom committee work, of being able with patience and forbearance to hear and distil the essence of what others were bringing to the table and then to forge statements or resolutions that carried forward this ecumenism, especially at the crucially important meeting at Bishopthorpe in 1933 where he brought representatives of the Protestant churches together to lay the groundwork for the World Council of Churches.

In his mature teaching ministry in the 1930s a collaborative approach was more and more apparent, with *Christian Faith and Life*, *Nature, Man and God* and *Readings in St John's Gospel* presenting the Christian faith in ways that did not attempt to put pressure on the sceptical to come to faith but invited his listeners and readers to open their inner eyes, the eyes of their imagination, to the person of Christ and to his way of life, and then to follow that way in their own lives, a leadership of open invitation and encouragement rather than of direct challenge and judgement. In the *Readings*, furthermore, Temple went even further and opened a window on to his own personal faith where fellowship, service and love were expressions of one compelling divine and human reality.

The outbreak of the Second World War propelled Temple on to a national and international stage. In his BBC broadcast at the outbreak of war in 1939 we saw him identify with and then articulate the mood of many within the nation, in a restrained yet positive way so that the requirements of justice would prevail over warmongering. It was, perhaps, his finest hour and reveals the leader that Temple had become, one wholly committed to the service of his fellow human beings. His lifestyle as Archbishop of Canterbury bore this out, seen in his travelling on buses and crowded trains during the war, expressed in a self-sacrificial and tireless ministry, seasoned with unflagging cheerfulness and that roisterous laugh, endlessly writing letters to all kinds of people and speaking all over the country conveying purpose and hopefulness, finally succumbing to illness and a premature death through overwork.

Temple's final act of political intervention, in support of Butler's education bill, was sophisticated, committed and ultimately successful. His approach in this was not simply to protect the interests of his own constituency, the Church of England and its schools, but to forge an alliance with the state so that there could be benefits all round, not least for all young people currently in education and all children about to embark on education. His intervention in the debate leading to the passing of the 1944 Education Act vividly showed how he put into practice his own famous saying that the church exists to serve the interests of those who are not its members.

How, then, to sum up William Temple's leadership? Was he a prelate or a servant? Technically he was a prelate or, rather, 'Primate of England' when Archbishop of York and 'Primate of all England' when Archbishop of Canterbury. But in terms of the spirit and manner in which he fulfilled his duties, this does not begin to do justice to what we have seen. Instead it is appropriate to recall Robert K. Greenleaf and Ken Blanchard's model of leadership, mentioned at the start of this book. For they propose a way of leading others which is intentional, dynamic and purposeful and yet, paradoxically, at the service of others, responsive and collaborative. This is the model of servant leadership. It is highly appropriate for Temple because he clearly and sacrificially made the service of others his main priority, caring for the spiritual and material needs of his neighbours and fellow citizens and helping them, in Greenleaf's language, to become healthier and wiser, guiding them towards self-improvement. He also clearly fulfilled both parts of Blanchard's description of the practice of servant leadership: first of offering insight into the way things are with a compelling and hopeful vision of the way they could be, with the principles, values and specific goals needed to get there, seen especially towards the end of his life within the strictures of wartime; and second in a whole host of ways in which he provided the hands-on leadership of encouraging others to turn that vision into reality, through responding to their needs, collaborating with them and encouraging them along the way. Temple offers a fine example of someone who came to embody servant leadership for his times, whose disposition, values and actions encouraged in others 'imitation and a certain mixture of aspiration and admiration'.[16]

But these chapters have also revealed a figure who in many ways transcends his own times to offer inspiration and encouragement for leadership in our time. This is because he was not just an academic and teacher, or an activist and campaigner, or a man of prayer and evident spirituality, or a larger-than-life and charismatic figure, or a person of unassuming humility who despite his privileged upbringing found his own way in life, but was all of these rolled into one, a person of simple integrity and holiness. He was both a prelate and a servant, a paradox and a gift. Bishop George Bell described Temple as having 'all the vividness and swiftness of a flame ... he communicated warmth and light to all who saw or heard him.'[17] That warmth and light can still be felt today through the servant leadership he gave to church and world.

Notes

1 F. A. Iremonger, *William Temple, Archbishop of Canterbury: His Life and Letters*, London: Oxford University Press, 1948, p. 10.

2 Iremonger, *William Temple*, p. 619.

3 Iremonger, *William Temple*, p. 506.

4 Iremonger, *William Temple*, p. 620.

5 Iremonger, *William Temple*, p. 508.

6 William Temple, *Some Lambeth Letters*, Oxford: Oxford University Press, 1963, p. 182.

7 Temple, *Some Lambeth Letters*, p. 185.

8 Archbishops' Commission on Evangelism, *Towards the Conversion of England*, London: The Church Assembly, 1945.

9 Temple, *Some Lambeth Letters*, p. 187.

10 Temple, *Some Lambeth Letters*, p. 190.

11 Iremonger, *William Temple*, p. 625.

12 Temple, *Some Lambeth Letters*, pp. 157–8.

13 Adrian Hastings, *The Shaping of Prophecy*, London: Geoffrey Chapman, 1995, p. 68.

14 'William Temple', *Dictionary of National Biography*.

15 Frances Knight, 'Why study William Temple?'

16 Malcolm Grundy, *Leadership and Oversight*, London: Mowbray, 2011, p. 115.

17 A. E. Baker, *William Temple and His Message*, London: Penguin, 1946, p. 47.

Bibliography

Books by William Temple (in chronological order)

The Faith and Modern Thought. Lectures. London: Macmillan, 1910
Principles of Social Progress, Melbourne: Australian Student Christian Union, 1910
The Nature of Personality. Lectures. London: Macmillan, 1911
The Kingdom of God. Lectures. London: Macmillan, 1912
Repton School Sermons: Studies in the Religion of the Incarnation. London: Macmillan, 1913
Studies in the Spirit and Truth of Christianity. Sermons. London: Macmillan, 1914
Church and Nation. Lectures. London: Macmillan, 1915
Plato and Christianity. Lectures. London: Macmillan, 1916
Mens Creatrix: An Essay. London: Macmillan, 1917
The Challenge to the Church. Mission account. London 1917
Issues of Faith. Lectures. London: Macmillan, 1917
Fellowship with God. Sermons. London: Macmillan, 1920
The Universality of Christ. Lectures. London: SCM Press, 1921. Reprinted in *About Christ*, London: SCM Press, 1962
Life of Bishop Percival, London: Macmillan, 1921
Christus Veritas: An Essay. London: Macmillan, 1924
Christ in His Church. Diocesan charge. London: Macmillan, 1925
Christ's Revelation of God. Lectures. London: SCM Press, 1925. Reprinted in *About Christ*, London: SCM, 1962
Personal Religion and the Life of Fellowship. London: Longmans Green and Co., 1926
Essays in Christian Politics and Kindred Subjects. London: Longmans Green and Co., 1927
Christianity and the State. Lectures. London: Macmillan, 1928
Christian Faith and Life. Oxford Mission addresses. London: SCM Press, 1931. Reissued 1963: page references are to this edition. New edition, ed. Susan Howatch, London: Mowbray, 1994
Thoughts on Some Problems of the Day. Diocesan charge. London: Macmillan, 1931
Nature, Man and God. Gifford Lectures. London: Macmillan, 1934
Basic Convictions. Addresses. London, 1936
Christianity in Thought and Practice. Lectures. London: SCM Press, 1936
The Church and its Teaching Today. Lectures. New York: Macmillan, 1936
The Preacher's Theme Today. Lectures. London: SPCK, 1936
Readings in St. John's Gospel. 2 vols. London: Macmillan, 1939–40. Complete edition 1945: page references are to this edition. Paperback edition 1961

Thoughts in War-Time. Sermons and addresses. London: Macmillan, 1940
The Hope of a New World. Sermons and addresses. London: SCM Press, 1940
Citizen and Churchman. London: Eyre and Spottiswoode, 1941
Christianity and Social Order, Harmondsworth: Penguin Special, 1942. New edition London: SCM, 1950. New edition: Shepheard-Walwyn and SPCK, 1976, with Foreword by the Rt Hon. Edward Heath and Introduction by Professor R. H. Preston, used here.
The Church Looks Forward. Sermons and addresses. London. Macmillan, 1944
Religious Experience and Other Essays and Addresses. Posthumous collection. London: James Clarke, 1958
Some Lambeth Letters, ed. F. S. Temple, Oxford: Oxford University Press, 1963

Other writings by William Temple

(Select list, in chronological order)

The Education of Citizens, Address, London, 1905
'The Church and the Labour Party: A Consideration of their Ideals', *The Economic Review* Vol. XVIII, 15 April 1908
'The Church', 'The Divinity of Christ' and 'Epilogue' in *Foundations. A Statement of Christian Belief in Terms of Modern Thought by Seven Oxford Men*. London: Macmillan, 1912
Competition: A Study in Human Motive. London: Macmillan, 1917. Written by a committee including Temple
'The Church and Labour', *Daily News*, 14 May 1918, reprinted in Spencer (ed.), *Christ in All Things*, pp. 81–3
'Introduction: The Christian Social Movement in the Nineteenth Century', *Christian Social Reformers of the Nineteenth Century*, ed., Hugh Martin, London: SCM Press, 1927
'Revelation', *Revelation*, ed., John Baillie and Hugh Martin, London: Faber and Faber, 1937
'Chairman's Introduction' in *Doctrine in the Church of England, The Report of the Commission on Christian Doctrine Appointed by the Archbishops of Canterbury and York in 1922*. London: SPCK, 1938
'Christian Faith and the Common Life' in *Christian Faith and the Common Life*, Vol. IV of the Oxford Conference, 1937, On Church, Community and State. London: Allen and Unwin, 1938
'Introduction', *Men Without Work. A Report made to the Pilgrim Trust*. Cambridge University Press, 1938
'Theology To-day', in *Theology* 39 (233), 1939, reprinted in *Thoughts in War Time*, 1940, and in *Theology*, Vol. 123 No. 4, July/August 2020
'The Chairman's Opening Address' and 'A Review of the Conference' in *Malvern, 1941. The Life of the Church and the Order of Society, Being the Proceedings of the Archbishop of York's Conference*. London: Longmans Green and Co., 1941
'Prologue', 'Pacifists and Non-Pacifists' with C. E. Raven, 'Christmas Broadcast to Germany', *Is Christ Divided?*, ed. William Temple, Harmondsworth: Penguin, 1943

Nazi Massacre of the Jews and Others: Some Practical Proposals for immediate rescue, The Archbishop of Canterbury and Lord Rochester, London: Victor Gollanz, 1943

Other Letters and Papers

The William Temple Papers at Lambeth Palace Library, in multiple volumes, contains his official correspondence as Archbishop of Canterbury as well as many letters from his earlier life. They also contain copies of many of his newspaper and magazine articles, and pamphlets, and some unpublished writings.

MS 1765 at Lambeth are the letters he wrote to his brother throughout his life, about 700 in all. There are also editorials and articles in *The Challenge*, *The Pilgrim* and *The Highway*, *The Listener*.

Monographs on William Temple (select list)

Carmichael, John D. and Goodwin, Harold S., *William Temple's Political Legacy*, London: A. R. Mowbray, 1963
Dackson, Wendy, *The Ecclesiology of Archbishop William Temple*, Lewiston, New York: Edwin Mellen Press, 2004
Fletcher, Joseph, *William Temple: Twentieth-Century Christian*, New York: Seabury, 1963
Grimley, Matthew, *Citizenship, Community and the Church of England: Liberal Anglican Theories of the State between the Wars*, Oxford: Oxford University Press, 2004
Iremonger, F. A., *William Temple, Archbishop of Canterbury: His Life and Letters*, London: Oxford University Press, 1948
Kent, John, *William Temple: Church, State and Society in Britain 1880–1950*, Cambridge: Cambridge University Press, 1992
Loane, Edward, *William Temple and Church Unity: The Politics and Practice of Ecumenical Theology*, Palgrave Macmillan, 2016
Padgett, Jack F., *The Christian Philosophy of William Temple*, The Hague: Martinus Nijhoff, 1974
Suggate, Alan D., *William Temple and Christian Social Ethics Today*, Edinburgh: T and T Clark, 1987
Spencer, Stephen, *William Temple: A Calling to Prophecy*, London: SPCK, 2001
Thomas, Owen C., *William Temple's Philosophy of Religion*, London: SPCK, 1961

Other books and articles

Anglican Communion, 'The Chicago-Lambeth Quadrilateral' of the 1888 Lambeth Conference, anglicancommunion.org/resources/acis/docs/chicago_lambeth_quadrilateral.cfm

Arendt, Hannah, 'The Concept of History: Ancient and Modern', in *Between Past and Future*, Harmondsworth: Penguin, 1977

Atherton, John, Christopher Baker and John Reader, *Christianity and the New Social Order*, London: SPCK, 2011

Avis, Paul (ed.), *Churches in a Pluralist World: The Thought and Legacy of John Neville Figgis, CR*, Leiden: Brill, 2022

—— 'William Temple: Pillar and Pioneer of Christian Unity', *Ecclesiology*, 12 October 2020, brill.com/view/journals/ecso/16/3/article-p401_401.xml?language=en

Baker, Chris, book review, williamtemplefoundation.org.uk/book-review-christ-in-all-things-spencer-william-temple, 2015

Beaken, Robert, *Cosmo Lang: Archbishop in War and Crisis*, London: I. B. Tauris, 2012

Begbie, Harold, 1920, 'Religion and Politics: A Talk with Canon Temple', *The Daily Telegraph*, 6 April 1920

Bell, G.K., 'Memoir', in *William Temple and His Message*, ed., A. E. Baker, Harmondsworth: Penguin, 1946

Berlin, Isaiah, *Karl Marx*, Oxford: Oxford University Press, 1935

Bosanquet, Bernard, *The Philosophical Theory of the State*, London: Macmillan and Co., 1923

Bradley, F. H., 'My Station and Its Duties' (1876), in *Ethical Studies*, Oxford: Oxford University Press, 1927

Brown, Malcolm, 'Politics as the Church's Business: William Temple's *Christianity and Social Order* Revisited', *Journal of Anglican Studies*, Vol. 5 (2), 2007

Bruce, Malcolm, *The Coming of the Welfare State*, London: Batsford, 1961

Caird, Edward, *Hegel*, Edinburgh and London: Wm Blackwood and Sons, 1883

—— *Lay Sermons and Addresses delivered in the Hall of Balliol College*, Glasgow: Wentworth Press, 1908

Carpenter, James, *Gore: A Study in Liberal Catholic Thought*, London: The Faith Press, 1960

Charry, Ellen T., 'The Beauty of Holiness: Practical Divinity', in *The Vocation of Anglican Theology*, ed. Ralph McMichael, London: SCM Press, 2014

Christensen, T., *Origins and History of Christian Socialism 1848–54*, Aarhus: Universitetsforlaget, 1962

Coutts, Jon, *SCM Studyguide to Church Leadership*, London: SCM Press, 2019

Dackson, Wendy, 'Archbishop William Temple and Public Theology in a Post-Christian Context', *Journal of Anglican Studies*, Vol. 4 (2), 2006

Emmet, Dorothy, 'The Philosopher', in F. A. Iremonger, *William Temple, Archbishop of Canterbury: His Life and Letters*, London: Oxford, 1948

Field, Frank, 'The Temple Family', *Saints and Heroes: Inspiring Politics*, London: SPCK 2010

Figgis, John Neville, *Churches in the Modern State*, London: Longmans Green and Co., 1913

Forbes, Duncan, *The Liberal Anglican Idea of History*, Cambridge: Cambridge University Press, 1952

Friere, Paulo, *Pedagogy of the Oppressed*, Eng. trans., London: Sheed and Ward, 1972

Galgalo, Joseph, 'Service to God and Humanity: Modelling cathartic sacrifice as the leitmotiv of authentic Christian service', in *Leadership with Integrity: Higher*

Education from Vocation to Funding, eds C. Stückelberger, J. Galgalo and S. Kobia, Globethics.net. 2021, www.globethics.net/documents

Gore, Charles, editor, *Property: Its Rights and Duties: Historically, Philosophically and Religiously Regarded*. London: Macmillan and Co., 1913

Greenleaf, Robert K., *Servant Leadership*, New York/Mahwah: Paulist Press, Inc., 1977, 1991, 2002

Grimley, Matthew, *Citizenship, Community and the Church of England: Liberal Anglican Theories of the State Between the Wars*, Oxford: Oxford University Press, 2004

—— 'Anglicans, reconstruction and democracy: the Cripps circle, 1939-52', in Tom Rodger et al., *The Church of England and British Politics since 1900*, Woodbridge: The Boydell Press, 2020

Grundy, Malcolm, *Leadership and Oversight: New models for episcopal ministry*, London: Mowbray, 2011

Guess, Deborah, 'The Eco-theological Significance of William Temple's "Sacramental Universe"', *Journal of Anglican Studies*, Vol. 18/No.1, May 2020, Cambridge: Cambridge University Press

Harris, Jose, *William Beveridge: A Life*, Oxford: Clarendon Press, 1997

Hastings, Adrian, *A History of English Christianity 1920–2000*, London: SCM Press, 2001

—— 'William Temple', in Adrian Hastings, *The Shaping of Prophecy*, London: Geoffrey Chapman, 1995

—— 'William Temple', in *The New Dictionary of National Biography*, Oxford: Oxford University Press, 2004

Hegel, G. W. F., *Lectures on the Philosophy of World History* (trans. H. B. Nisbet), Cambridge: Cambridge University Press, 1975

—— *Philosophy of Right* (trans. T. M. Knox), Oxford: Oxford University Press, 1952

Hinchliff, Peter, *God and History: Aspects of British Theology 1875–1914*, Oxford: Clarendon Press, 1992

—— *Frederick Temple, Archbishop of Canterbury, A Life*, Oxford: Clarendon Press, 1998

Hoare, Rupert, 'William Temple's *Readings in St John's Gospel* and Social Ethics', *Crucible: The Journal of Christian Social Ethics*, Jan.–Mar. 2003, Norwich: Hymns Ancient and Modern

Jasper, R. C. D., *George Bell*, Oxford: Oxford University Press, 1968

Jenkins, David, 'Editorial: Christianity, Social Order and the Story of the World', *Theology*, London: SPCK, September 1981

Jones, P. d'A, *The Christian Socialist Revival 1877–1914*, Princeton: Princeton University Press, 1968

Knight, Frances, 'Why study William Temple?', 2015, mediaspace.nottingham. ac.uk/media/Why+Study+William+Temple+with+Frances+Knight/1_beved8tj

Lowry, Charles, 'William Temple after Forty Years', *Theology*, January 1985

Macquarrie, John, 'William Temple: Philosopher, Theologian, Churchman', *The Experiment of Life: Science and Religion*, ed. F. Kenneth Hare, Toronto: University of Toronto Press, 1983

Maurice, F. D., *Tracts on Christian Socialism*, London: Bell, 1850

Munby, D. L., *God and the Rich Society*, Oxford: Oxford University Press, 1960

Niebuhr, Reinhold, 'Dr. William Temple and His Britain', *The Nation*, New York, 11 November 1944

Norman, E. R., *Church and Society in England, 1770–1970: A Historical Study*, Oxford: Clarendon, 1976

Oliver, John, *The Church and Social Order: Social Thought in the Church of England 1918–1939*, London: A. R. Mowbray, 1968

Padfield, Jude, *Hopeful Influence: A Theology of Christian Leadership*, London: SCM Press, 2019

Parker, Stephen G., and Rob Freathy, 'The Church of England and religious education during the twentieth century', in Tom Rodger et al., *The Church of England and British Politics since 1900*, Woodbridge: The Boydell Press, 2020

Peacocke, A. R., 'The New Biology and *Nature, Man and God*', in *The Experiment of Life: Science and Religion*, ed. F. Kenneth Hare, Toronto: University of Toronto Press, 1983

Preston, Ronald H., 'Thirty-Five Years Later: 1941–1976: William Temple's *Christianity and Social Order*', in *Explorations in Theology* 9, London: SCM, 1981

—— 'Middle Axioms in Christian Social Ethics', in *Explorations in Theology* 9, London: SCM, 1981

—— 'William Temple as a Social Theologian', *Theology*, London: SPCK, September 1981

Ramsey, A. M., *From Gore to Temple: The Development of Anglican Theology between Lux Mundi and the Second World War*, London: Longmans, 1960

Reeves, Marjorie, ed., *Christian Thinking and Social Order: Conviction Politics from the 1930s to the Present Day*, London: Cassell, 1999

Rogerson, J. W., 'William Temple as Philosopher and Theologian', *Theology*, London: SPCK, September 1981

Sadler, John, 'William Temple's Educational Work and Thought', Taylor and Francis Online, https://doi.org/10.1080/0141620850080102

Skidelsky, Robert, *John Maynard Keynes 1883–1946: Economist, Philosopher, Statesman*, New York: Penguin, 2003

Suggate, Alan D., 'William Temple and the Challenge of Reinhold Niebuhr', *Theology*, London: SPCK, November 1981

Spencer, Stephen, 'William Temple's *Christianity and Social Order* after Fifty Years', *Theology*, London: SPCK, January/February 1992

—— 'History and Society in William Temple's Thought', *Studies in Christian Ethics*, Edinburgh: T and T Clark, Vol. 5, No. 2, 1992

—— 'William Temple', ed., a themed edition of *Crucible: The Journal of Christian Social Ethics*, with articles by John Atherton, Frank Field, Jane Shaw, Rupert Hoare and Chris Baker, January–March 2003, Norwich: Hymns Ancient and Modern

—— *Christ in All Things: William Temple and His Writings*, Norwich: Canterbury Press 2015

—— 'William Temple and the "Temple Tradition"', in *Theology Reforming Society: Revisiting Anglican Social Theology*, Scott Holland Lectures 2017, London: SCM Press, 2017

—— 'R. H. Tawney and Anglican Social Theology', *Crucible: The Journal of Christian Social Ethics*, January 2018, Norwich: Hymns Ancient and Modern

—— 'John Neville Figgis and William Temple: A Common Tradition of Anglican Social Theology?', in *Churches in a Pluralist World: The Thought and Legacy of John Neville Figgis, CR*, ed. Paul Avis, Leiden: Brill, 2021

—— 'William Temple and the Beveridge Report', *Crucible: The Journal of Christian Social Ethics*, July 2022, Norwich: Hymns Ancient and Modern

—— '*Christianity and Social Order* as a model of collaborative leadership in the public arena', *Theology*, July 2022, London: SPCK

Tawney, R. H., 'William Temple: An Appreciation', *The Highway*, January 1945

Taylor, Charles, *Hegel*, Cambridge: Cambridge University Press, 1975

Vidler, A. R., 'The Limitations of William Temple', *Theology*, London: SPCK, January 1976; reprinted in *Theology*, Vol. 123 No. 4, July/August 2020

Visser 't Hooft, Willem Adolf, 'The Genesis of the World Council of Churches', in *A History of the Ecumenical Movement 1517–1948*, ed. Ruth Ronse and Stephen Neill, second edn, Philadelphia: Westminster Press, 1968

Warner, Hugh C. (ed.), *Daily Readings from William Temple*, London and Oxford: Mowbray, 1981

Wilkinson, Alan, *Christian Socialism: Scott Holland to Tony Blair*, London: SCM Press, 1998

Williams, Canon G.A., *Viewed from the Water Tank: A History of the Diocese of Blackburn*, Preston: Palatine Books, 1993

Williams, Rowan, 'Anglican approaches to St John's Gospel', *Anglican Identities*, London: DLT, 2004

—— *Christian Imagination in Poetry and Polity: Some Anglican Voices from Temple to Herbert*, Oxford: SLG Press, 2004

—— 'From Welfare State to Welfare Society: the contribution of faith to happiness and well-being in a plural civil society', *Crucible: The Journal of Christian Social Ethics*, January–March 2009

—— 'The challenge of affluence: lessons for a parish from the life of Conrad Noel', lecture, RWLB-190712.pdf (saintanne-kew.org.uk) 2019

Index